PLAYFUL
TEACHING AND
LEARNING

Sara Miller McCune founded SAGE Publishing in 1965 to support the dissemination of usable knowledge and educate a global community. SAGE publishes more than 1000 journals and over 800 new books each year, spanning a wide range of subject areas. Our growing selection of library products includes archives, data, case studies and video. SAGE remains majority owned by our founder and after her lifetime will become owned by a charitable trust that secures the company's continued independence.

Los Angeles | London | New Delhi | Singapore | Washington DC | Melbourne

PLAYFUL
TEACHING AND
LEARNING

EDITED BY

GLENDA WALSH, DOROTHY MCMILLAN & CAROL MCGUINNESS

Los Angeles | London | New Delhi
Singapore | Washington DC | Melbourne

Los Angeles | London | New Delhi
Singapore | Washington DC | Melbourne

SAGE Publications Ltd
1 Oliver's Yard
55 City Road
London EC1Y 1SP

SAGE Publications Inc.
2455 Teller Road
Thousand Oaks, California 91320

SAGE Publications India Pvt Ltd
B 1/I 1 Mohan Cooperative Industrial Area
Mathura Road
New Delhi 110 044

SAGE Publications Asia-Pacific Pte Ltd
3 Church Street
#10-04 Samsung Hub
Singapore 049483

Editor: Jude Bowen
Associate editor: George Knowles
Production editor: Tom Bedford
Copyeditor: Catja Pafort
Proofreader: Andy Baxter
Indexer: David Rudeforth
Marketing manager: Dilhara Attygalle
Cover design: Wendy Scott
Typeset by: C&M Digitals (P) Ltd, Chennai, India
Printed by CPI Group (UK) Ltd, Croydon, CR0 4YY

Library of Congress Control Number: 2016949389

British Library Cataloguing in Publication data

A catalogue record for this book is available from
the British Library

ISBN 978-1-4739-4880-8
ISBN 978-1-4739-4881-5 (pbk)

At SAGE we take sustainability seriously. Most of our products are printed in the UK using FSC papers and boards.
When we print overseas we ensure sustainable papers are used as measured by the PREPS grading system.
We undertake an annual audit to monitor our sustainability.

To Our Mothers – who knew all about Playful Learning

Contents

List of Figures

List of Tables

About the Editors and Contributors

Editors

Glenda Walsh is Head of Early Years Education and principal lecturer at Stranmillis University College, Belfast. Her research interests centre on quality issues in Early Childhood Education, particularly in the field of pedagogy and curriculum. Her PhD thesis focused on an evaluation of play versus formal experiences for 4–5 year old children in Denmark and Northern Ireland, and for the purposes of her doctoral study she designed an observation tool, known as the Quality Learning Instrument. Subsequently she has been involved in many major research projects such as the longitudinal evaluation of the Early Years Enriched Curriculum Project in Northern Ireland and she also headed a major project on examining pedagogy in Early Childhood Education for the Department of Education in the Republic of Ireland. Her publications reflect her interest in curriculum and pedagogy, focusing in particular on resolving the dilemmas associated with play as learning and teaching in practice.

Dorothy McMillan was, until recently, a senior lecturer in Early Childhood Education at Stranmillis University College, Belfast, teaching on the PGCE (Early Years), BA and MA in Early Childhood Studies degree programmes. She has wide experience of working with children, as a former primary school teacher, nursery school principal and playgroup leader, and has also been involved in setting up and running parent and toddler groups.

Her doctoral thesis centred on the conceptual notion of 'educare' in preschool settings and its implications for early years training. Her research interests are focused on training and early years professionalism issues, including management and leadership. Dorothy recently moved to live in The Netherlands where she has joined the staff team at the International Baptist Theological Study Centre in Amsterdam.

Carol McGuinness is Professor Emerita at Queen's University Belfast. Her main research interest is the application of cognitive and developmental psychology to classroom learning, specifically, how teachers can promote the development of children's thinking skills. She authored the influential Department of Education (then DfEE) report *From Thinking Skills to Thinking Classrooms* (1999), and directed the Activating Children's Thinking Skills (ACTS) project, funded by the ESRC's Teaching and Learning Research Programme (2002–2005). Working with Glenda Walsh and colleagues, she led the longitudinal evaluation of the play-based curriculum in the early years of primary school in Northern Ireland, the Enriched Curriculum (2000–2009). Both these strands of research have had significant influence on education policy in Northern Ireland and elsewhere. More recently, with Robert Swartz (Center for Teaching Thinking, Boston), she is advising the International Baccalaureate on the development of thinking in their curriculum (2014–2016).

Contributors

Andrea Doherty is a senior lecturer in Early Years Education at Stranmillis University College, Belfast. She specialises in STEM within the early years, with research interests in the fields of playful pedagogy, cultural-historical theory, outdoor education, science education, and co-teaching in teacher education. With a BEd in primary science and a PhD on play theory and practice in Northern Ireland, Andrea's research interests fuel and are fuelled by her work with undergraduate, postgraduate and practising teachers. As a co-director of the Primary Science Teaching Trust Hub at Stranmillis University College, Andrea leads projects promoting playful approaches in primary science and technology.

Marion Dowling has had a wonderful and varied career in early years. She was involved in the pre-school playgroup movement, taught in London and was headteacher of a maintained nursery school. Marion worked as an educational adviser in two local authorities, was a member of Her Majesty's

Inspectorate of Education, and participated in a number of national working parties on early years matters. She now works as a trainer and consultant in the UK and overseas and keeps closely in touch with the workforce through regular and frequent visits to early years settings. Marion is an experienced author and has published widely on early years issues. Her main interests are young children's thinking and their personal, social and emotional development. She was formerly president and is now vice-president of Early Education, a national charity.

Liz Dunphy teaches and co-ordinates a range of undergraduate and postgraduate early childhood education courses in her role as a senior lecturer in Early Childhood Education at St Patrick's College, Dublin City University. Her research interests include young children's mathematics, early childhood curriculum and pedagogy and the assessment of early learning. Her recent publications include 'Supporting children's engagement in mathematical thinking processes' in A. Gervasoni, A. MacDonald and B. Perry (eds) (2015) *Mathematics and Transition to School: International Perspectives*. London: Springer. pp. 295–312.

Jacqueline Fallon is a lecturer in Early Childhood Education in the Church of Ireland College of Education, Dublin. She is a former primary school teacher with over 20 years' experience, primarily with 3–6 year old children. In 2002 she joined the Centre for Early Childhood Development and Education where she co-authored *Síolta, The National Quality Framework for Early Childhood Education* (2006). As a long-standing member of the National Council for Curriculum and Assessment's Board of Early Childhood and Primary Education, she has contributed to the development of policy in the area of Early Childhood Education, including *Aistear, The Early Childhood Curriculum Framework* (2009). Her doctoral research focused on primary school teachers' beliefs about play in infant classes, and her research interests centre on practice in the early years of primary schooling. A particular interest is the provision of continuous professional development (CPD) as part of her commitment to supporting both serving teachers and students in making provision for children's play in primary schools.

Catherine Gilliland is an experienced senior lecturer in Language and Literacy at St Mary's University College, Belfast. Her students describe her as a highly inspiring, passionate and enthusiastic lecturer who uses visual imagery and story to connect them to the Literacy concepts. She has a real commitment to storytelling, children's literature, puppets and film as conduits for getting children addicted to Literacy. Her research is school-based and stimulates discussion about what can be achieved within the classroom context. Catherine's work has taken her to speak at conferences across Europe and Ireland, including delivering the keynote address at the Literacy Association of Ireland Annual Conference in September 2015.

Richard Greenwood is a senior lecturer in Primary Education at Stranmillis University College, Belfast. Since 1990 he has taught on the BEd Primary degree course as well as the PGCE (Early Years), MA and MEd programmes. His main areas of interest are the teaching of geography in primary schools, outdoor learning, ICT and preparation of students for school placements. He has published and presented at conferences on thematic approaches to teaching in primary schools. His PhD with Queen's University, Belfast, looked at teachers' implementation of and opinions on the cross-curricular 'World Around Us' area of the Northern Ireland Primary Curriculum. Recent papers have included 'Subject-based and cross-curricular approaches within the revised primary curriculum in Northern Ireland: Teachers' concerns and preferred approaches' (*Education 3–13*, 2013).

John McCullagh is a senior lecturer in Primary Science at Stranmillis University College, Belfast. His research interests include developing effective strategies for developing pre-service and in-service teachers' practice in enquiry-based science. Through his work with the Primary Science Teaching Trust, John has led projects on the use of children's story books and the use of digital technology to promote engagement and enjoyment in science education. John's research in initial teacher education includes co-teaching and the use of video to enhance teachers' reflective practice.

Ross Ó Corráin is a primary school teacher working in Dublin. He teaches part-time on Early Childhood Education modules at St Patrick's College, Dublin City University as well as providing continuous professional development for in-service teachers on aspects of early years teaching. Ross has a degree in Drama and Theatre Studies from Trinity College, Dublin, and has worked extensively on arts education projects across Ireland. His research interests include young children's mathematics, pedagogy for teaching English as a second language to young children and early years teaching and learning.

Liz Sproule is a visiting fellow in the School of Psychology at Queen's University Belfast. She specialises in early years pedagogy. Liz was previously

Project Co-ordinator for the Early Years Enriched Curriculum Evaluation Project in Queen's, a major study of a play-based early years curriculum conducted in Northern Ireland over eight years. Her research interests include mathematics education and teaching thinking.

Christine Stephen is a research fellow in the Faculty of Social Sciences, University of Stirling. The focus of her research is children's learning in the early years and the ways in which this is supported in preschool settings and at home. Evaluating the impact of innovations and interventions, investigating pedagogic actions and interactions and the everyday experiences of children, parents and practitioners is at the centre of her work, along with ensuring that the perspectives of children are included in her research. Her studies have included exploring children's engagement with technologies in their homes and educational active learning at the beginning of primary school. Christine's research has been funded by the Economic and Social Research Council, the Scottish Government and other government and third sector agencies. She is a member of a number of Scottish Government advisory groups.

Foreword

This book draws on a wealth of research on play, learning, pedagogy and curriculum in early childhood education. The contributors rightly emphasise the importance of play to children, and the opportunities that play provides for learning and development. Each of the chapters is informed by international research, and offers contrasting perspectives about different forms of play, and the challenges that practitioners face day to day.

What makes this book distinctive is that the authors do not shy away from the controversial issues surrounding play in early childhood settings. The substantial research evidence regarding the connections between play and learning is consistently counterbalanced by evidence from practice: play can be lacking in richness, challenge and adventure, adults remain confused about their roles, and assessment and progression in play remain problematic. These are all significant challenges for practitioners, particularly within contemporary policy frameworks for early childhood education (ECE). In many countries we continue to witness a narrowing of ECE curricula, a focus on school readiness, and the push-down effects of the primary school curriculum. Assessment practices are often conscripted to reinforce these trends, for example by focusing on Literacy and Mathematics, and by valuing those outcomes that construct the 'school-ready child'.

The contributors embrace these controversies as provocations, in order to create spaces for discussion, reflection and critical engagement. The authors address one of the main challenges around play and learning. Freely chosen play does provide children with rich and diverse spaces for learning, which incorporates many varied dimensions: exercising agency, developing their identities, forming social relationships, incorporating popular culture, and mixing traditional and digital forms of play. As such, freely chosen play creates spaces of emergence, possibility and creativity, in which children reveal their funds of knowledge and working theories. However, this flexibility is also problematic when it comes to linking play with defined learning outcomes, because play 'in the moment' rarely resembles what it might actually lead to in the longer term. The counter-position, which is structured play, can become so structured that it is not really play, but play disguised as work, which rarely fools children.

So, can these two seemingly polarised positions be bridged? The focus on Playful Teaching and Learning offers some practical ways forward for practitioners, though not by promoting narrow versions of 'educational play', or 'eduplay' as the solution. The authors focus on playful structure, which incorporates playfulness and playful interactions as the means to sustain the intrinsic and affective qualities of play – such as motivation, engagement, enthusiasm, open-endedness, risk-taking and problem-solving. They link these qualities with playful pedagogical approaches and the characteristics of effective pedagogy. Unexpected turns and directions are accommodated, and practitioners remain tuned in to children's interests and to working theories. Playful learning and teaching thus create spaces for collaboration, interactions and ethical relationships. The model of play-ful pedagogies promoted here is aspirational, and requires deep attention to the knowledge bases that underpin practitioners' professionalism in ECE. To this end, subject knowledge is addressed within a broadly socio-cultural theoretical orientation to learning and development.

This book offers theoretical justifications for playful teaching and learn-ing, a strong international evidence base, and short vignettes from research studies for discussion and critical reflection. This is not a 'how to' book, but a 'think about' book, where the vignettes provoke engagement with contra-dictions and dilemmas. The authors engage critically with the pedagogical work that needs to be done in order to develop playfulness in leadership, in relationships with adults and children, and in the ability to think creatively about roles and responsibilities towards children, families and communities. The authors provide thoughtful counterpoints to dominant policy narratives, not by rejecting them, but by engaging creatively with possible alternatives.

Professor Elizabeth Wood
School of Education
University of Sheffield

Acknowledgements

This book could not have been completed without the help of a number of people.

First, we would like to thank all our colleagues who gave up their precious time to contribute a chapter to the book. We are immensely grateful to them. We would also like to thank the team at SAGE, namely Jude Bowen, Amy Jarrold and George Knowles for their support and advice throughout. We greatly appreciated feedback from the reviewers at various stages and trust that we acted on the feedback in ways that have improved the text. Particularly we wish to mention the early years practitioners and young children whose voices can be heard throughout the Case Studies.

Last, but not least, a special thank-you to our long suffering husbands and families. Without their support this book would not have happened.

Introduction

Glenda Walsh, Carol McGuinness and Dorothy McMillan

This book grew out of several kinds of oppositional thinking that we – as early years researchers, practitioners and educators – have been struggling with over the past ten years or so; for example, the tension between informal and formal approaches for early years practice, the significance of play versus work for children, and the relative merits of child-initiated versus adult-initiated activities for children's learning. Our main goal in trying to resolve these apparent oppositions and tensions is to ensure that early years professionals can captivate and maintain the interest of young children through the provision of a playful learning experience, while at the same time ensuring that effective learning is taking place. Research evidence has consistently shown how play in practice is highly problematic, irrespective of context, where early years professionals are uncertain about how to advance children's learning through play and how to effectively translate a playful learning experience into practice. Similar challenges emerge for early years students. Some see play simply as an addition to the curriculum rather than a pedagogical approach to enhance children's thinking and learning. Others see playful learning as a central tenet in the early years classroom but are confused about their own role in children's play and about how to ensure that all aspects of the curriculum are effectively addressed.

The first attempt to articulate the position on Playful Teaching and Learning (PTL), which underpins this book, was in the paper entitled 'Playful structure' (Walsh et al., 2011). The core idea was that if play-based curricula were to fulfil their promises, more nuanced understandings of play in practice were required. Thus the idea of play as a mere activity was replaced by the infusion of playfulness across the entire early years day, perceived as a characteristic of the interaction between the adult and the child, rather than the characteristic of child-initiated versus adult-directed or play time versus task time. The notion of playfulness and learning being intertwined promises a more integrated pedagogical approach in the early years of education that honours the interests and autonomy of young children, while also accommodating new thinking about the role of the teacher in scaffolding and co-constructing children's learning. This textbook therefore focuses directly on this playful teaching and learning point of view. It does not claim to present all viewpoints on play and playful learning as might be found in other edited handbooks or volumes.

Our theoretical position has also grown and become more refined over the years. It can now be characterised as largely post-Vygotskian in perspective, drawing on a range of socio-cultural ideas (e.g., cultural tools, scaffolding) where the emphasis on participatory learning methods between the adult and the child comes to the fore. Such thinking is visible throughout the entire book and will be seen in most of the chapters. Consequently, the focus of the book is as much about teaching and learning as it is about play. The aim of the book is to provide an innovative and creative take on how play as learning and teaching can become a reality in early years settings and classrooms. For these reasons, we feel that the primary audience of the book is practising early years teachers, professionals and, in particular, students, with a focus on children aged 3–8 years. We also feel that the book will be useful for early years educators.

We have drawn together a group of contributors particularly in the practice field with the objective of illustrating how broad the scope of playful teaching and learning can be for learning across the early years context. Some chapters focus on promoting playful teaching and learning in curricular areas such as Literacy, Numeracy, Science, ICT; others deliberate on broader skills and competences such as Thinking Skills, Growing the Child and Outdoor Learning, while also concentrating more directly on the pedagogical strategies of observation and assessment.

The book is constructed in three parts. The first section entitled 'Principles of Playful Teaching and Learning' consists of three chapters and provides an evidence-based background on the underpinning principles of PTL. The middle section is more practice-based in perspective. Entitled 'Playful Teaching and Learning across the Curriculum', it consists of seven individual chapters. Drawing on recent and innovative research, each chapter sets out to help the reader to better understand how playfulness and aspects of the curriculum can become effectively intertwined to meet the needs and interests of all children between the ages of 3 and 8 years. The last section of the book,

'The Role of the Playful Professional', initially rehearses some familiar but pertinent issues in early years practice such as observing, planning and assessing within the PTL experience. The final chapter opens up new thinking about the personal qualities required of an early years educator, with an additional focus on innovative thinking centring on the idea of educating a workforce for 3–8 year old children, known as Playful Professionals.

In conclusion, the general theoretical underpinnings advanced in this book do not stand alone in the early years literature. We are part of a growing community of scholars across the globe who are also trying to resolve the oppositions that we have been talking about. For example, in the USA, Weisberg et al. (2013) are trying to carve out a middle ground in the early years context known as 'Guided Play', which sits between free play and direct instruction. Similarly, Van Oers and Duijkers (2012) in The Netherlands present the dilemma many early years educationalists and practitioners face about "both the child-centred approach which in their view does not foster all children's developmental potentials, and the teacher-driven approach that allegedly reduces children to trainable production factors in an economically driven society" (2012: 2). In response they promote the concept of 'Developmental Education' for 4–8 year old children, where the role of the teacher in children's play is granted greater importance. And, as a final comment, the work of Elizabeth Wood (2014) in the United Kingdom with regard to the policy–practice interface has particular relevance to this debate. She too emphasises the need for an "expansive understanding of play and pedagogy and to hold that space against reductionist policy discourses" (2014: 155).

This book is to help early years practitioners and, ultimately, to help children's learning. We hope you enjoy your reading and find it of benefit to your early years practice. Happy Reading!

References

van Oers, B. and Duijkers, D. (2012) 'Teaching in a play-based curriculum: Theory, practice and evidence of developmental education for young children', *Journal of Curriculum Studies* 45 (4): 511–34.

Walsh, G., Sproule, L., McGuinness, C. and Trew, K. (2011) 'Playful structure: A novel image of early years pedagogy for Primary School classrooms', *Early Years* 31 (2): 107–19.

Weisberg, D.S., Hirsh-Pasek, K. and Golinkoff, R.M. (2013) 'Guided play: Where curricular goals meet a playful pedagogy', *Mind, Brain, and Education* 7: 104–12. doi:10.1111/mbe.12015.

Wood, E. (2014) 'The play–pedagogy interface in contemporary debates', in L. Brooker, M. Blaise and S. Edwards (eds), *The Sage Handbook of Play and Learning in Early Childhood*. Los Angeles: Sage. pp. 145–56.

Section 1
Principles of Playful Teaching and Learning

Why Playful Teaching and Learning?

Glenda Walsh

Chapter Overview

This chapter will take you on an evidence-based journey to show you why play in practice needs to be reconceptualised. To ensure that 3–8 year old children learn more effectively in setting-based contexts, we need to think differently about play and what it means for learning – and that is the purpose of this first chapter. Before embarking on the substance of the chapter, take time to read the introductory case study as it presents the essence of what the chapter is about.

Case Study 1.1: Lillyfield Primary School's Playtime

Like every morning, Mrs B got the children around her and began to recite the different play areas that were available for the children to play with that morning. "Today, boys and girls, you have the house corner, but I don't want to see the same silliness as yesterday - no bringing in the dough or water - you can pretend to wash the dishes and to make cakes - sure that is what it is all about". She then continued to

(Continued)

(Continued)

explain where else the children could play including small world dinosaur play, construction using Lego, making birthday cakes with the dough and the writing corner where today children were having the opportunity to make Mother's Day cards. After approximately 20 minutes sitting and waiting, the 26 children were finally released to go and play in the area to which they had been assigned. Bertie and Bob were at the dinosaurs – the area they had been waiting for all week – six dinosaurs of different shapes and sizes set inside a shoe box, filled with some leaves. The boys started off making roaring sounds and then bouncing the dinosaurs in the shoebox as if they were ready to attack. The play soon developed into a dinosaur fight, becoming raucous and noisy. At first Mrs B tried to ignore what they were doing, but soon realised that she would have to intervene by asking the boys to play more quietly or she would have to move them elsewhere. In an attempt to bring them back on task, she asked then to name each dinosaur in turn and then to count how many there were. After she moved on, the boys returned to their loud and somewhat aggressive and chaotic play, but after 5 minutes they then decided to move to the dough table, where they rolled out a circle shape and stuck a candle on the top. Mrs B then called them over to the writing table to make a Mother's Day card, with the help of Miss F (the classroom assistant), as there was only 5 minutes until tidy up time.

This is the story of playtime at Lillyfield primary school. Although the observation took place some years ago (in 2010), the story is still very relevant today in many of our early years settings. Play *is* taking place and, as early years educationalists, we should be delighted about this; but in many cases the play lacks richness, challenge and adventure. In many of our educational settings, play has become reduced to routine and mundane practical tasks, where educators appear confused and lack understanding about what their role in play should be in an effort to foster learning and indeed what play as learning should look like in practice. In this chapter I intend to examine more carefully why many early years educators face these dilemmas and then create a rationale for why play in practice needs to be reconceptualised as pedagogy – moving away from an overly maturistic and child-led approach to play towards aligning play, learning and teaching more closely and proposing the concept of Playful Teaching and Learning as the way forward.

Origins of Play as Learning

The importance of play for young children's learning and development has long been recognised, emanating from the pioneering work of eminent scholars and philanthropists such as Rousseau, Fröbel and Pestalozzi. From as early as the eighteenth century, play has been deemed as highly serious and of deep significance for children. It has been promoted as the medium through which young children learn best and through which the 'whole' child is fully developed. Contemporary research confirms the thinking of these early pioneers, drawing on a range of evidence that suggests that play educates emotionally, socially, cognitively and physically (e.g., Whitebread et al., 2012). The lasting social and emotional benefits of play have long been established in a number of longitudinal experimental studies (e.g., Schweinhart and Weikart, 1997). These studies demonstrate that engaging in more play-based and developmentally appropriate curricula in those formative early years of education has positive effects on children's inter-personal and negotiation strategies, on their personal relationships and community behaviour, on their ability to deal with stress and emotional issues, as well as their overall academic aspirations.

More recent evidence has also been accruing on the power of play-based activity in fostering children's dispositional and cognitive skills. Play, it appears, can provide opportunities for children to engage in self-regulation, to solve problems, to advance their motivation and concentration and to develop their independence and metacognitive powers (e.g., Walsh et al., 2006). A further small but growing body of evidence links play directly to children's ability to master academic skills such as literacy and numeracy. For example, researchers have found that engagement in dramatic play and acting out stories prompted their metalinguistic ability, helping children to recognise the components of stories and improve their text comprehension (Christie and Roskos, 2006). Likewise, evidence would suggest that children's early experimentation, observation and comparison in their play impacts on children's later learning of STEM (Science, Technology, Engineering and Maths) (Bergen, 2009). With regard specifically to mathematics, research by Carruthers and Worthington (2006) has highlighted that play involving counting and other basic mathematical operations supports young children's ability to engage in formal mathematics more confidently.

The physicality associated with play-based activity has also received growing significance in terms of children's health, well-being (Hope et al., 2007) and cognitive development (Pellegrini and Holmes, 2006). Jarvis' findings (2010) (focusing particularly on rough and tumble play) reveal that much social and gender role development is mediated through physical play experiences, while a literature review by Campbell and Hesbeth (2007) proposes a link between physical activity beginning in early childhood and the prevention of obesity in later years.

In this way, it could be argued that play, in its highest form, can provide for the holistic development of the young child in its widest sense, that is, socially, emotionally, cognitively and physically.

Pause for Thought

The evidence described above emphasises the many benefits of play in practice for young children's learning and development. Why, in your opinion, can play be such a powerful learning medium for young children?

Challenges of Play as Learning in Practice

Against this understanding of play being beneficial for young children's learning and development, is a portrayal of play in practice that is highly controversial and problematic (Hunter and Walsh, 2014; Wood, 2014). Substantial research evidence across the globe has presented a picture of play in practice as largely superficial, lacking depth and challenge, where practitioners appear to lack the skills and competence to ensure effective play-as-learning in practice (Hunter and Walsh, 2014). The quality of the provision, the role of the adult, parental expectations, and top-down pressures are some of the reasons why play in practice is perceived principally as an accessory to the learning experience, rather than the medium through which young children learn best. In many cases, play is considered little more than a means of settling children into the school day before the real work begins.

As a result, it would seem that children's play has been declining both in terms of quantity and quality over recent years. Children's ability to engage in high level play, according to Bodrova (2008), is less well developed than it should be for their age. She argues that even 5–6 year old children often display signs of immature play, typical of much younger children, where their powers of imagination are limited and the scenarios they create are quite stereotypical in perspective. The research findings from a small-scale study on the reality of play in Northern Ireland primary schools reveals a similar picture. Although the observations suggest that at least play is taking place in the early years of primary schooling (called

Foundation Stage classes in Northern Ireland for 4–6 year old children), higher levels of challenge and extension were not immediately guaranteed. It appears that complex and sophisticated play as a medium to develop children's intellectual skills and creativity was not fully understood by the practitioners involved (Hunter and Walsh, 2014).

More rigorous supporting evidence has emerged from an extensive long-itudinal evaluation of a play-based intervention, known as the Early Years Enriched Curriculum (Walsh et al., 2010). Despite the increased benefits associated with the play-based approach in terms of the children's socio-emotional and dispositional aspects of learning, when compared to a more traditional and formal approach, the findings regarding their more cognitive and intellectual behaviours such as problem solving, logical reasoning and creativity, were less positive. These findings signal a warning that simply providing more play-based activities does not necessarily promote chil-dren's cognitive and metacognitive processes (Walsh et al., 2010).

Further perusal of the evidence base suggests that some teachers adopt an overly maturistic approach to play in practice, an issue that Liz Sproule will develop more fully in Chapter 2 entitled 'Mental Models of Playful Practice: Digging Deeper'. Some early years educators seem reluctant to interfere with children's play space due to a pre-conceived child-centred notion that is normally associated with Piagetian perspec-tives on child development. According to this viewpoint, the role of the adult is perceived principally as facilitative, where children are believed to be active agents of their own learning and construct meaning for themselves with little outside intervention (Walsh et al., 2010). As schol-ars such as Grieshaber (2008) argue, many play-based experiences have now become associated with laissez-faire teaching, with an over-emphasis on developmental perspectives with educators waiting for children to grow up and learn on their own.

Drawing on such an evidence-base it could be argued that early years practitioners appear much more comfortable when promoting the social and emotional aspects of children's learning within play, but, when it comes to the more academic aspects of learning, the findings suggest that reconciling play with educational values is a much more complex task for early years educators (Walsh and Gardner, 2006; McInness et al., 2011; Hunter and Walsh, 2014). As Fisher et al. (2010) emphasise, many early years educators have come to believe that play and academic learning are at polar extremes and fundamentally incompatible, where they must either choose to engage in direct instruction to ensure intellectual gains or let children play to enable their holistic development.

But the question is: how can we ensure a closer alignment between play and learning without subordinating play to policy directives and making it compliant with a narrow set of educational goals and targets? Recently there has been an uneasiness expressed about the over-emphasis being placed on formal methods of teaching in early years education to address the more academic aspects of learning. In particular, concerns have been voiced about the over-emphasis being placed on a schoolification model of practice, where the main focus of early years education is becoming associated with getting children ready for formal school (Fisher et al., 2010; Russo, 2012). As Whitebread and Bingham maintain:

> The model of 'readiness for school' is attractive to governments as it seemingly delivers children into primary school ready to conform to classroom procedures and even able to perform basic reading and writing skills. However, from a pedagogical perspective this approach fuels an increasingly dominant notion of education as 'transmission and reproduction', and of early childhood as preparation for school rather than for life. (2011: 2–3)

Yet to deprive children of academic content knowledge and skills in the so-called 'knowledge age' that we live in would be highly detrimental for their overall learning and development (Fisher et al., 2010). In addition, to argue that play has no place in the enhancement of children's academic learning would be misinformed and would run counter to the underpinning principles of play scholarship in its entirety (Hunter and Wash, 2014). The time is ripe, therefore, to challenge this disjuncture between play and education and to place renewed emphasis on reconceptualising play as a form of pedagogy in practice, where the adult takes a more active role in the playful experience. As Russo (2012) maintains, "the challenge for teachers is to find the appropriate balance between academic engagement and academic challenge, while providing a learning environment that encourages and supports exploration and discovery without the stress of competition, standardization and testing" (2012: 10) – the essence of what this book is about.

Pause for Thought

In your opinion, why might play and academic learning appear incompatible?

What needs to be done to ensure a closer alignment between play and learning in practice?

What challenges might you face in the process?

Reconceptualising Play as Pedagogy

In an effort to help early years educators to resolve some of these dilemmas in practice, there is a growing evidence base that is beginning to create bridges between ideas and to open up conceptual boundaries that were previously thought to be impenetrable, that is, aligning play and play-related activities more closely with a proactive and intentional pedagogy, where playing, learning and teaching are becoming more fully synchronised (Wood, 2013). There is growing acceptance that allowing children to make their own meanings through play does not mean that teachers abandon their responsibility to teach (Brooker, 2010). Such thinking, it could be argued, originated in the findings of the project known as Researching Effective Pedagogy in the Early Years (REPEY) (Siraj-Blatchford and Sylva, 2004), as part of their major longitudinal EPPE (Effective Provision for Pre-school Education) study in England and EPPNI in Northern Ireland. From case studies that were carried out in preschool settings in England, Siraj-Blatchford and Sylva (2004) concluded that the most effective teachers/practitioners:

- engaged children in interactions that showed sustained shared thinking;
- showed a good understanding of the content of curriculum areas;
- encouraged children to engage with cognitive challenge;
- had a repertoire of pedagogical activity (including direct instruction) that they drew on as appropriate;
- differentiated the curriculum to match activities and level of challenge to the children's needs;
- showed an equal balance between child-initiated and adult-initiated activities; and
- had clear behaviour and discipline policies, supported by facilitating children to talk through conflicts, which benefited social skills.

From their extensive analyses of adult/child pedagogical interactions in the pre-school settings, they deduced that the most effective preschool settings (in terms of intellectual, social, and dispositional outcomes) achieved a balance between the opportunities provided for children to benefit from teacher-initiated group work and the provision of freely chosen yet potentially instructive play activities. In addition, they argue that the best practitioners use a mixture of pedagogical approaches – for example, scaffolding, extending, discussing, monitoring and direct instruction – to fit both the concept or skill and the developmental zone of the children. They also highlight the importance of "sustained shared thinking", where adults and children work together "to solve a problem, clarify a concept, evaluate activities or extend a narrative." (Siraj-Blatchford and Sylva, 2004: 718)

More recent work by Hedges et al. (2011) in New Zealand also draws attention to the proactive pedagogical strategies the teacher can employ in children's play. Drawing on a qualitative study in two early childhood settings, their findings suggest that practitioners need to look beyond the tradition of well-resourced, child-centred, play-based environments, to engage more fully with children's own interests and the already-acquired knowledge that children bring from home to enable a richer extension of children's learning. In this way they are calling for teachers to be conscious of how young children learn and develop, but simultaneously keep in mind the concepts that they as teachers wish young children to learn and understand (Hedges and Cullen, 2012). Such thinking resonates with the work of Pramling-Samuelsson and Asplund Carlsson (2008) on the "playing learning child" which argues that teachers need to be both child-centred but also directed towards learning objectives simultaneously.

The significance of this more proactive and intentional play pedagogy on children's learning has been clearly evidenced within the Tools of the Mind programme in the USA (Bodrova, 2008). In this programme, teachers are specifically encouraged to help children use toys and props in a symbolic way; for example, rather than using a toy telephone, encouraging children to represent the telephone with an object such as a rectangular block, which bears only the most superficial resemblance to it. Gesture is also encouraged to stand for action. Activities are designed to develop extended play scenarios, to discuss roles and to plan future scenarios, called 'play plans'. Although the activities in the Tools of the Mind programme involve teachers to a greater extent than is generally expected for role play, Bodrova points out that their involvement should last only for a short time; the children should quickly learn how to build their own roles and rules, and then require much less support. Comparing the Tools of the Mind programme with a more traditional early years curriculum, Barnett et al. (2008) found that this more systematic pedagogical approach to play improved overall classroom quality and children's executive functioning. The programme, in this case, also had some positive effects on the children's language (though these effects did not reach statistical significance).

This renewed emphasis on championing the role of the teacher in children's play portrays a distinct shift in conceptual framing beyond the confines of Piaget's developmental ages and stages approach towards Vygotskian and post-Vygotskian notions of socio-culturalism and participatory learning theories. Through appropriate interaction with adults and more knowledgeable peers, children's learning, it appears, can be nudged forward in new directions that may not be possible by waiting for children to develop at their own pace. However, it is important to note that such 'pushing' is not to be conceived as an "acceleration of development", that is, a push down of inappropriate instruction and activities (Grieshaber, 2008: 6). Instead, by actively participating with children in a playful manner, teachers can encourage children to explore and construct new knowledge, skills and understanding, opening up genuine learning opportunities. In so doing, "buds of development" (Vygotsky, 1978: 86) will blossom.

Pause for Thought

Why is the role of the teacher so important in the play experience?
    What, in your opinion, makes the difference between a practitioner who interacts appropriately in children's play to extend learning as opposed to one who does not?

Towards Playful Teaching and Learning

It is from this theoretical perspective and evidence base that the concept of 'Playful Teaching and Learning' emerges. Interpreting the pedagogical lessons learned from the Early Years Enriched Curriculum evaluation, Walsh et al. (2011) point towards a new integrated early years pedagogy known as 'playful structure' which promotes playful teaching and learning in practice. Playful structure invites teachers and children to initiate and maintain a degree of playfulness in the learning experience, while at the same time maintaining a degree of structure to ensure that effective learning takes place. The idea of play becomes a characteristic of the interaction between the adult and the child and not just a characteristic of child-initiated versus adult-initiated activities. In this way it is thought the interaction adopts playful characteristics; for example, the tone is light-hearted, the activity becomes self-sustaining because both partners are enjoying it, and unexpected turns and directions are allowed.

Such thinking builds on the recent work of Howard and McInnes (2013) who associate children's feelings of playfulness with increased performance. They argue that it is the internal and affective qualities of play such as motivation, enthusiasm, and willingness that make it so vital for development, rather than the act of play itself. Consequently, they believe that it is the practitioners' responsibility to tune into "children's cues and so enable them to take a playful approach and attitude to activities" (Howard and McInness, 2013: 48). That said, it is important to emphasise that the infusion of playfulness is not perceived as mere frivolity, simply donning a childish and immature persona and trying to make learning silly and fun. Instead, the concept of playful teaching and learning conjures up an experience, an interaction, a relationship and ethos between children and adults which results in motivation, enthusiasm, engagement, trial and error and thinking outside the box.

Enriched Curriculum teachers who provided the highest quality teaching and learning experiences were able to infuse such playfulness into a learning situation without it appearing contrived, allowing children to try out new ideas without fear of failure. They made use of an array of tools and pedagogical approaches – using role play, drama, stories, puppets, the outdoors, problem-solving, popular culture, topics, questions, ideas and suggestions. All classroom activity, not only free play, assumed playful characteristics. Read the following case study and consider how it illustrates such thinking in practice:

Case Study 1.2: The Magic Wand

The teacher is giving a lesson on partitioning sets to a group of children aged six years. The six children have all been given a set circle and a set of five objects. The teacher, wearing a wizard's hat, employs a 'magic wand' wooden spoon to demonstrate partitioning the set. She says, "Here's my magic wand. Watch carefully!". She brings the spoon back over her head and moves it forward saying dramatically, "Magic wand, magic wand, split the set", as she splits the objects into two sets. She demonstrates this twice more, including "splitting the set a different way". The children are encouraged to use their own magic wands to split the set for themselves and then move on to describing in words what they have done. Finally, they are offered a choice of recording what they have done in words or in informal numerical style.

In addition, evidence suggests that an important role of the playful teacher is to interact with the children when appropriate, structuring the task if required or simply observing, listening and tuning into what is taking place in order to ensure effective learning is taking place in practice (see Walsh et al., 2010). Playful teachers require a sound knowledge and understanding about how young children learn and develop but are also capable of letting down their guard and playing alongside the children and (on occasions) following their lead, encouraging creativity, imagination, spontaneity and ambiguity in the learning experience. In this way the playful experience might be something as simple as encouraging children to paint pictures with milk or white chocolate, searching for money in a basin of Coco Pops, creating a castle from an array of cardboard boxes or imagining that you are one of Santa's little helpers and helping to create a factory line of toys. In these examples cross-curricular skills are being fostered in abundance but in a playful and engaging manner. The following case study helps to showcase how a teacher can drip-feed learning into a playful experience. Consider the learning that is being fostered in the following case study:

Case Study 1.3: A Re-enactment of Daisy Hill Farm

Having visited Daisy Hill Farm the previous Friday, the 3–4 year old children at Meadow Green nursery school were enthralled to learn on Monday morning that they were going to set up their own farm in the nursery. Using a planning board, they explored ideas about what they would want to call their farm, what they would want to see there and what they would want to do there. The children were full of ideas from milking cows, driving the tractor to baking their own bread in the farmhouse oven. Mrs Harmony was delighted with their ideas and set to task finding materials and resources to ensure that the children's interests were built upon, but at the same time that her overarching learning intentions, focusing on "people who help us" – in this case "the farmer" and the story of milk – were fully met. On Tuesday morning, when the children arrived into class, the nursery was transformed. Daisy the cow was waiting to be milked with glove attached, the water in the water tray was now white and several different sized bottles were waiting to be filled and brought to the nearby farm shop. In the junk area, large cardboard boxes were waiting for children's eager hands to be transformed into some form of farm machinery and the smell of flour, margarine and sugar filled the air as Mrs Harmony awaited the children's help to get some soda bread in the oven.

Key Messages

In this chapter we learned that:

- High-quality play has many benefits for young children's learning and development.
- The play that we see in practice, in many cases, is low key and mundane, offering little opportunity for cognitive challenge.
- Many practitioners appear confused about what their role in play should be and undervalue the potential of play as learning in practice.
- An integrated early years pedagogy, known as Playful Teaching and Learning (PTL) has been proposed as the way forward.
- PTL honours the interests and autonomy of young children and accommodates new thinking about the role of adults in scaffolding and co-constructing children's learning, in order to move beyond the confines of play and academic learning as separate entities.
- Infusing playfulness into the teaching and learning experiences is perceived as a novel way of bridging previously held dichotomies between formal and informal, work and play, child-initiated and adult-led activities in early years classrooms.
- PTL can provide the appropriate balance between enabling young children to be autonomous and creative while ensuring genuine progression in children's cognitive skills and content knowledge.

Further Reading

Hirsh-Pasek, K., Golinkoff, R., Berk, L. and Singer, D. (2009) *A Mandate for Playful Learning in Preschool: Presenting the Evidence.* New York: Oxford University Press.

Rogers, S. (2010) *Rethinking Play and Pedagogy in Early Childhood Education: Concepts, Contexts and Cultures.* Oxford: Taylor and Francis.

References

Barnett, W., Jung, K., Yarosz, D., Thomas, J., Hornbeck, A., Stechuk, R. and Burns, S. (2008) 'Educational effects of the tools of the mind curriculum: A randomised trial', *Early Childhood Research Quarterly* 23 (3): 299–313.

Bergen, D. (2009) 'Play as the learning medium for future scientists, mathematicians and engineers', *American Journal of Play* 1: 413–28.

Bodrova, E. (2008) 'Make-believe play versus academic skills: A Vygotskian approach to today's dilemma of early childhood education', *European Early Childhood Education Research Journal* 16 (3): 357–69.

Brooker, L. (2010) 'Learning to play in a cultural context', in P. Broadhead, J. Howard and E. Wood (eds), *Play and Learning in the Early Years*. London: Sage. pp. 27–42.

Campbell, K.J. and Hesketh, K.D. (2007) 'Strategies which aim to positively impact on weight, physical activity, diet and sedentary behaviours in children from zero to five years. A systematic review of the literature', *Obesity Reviews* 8 (4): 327–38.

Carruthers, E. and Worthington, M. (2006) *Children's Mathematics*. London: Sage.

Christie, J. and Roskos, K. (2006) 'Standards, science, and the role of play in early literacy education', in D. Singer, R. Golinkoff and K. Hirsh-Pasek (eds), *Play=Learning: How Play Motivates and Enhances Children's Cognitive and Socio-Emotional Growth*. New York: Oxford University Press. pp. 57–73.

Fisher, K., Hirsh-Pasek, K., Golinkoff, R.M., Berk, L. and Singer, D. (2010) 'Playing around in school: Implications for learning and educational policy', in A. Pellegrini (ed.), *Handbook of the Development of Play*. New York: Oxford University Press. pp. 341–63.

Grieshaber, S.J. (2008) 'Interrupting stereotypes: Teaching and the education of young children', *Early Education and Development* 19 (3): 505–18.

Hedges, H. and Cullen, J. (2012). 'Participatory learning theories: A framework for early childhood pedagogy', *Early Child Development and Care* 182 (7): 921–40.

Hedges, H., Cullen, J. and Jordan, B. (2011) 'Early years curriculum: Funds of knowledge as a conceptual framework for children's interests', *Journal of Curriculum Studies* 43: 185–205.

Hope, G., Austin, R., Dismore, H., Hammond, S. and Whyte, T. (2007) 'Wild woods or urban jungle: Playing it safe or freedom to roam', *Education 3–13* 35 (4): 321–32.

Howard, J. and McInnes, K. (2013) The *Essence of Play*. London: Routledge.

Hunter, T. and Walsh, G. (2014) 'From policy to practice? The reality of play in primary school classes in Northern Ireland', *International Journal of Early Years Education* 22 (1): 19–36.

Jarvis, P. (2010) 'Born to play: The biocultural roots of rough and tumble play and its impact upon young children's learning and development' in E. Wood, P. Broadhead and J. Howard (eds), *Play and Learning in the Early Years*. London: Sage. pp. 61–77.

McInnes, K., Howard, J., Miles, G. and Crowley, K. (2011) 'Differences in practitioners' understanding of play and how this influences pedagogy and children's perceptions of play', *Early Years* 13 (2): 121–33.

Pelligrini, A.D. and Holmes, R.M. (2006) 'The role of recess in primary school', in D. Singer, R. Golinkoff and K. Hirsh-Pasek (eds), *Play=Learning: How Play Motivates and Enhances Children's Cognitive and Socio-Emotional Growth*. New York: Oxford University Press. pp. 36–53.

Pramling-Samuelsson, I. and Asplund Carlsson, M. (2008) 'The playing learning child: Towards a pedagogy of early childhood', *Scandinavian Journal of Educational Research* 52 (6): 623–41.

Russo, H.L. (2012) 'Rethinking the role of play and creativity', *ICCP World Conference*, Estonia: Tallinn University, June. http://www.iccp-play.org/documents/tallinn/russo.pdf (accessed 26 August 2016).

Schweinhart, L. and Weikart, D. (1997) *Lasting Differences*. Ypsilanti, MI: HighScope Press.

Siraj-Blatchford, I. and Sylva, K. (2004) 'Researching pedagogy in English pre-schools', *British Educational Research Journal* 30 (5): 713–31.

Vygotsky, L.S. (1978) *Mind in Society: the Development of Higher Psychological Processes*. Cambridge, MA: Harvard University Press.

Walsh, G. and Gardner, J. (2006) 'Teachers' readiness to embrace change in the early years of schooling', *European Early Childhood Education Research Journal* 14 (2): 127–40.

Walsh, G., Sproule, L., McGuinness, C., Trew, K., Rafferty, H. and Sheehy, N. (2006) 'An appropriate curriculum for the 4–5 year old child in Northern Ireland: Comparing play-based and formal approaches', *Early Years* 26 (2): 201–21.

Walsh, G., McGuinness, C., Sproule, L. and Trew, K. (2010) 'Implementing a play-based and developmentally appropriate curriculum in Northern Ireland primary schools: What lessons have we learned?', *Early Years* 30 (1): 53–66.

Walsh, G., Sproule, L., McGuinness, C. and Trew, K. (2011) 'Playful structure: A novel image of early years pedagogy for primary school classrooms', *Early Years* 31 (2): 107–19.

Whitebread, D. and Bingham, S. (2011). 'School readiness: A critical review of perspectives and evidence', *TACTYC Occasional Paper No. 2*. http://tactyc.org.uk/occasional-paper/occasional-paper2.pdf (accessed 26 August 2016).

Whitebread, D., Basilio, M., Kuvalja, M. and Verma, M. (2012) *The Importance of Play: A Report on the Value of Children's Play with a Series of Policy Recommendations*. Brussels, Belgium: Toys Industries for Europe.

Wood, E. (2013) *Play, Learning and the Early Childhood Curriculum* (third edition). London: Sage.

Wood, E. (2014) 'Free choice and free play in early childhood education: Troubling the discourse', *International Journal of Early Years Education* 22 (1): 4–18.

Mental Models of Playful Practice: Digging Deeper

Liz Sproule

Chapter Overview

Two pedagogies are often contrasted in early years practice. One is characterised as practitioner-led with a clear focus on external curriculum goals, while the other can be described as child-initiated and play-based. The purpose of this chapter is to explore a middle ground, drawing on case studies of classroom observations and interviews with early years practitioners who were shifting their practice from a previous practitioner-led and formal pedagogical approach towards a more play-based approach. The children in their classes were aged 4–8 years of age in the Northern Ireland primary school system.

This chapter explores the mental models of early years professionals and how they can influence classroom practice. By the end of it, I hope that you will be able to:

- Understand the concept of mental models and how they can shape early years classroom practice;
- Reflect on, and explore, your own mental model(s) of early years practice;
- Appreciate that you might be able to integrate a playful approach into your practice to achieve a broad range of learning outcomes for young children, including literacy and numeracy;
- Be able to explain and justify your practice if called upon to do so.

The Importance of Mental Models

Practitioners' classroom practices are influenced by many factors: their professional education and training; their experience as a practitioner – and previously as a learner; knowledge of children's development and different pedagogical approaches; personal values; school norms; prevailing educational policies; as well as cultural expectations about learning and teaching, among others. For practitioners, these influences converge into a mental framework or viewpoint on what is 'best' for children's learning in their classrooms. This messy confluence of knowledge, values, beliefs, assumptions and personal experiences are called mental models (sometimes called conceptions of teaching or just teachers' thinking). Professionals are not always aware of their own mental models and, unless they are deliberately prompted to articulate and reflect on them, these models can often remain implicit or tacit.

Mental models are not static, they can shift and develop. Indeed, one of the primary goals of professional development is to shift implicit mental models in the direction of best practice based on best evidence (Fisher and Wood, 2012), thus making them more explicit. Also, we can hold several mental models at the same time. Sometimes these can be consistent with one another; they can also be in conflict. For example, in their study Bennett et al. (1997: 117) offer additional support for Clark's (1986) characterisation of the typical mental model of practitioners' thinking about play as an eclectic collection of "rules of thumb, generalizations from personal experience, beliefs, biases and prejudices" – mental *muddles* rather than mental *models*. Whatever their characteristics, in the moment-to-moment dynamic of the classroom, they can exert considerable influence on what practitioners do and how they interact with children.

Pause for Thought

Before reading further, here are some exercises to help you to articulate your mental model of early years 'best practice'. Think specifically about the children that you teach (or will teach).

Complete the following sentences – follow your gut feeling in the first instance.

I think children learn best when ....

The best kind of teaching in the early years is ....

The biggest challenge for me is ....

Now, reflect on the meaning of what you have written and see if it fits together.

Compare your responses with a colleague or fellow student.

Mental Models and a Play-based Curriculum

There are three main reasons why it might be particularly important to understand practitioners' mental models of early years practice in a play-based curriculum:

- to enable them to embrace their greater responsibility for curriculum delivery in a play-based curriculum compared to a more prescribed programme;
- to clarify issues around the practitioner's role during play;
- to help practitioners develop a more coherent mental model that is evidence-informed and gives them confidence to develop professionally.

Practitioner Responsibility in a Play-based Curriculum

In a more formal early years curriculum much of the teaching tends to have a degree of external structure imposed through a more prescribed programme or through the use of reading, mathematics or other work schemes. The schemes dictate what to teach next and often how it should be taught. Such schemes allow little child autonomy and are focused on specific curriculum goals. By contrast, the greater flexibility available to practitioners in a play-based milieu also places a greater responsibility on them for shaping the child's experience. In a play-based curriculum, the practitioners spend much of their time interacting with the children individually and in small groups. The expectation of being developmentally appropriate, which frequently goes hand-in-hand with the play-based model, suggests that during these interactions, the practitioner is continually assessing the child's current level of progress and crafting an appropriate response. Because of the degree of professional autonomy, flexibility and responsiveness to individual children that a play-based curriculum demands, practitioners are likely to draw more deeply on their own mental model(s) of early years practice than might be the case in a more prescribed curriculum.

Understanding Adult Roles in a Play-based Curriculum

Despite the general acceptance that both child-initiated and adult-initiated/led activities are important for children's learning (Siraj-Blatchford and Sylva, 2004), getting the balance right for specific contexts – age-groups, tasks, individual children – may not be straightforward. While general Vygotskian ideas such as scaffolding can be helpful, Verenikina (2004) cautions that the educational meaning of scaffolding is drifting to include almost any kind of adult intervention, including direct instruction, rather than staying true to its original meaning of co-construction in the context of child-initiated activity.

Also, practitioners may not have a sufficiently rich repertoire of play roles to draw upon in their interactions with young children – such different roles exemplified by Dunkin and Hanna (2001: 15–36) as play-partner, co-learner, listener-decoder, planner, facilitator, etc.

Practitioners can also have different perspectives on what child- or adult-initiated activity means for children's learning. McInnes et al. (2011) report that practitioners think differently about when it is appropriate for an adult to intervene in children's play. For example, some practitioners in her study seemed willing to 'play' with the children if the activity was adult-initiated but not if it was child-initiated. Observing practitioners introducing a more active play-based curriculum in Scottish schools, Martlew et al. (2011) concluded that practitioners' mental models of learning seem to influence their practice. They suggested that nursery practitioners were more likely to see child-initiated activities as progressing the child's learning, compared to early years practitioners in schools who were more likely to favour adult-initiated activities as the main vehicle for learning. Regardless of the likely origins of these differences in education and training, the immediate influence can probably be attributed to the practitioners' mental models of good early years practice.

Coherent Evidence-informed Mental Models

Irrespective of their mental model, a practitioner's practice is subject to many constraints from outside influences (Bennett et al., 1997: 119). Their mental model and/or professional training may be at odds with the wishes of parents, colleagues or school inspectors, which may in turn be culturally influenced or value driven and not fully informed by the available evidence. For example, Jiang and Han (2015) and Fung and Cheng (2012) have highlighted the resistance of ethnic Chinese parents to a play-based pedagogy, even when they live in the United States or Hong Kong where much practitioner guidance endorses learning through play. If practitioners cannot articulate a coherent mental model of their own practice they are neither in the best position to be reflective in a constructive way nor well prepared to explain and justify their approach in the face of external pressures. This situation is likely to increase the practitioner's anxiety and create tensions in their practice that cannot be resolved.

Learning about Early Years Practice and Mental Models from the Practitioners

In this section we draw on classroom observations and interviews with a group of practitioners who were involved in an innovative project to shift their pedagogy from a more formal approach to a more play-based and developmentally appropriate curriculum during the first two years of primary school (for a full account of this project, see McGuinness et al., 2009). As the researchers observed their efforts and discussed their concerns, we gained a rich understanding of the challenges and dilemmas facing them. Some practitioners were uncertain as to how the *educational* value of play could be guaranteed. They struggled to see the connection between play as pedagogy and play as the medium to ensure a high level of interest, confidence and overall well-being for children. In order to capture their experiences, I will first describe the classroom practices of the practitioners who were rated as maintaining the highest quality of learning for the children through the use of the Quality Learning Instrument (see Chapter 12). Let's call that group the *play-rich* practitioners; the exact meaning will become clearer as you read on.

Compared to the previous formal approach, the children's day was broken into shorter and more active periods with less emphasis on written work and more opportunities for practical activities (Walsh et al., 2006). For some practitioners, how to divide their time between child-led and adult-led activities became the main issue. In contrast, the play-rich practitioners seemed to resolve this tension by transforming their pedagogy more generally in the direction of playful*ness* across the whole day. For example, although they had designated playtimes, they made great use of play-like activities, such as children playing mathematical games during other, more curriculum-focused tasks. We observed children to be just as engaged during these activities as they were during playtime – indeed one second-year teacher was initially astounded to find that the children celebrated when told it was mathematics task time. These practitioners also encouraged children to view finding information for themselves in books as a valid part of playtime, for example, to find ideas for a guided role play or construction toys. They also had occasional practitioner-directed sessions, but these sessions were short and as playful as they could make them. For example, a whole-class session in story writing led by the practitioner writing on the whiteboard included deliberate mistakes by her that children enjoyed correcting as well as opportunities for the children to suggest humorous aspects of the story.

In contrast, other practitioners did not see how such structured and non-play activities were compatible with a play-based curriculum; they held on to a firmer division between work and play, and had more difficulty apportioning time to practitioner-led versus child-led activities. As explained in Walsh et al. (2011), the play-rich practitioners reconciled their practice with the play-based nature of their developmentally appropriate curriculum by adopting a playful demeanour and low-stakes atmosphere; for a considerable part of the timetable, the emphasis was on playful*ness*, rather than only on play. These practitioners reported that much of the children's time during play sessions was similar to 'free' play. They commented that a practitioner might be interacting with one group to ensure that they made progress or that there was educational value in what they were doing, while at the same time, the majority of children were free from any adult input and children were regulating their own play and progress. Nevertheless, they felt justified in employing more focused and structured activities as long as children remained highly engaged. Children in classes with a greater balance in activities were observed to maintain high levels of engagement, irrespective of the type of activity. It was from these classrooms that the first image of Playful Teaching and Learning (PTL) – that underpins this book – grew.

Dominant Mental Models

This variation in how the early years professionals responded to the challenges of shifting to a more play-based pedagogy led us to look beyond their immediate classroom behaviour and to probe more deeply into what they understood a play-based pedagogy to mean. We began to ask what images of young children's learning and their own role as practitioners might be influencing their classroom behaviour and their interactions with the children. So we began to examine the practitioner interviews for evidence of statements on these issues.

Typically, we found that the practitioners in our study did not adhere to a single coherent mental model of early years practice. They were influenced by a number of perspectives that they had encountered during their specific training for the project, through talking to colleagues, reading relevant research, and most importantly, through their own previous experience as early years educators, as many of them were highly experienced. Nevertheless, their mental models were particularly informed by two dominant perspectives that have been widely observed and indeed critiqued in the early years literature – a maturationist model of child development and a child-led model of early years pedagogy. We will explore these two in greater detail as they have considerable importance for potential roles for the adult in early years pedagogy, and because they are at the heart of developmentally appropriate practice (for a full review of relevant literature, see Walsh et al., 2010).

Example 2.1: It All Depends on the Brain ...

Here are some statements from practitioners, collected in the context of the McGuinness et al. (2009) research, who are expressing their thoughts about the importance of brain maturation.

One practitioner was clearly surprised that the new curriculum was her first introduction to the importance of brain development.

> ... this had never been pointed out to me before – that there were certain channels in a child's brain that hadn't even started to develop (at this age)!

She goes on to suggest that there is some development happening in the child's brain over which she has no direct influence but which will have consequences for what the child can learn. She understands that the child's brain is developing physically in some way and that she will need to recognise that as a limiting factor; the child may not be ready for some kinds of practitioner input, *no matter how skilfully delivered.*

Here is another example of a practitioner revising her previous views with regard to teaching young children and recognising the importance of readiness.

> When I left teacher training college I would have felt that constant practice would have worked wonders with the weaker children and if you just kept going a little bit each day and practised and practised and practised it would get better – but now I can see if children are not ready then there is no point.

These statements point to a maturationist model of early years practice, a model that has been recognised and critiqued by Dickinson (2002) and NAEYC (2009). The main issue with waiting for a child to be ready to learn is that it can lead to an overly passive role for the adult. Table 2.1 summarises both the likely positive and negative outcomes for this approach.

For example, on the positive side, children can experience a gentle transition from pre-school into primary school because the emphasis is on the child's level of development, thus resulting in less pressure for children. On the other hand, children can be just marking time when they could be making progress because the emphasis is all on *waiting* for children to be ready to move on rather than preparing them to be ready. Furthermore, practitioners agonised over the question of identifying when children were ready and hesitated to move them on.

Pause for Thought

What are your thoughts about brain development and children's learning? To what extent is your classroom practice influenced by what you know about brain development?

Example 2.2: Follow the Child …

Here is an example of a practitioner reflecting on the benefits of feeling free to follow the children's own interest rather than pursuing externally imposed learning goals.

> In some of my previous Year 1 classes, you really did get into a battle with some children over doing different things – and that hasn't happened this year (in the new curriculum). I haven't got into that situation because we are not under the same pressure to make children do things.

The above quotation points to a positive outcome from the practitioner's conception of a child-led approach. The practitioner is thinking about whether she really needs to insist on a child undertaking some task or activity, implying that she is willing to consider whether the time is right or that it may be possible for the child to learn by alternative means.

In this next example, the practitioner is saying that she considered it worthwhile to miss out her planned session on phonics in order to follow the children's engagement.

> Today we were doing a literacy activity, 'The World Around Us', and we carried on for longer with it than I had intended because the children were getting so much out of it, which meant we missed out on phonics.
>
> These statements were typical of a more child-led mental model held by the practitioners who were building on the children's interests and allowing the children to make choices about what and when to learn, especially during play.

From the classroom observations, it was clear that children frequently showed high levels of engagement as a result of a child-led approach, enabling them to build on their strengths. Practitioners were often surprised at what they could achieve and realised that in some respects, they had been underestimating children's capabilities. They were thus able to see the value of high levels of engagement in enabling learning to progress. On the other hand, children's learning was also sometimes limited by their choices, for example, when some wanted to spend all of playtime at the computers. Moreover, the play we observed often lacked challenge because the practitioner felt that she could not intervene to give it a new direction, as that would not be consistent with her dominant child-led mental model. Table 2.1 overleaf shows the possible positive and negative consequences of following the child-led approach.

Pause for Thought

To what extent is your classroom practice child-led? What constraints do you experience in shifting your practice to being more or less child-led?

Mental Models Held by Play-rich Practitioners

When we examined the interviews of play-rich practitioners for evidence of mental models, we found that they drew on a wider range of

Table 2.1 Mental models of early years practice

Dominant models	Possible positive implications	Possible negative implications	Finding the balance: Play-rich model
Strong maturationism Progress in the early years depends on, and must wait for physical developments in the brain	Gentle transition into school	Passive teacher role: *Waiting* for children to be ready to learn more rather than *preparing* them to be ready	**Weak maturationism** Physical brain development and learning are seen as interactive, interdependent processes
	Slower pace for late developers so that no child experiences persistent early failure	A facilitating rather than an interventionist approach	Preserves the gentler transition and rich assessment
	Less fixed model of ability because of the possibility of brain development spurts	Teachers not recognising when children are ready to learn more, resulting in children losing interest	A more pro-active pedagogy preparing children to be ready to move forward
	Improved learning dispositions because children have experience of success	Teachers not understanding their role during play	
	Rich and deep assessment		
Child-led model Progress in the early years works best by following children's interests and allowing them to make choices about what and when they learn	Children have improved levels of engagement with activities, leading to better dispositions for learning	Learning is limited by the child's range of experiences and interests	**Child-progress model** A balance between child autonomy/agency and teacher scaffolding
	Teachers learn the value of high engagement in learning	Lack of challenge and experience of struggling to learn	Builds on children's strengths where possible but encourages children to welcome challenge and broaden interests
	Children can display their strengths	Some children display butterfly behaviour, not settling to any activity	High level of teacher skill needed to persuade the child to change behaviour without losing motivation
	Lack of confrontation between teacher and child	Children find it difficult to adjust to a higher level of teacher direction as they move up through school	

perspectives than those discussed above, making more reference to ideas about the positive role of adults through practices such as scaffolding and having conversations with children. They also had a strong sense of *what worked* to progress the children's learning. Moreover, these practitioners had modified the influence of the dominant perspectives in their mental models in ways that seemed to preserve the positive outcomes but not the negative ones. These modified approaches are summarised in the last column of Table 2.1.

Thus, instead of the strong model of maturationism summarised in the first column of Table 2.1, the play-rich practitioners expressed a weaker version. Their preparation for a more developmentally appropriate curriculum had given them a new understanding of brain development. They reported thinking more deeply than before about physical brain development being a limiting factor in what the child was ready to learn, thus recognising the need to give some children more time to progress than they would have previously. For example, they appreciated fully the desirability of establishing good language and emergent reading skills before children were asked to undertake more structured reading sessions. On the other hand, they correctly saw brain development and learning as *interactive* processes (Johnson, 2001), with learning being able to *stimulate* brain development as well as vice versa. Thus, their pedagogical role was to *prepare* children to be ready to move on rather than *waiting* for them to be ready – a much more proactive pedagogy.

Rather than being exclusively child-led, these practitioners focused on what was needed for the child to make progress. While there were many opportunities in their classrooms to allow the children autonomy and while they often responded to the children's interests by being flexible with their lesson plans, they also did not hesitate to gently insist on a child's change of activity if they felt that was appropriate. However, their approach tended to be subtle rather than heavy-handed, to avoid negatively affecting the child's motivation. For example,

> the practitioner might ask a child, 'Have you painted a picture for me yet?' The inclusion of the word 'yet' in this question conveyed the idea that the child had already decided to paint a picture but that the decision as to when it was painted was up to the child. (Walsh et al., 2011: 113)

Children readily fell in with similar delicate suggestions with every appearance of high enthusiasm.

Play-rich practitioners were also able to structure children's role play in the manner described by Leong and Bodrova (2012), who advocated a more Vygotskian approach to early years pedagogy, in which practitioner intervention is actively encouraged. By 'setting the stage' for the children's role play, using stories and discussion beforehand and scaffolding the action only when required, practitioners can support progress in role play without dominating the action. Thus, over time, children become better able to sustain role play/drama and become more sophisticated in the use of props. These writers argued that role play *progressed* through a series of well-defined stages, developing increasing degrees of abstraction that are hypothesised to further symbolic thinking. During these and other types of structured sessions, the play-rich practitioners maintained a playful tone, showing a ready understanding of young children's humour and keeping the atmosphere light.

Throughout, play-rich practitioners assessed the situation before crafting any intervention with a child who was highly engaged. Such assessments weighed the possible benefit of an intervention against the possibility that the flow of the play or activity might be lost. Where possible, the intervention was also playful. By this sensitivity, these practitioners showed how much they valued play and believed that their pedagogy enhanced it – to the extent of claiming that their children "really know how to play" – while at the same time believing in the balance between play and more structured activities. These practitioners also had firm ideas about how, as children progressed up through school, activity-based learning should continue to retain an element of playfulness but gradually of a more adult kind, such as playing with ideas. Thus, children would experience less discontinuity as they transition between classes.

Mental Models and Balance

While much of previous discussions about balance have been about balance between types of learning activities (child-initiated versus adult-initiated, teaching versus play) and the time spent on them, this chapter has sought to draw attention to the importance of balance in what early years practitioner *think* about early years practice – their mental models – and how these can shape what they do in classrooms and thus shape the child's learning and experience.

We drew on the stories of early years practitioners in primary schools who were embracing a change in classroom practice, particularly on the group who were identified as being play-rich. These practitioners who have developed more coherent, balanced mental models of early years pedagogy were able to access the full range of pedagogical approaches; relatively free play, more structured play (e.g., the role play described above), play-like activities such as mathematical games, short didactic sessions, very short repetition sessions and interactive story sessions. Rather than their mental models being dominated by a single perspective, they were open to new ideas; they were always considering the outcomes for the children in order to reflect on any changes that might be needed. At the same time, they strove to be playful, whether during play episodes or during other activities.

Practitioners who developed more balanced models were confident in their pedagogy and in its outcomes for children. They were following a flexible interpretation of a play-based curriculum. They were thus less prone to stress than those whose practice was shaped by the dominant models. The balanced models had other very clear benefits. Their more elastic interpretation made for an easy transition from the earliest early years towards the later ones. Being willing to be flexible, practitioners with a balanced approach had little difficulty with a gradual change from longer periods spent in relatively free play towards the activity-based learning and written work that would gradually become more prevalent as children moved towards the later years of primary school. Equally, they could allow for individual differences in development by adjusting the balance according to the needs of the individual. Their guiding star was not a prescriptive curriculum, either in content or in pedagogy; it was being responsive to the needs of each child with every pedagogical skill at their disposal within the playful learning approach.

Key Messages

- What early years practitioners **think** about early years practice – their mental models – is an important factor in shaping what they do in the classroom.
- Mental models are particularly important for a play-based curriculum as practitioners have more autonomy in shaping children's experiences compared to a more prescribed curriculum.
- Early years professionals can develop mental models dominated by a single perspective or they can have more balanced and coherent models drawn from several perspectives, as in the example of the play-rich practitioners.
- Articulating mental models is very important for professional learning and development.

Further Reading

Dunkin, D. and Hanna, P. (2001) *Thinking Together: Quality Child Interactions*. Wellington, New Zealand: New Zealand Council for Educational Research.

Leong, D.J. and Bodrova, E. (2015) 'Assessing and scaffolding: Make-believe play', *Young Children* 67 (1): 28-34. https://www.naeyc.org/files/yc/file/201201/Leong_Make_Believe_Play_Jan2012.pdf (accessed 30 August 2016).

Walsh, G., Sproule, L., McGuinness, C. and Trew, K. (2011) 'Playful structure: A novel image of early years pedagogy for primary school classrooms', *Early Years*, 31 (2): 107-19.

References

Bennett, N., Wood, E. and Rogers C. (1997) *Teaching through Play: Teachers' Thinking and Classroom Practice*. Buckingham: Open University Press.

Clark, C. M. (1986) 'Ten years of conceptual development in research on teachers' thinking', in M.B. Peretz, R. Bromme and R. Halkes (eds), *Advances of Research on Teacher Thinking*. Lisse, Netherlands: Swots and Zeitlinger.

Dickinson, D.K. (2002) 'Shifting images of developmentally appropriate practice as seen through different lenses', *Educational Researcher* 31: 26–32.

Dunkin, D. and Hanna, P. (2001) *Thinking Together: Quality Child Interactions*. Wellington, New Zealand: New Zealand Council for Educational Research.

Fisher, J. and Wood, E. (2012) 'Changing educational practice in the early years through practitioner-led action research: An adult–child interaction project', *International Journal of Early Years Education* 20 (2): 114–29.

Fung, C. and Cheng, D. (2012) 'Consensus or dissensus? Stakeholders' views on the role of play in learning', *Early Years: An International Research Journal* 32 (1): 17–33.

Jiang, S. and Han, M. (2015) 'Parental beliefs on children's play: Comparison among mainland Chinese, Chinese immigrants in the USA, and European-Americans', *Early Child Development and Care* 186 (3): 341–52.

Johnson, M.H. (2001) 'Functional brain development in humans', *Nature Reviews Neuroscience* 2 (7): 475–83.

Leong, D.J. and Bodrova, E. (2012) 'Assessing and scaffolding: Make-believe play', *Young Children* 67(1): 28–34.

Martlew, J., Stephen, C. and Ellis, J. (2011) 'Play in the primary school classroom? The experience of teachers supporting children's learning through a new pedagogy', *Early Years: An International Journal of Research and Development* 31 (1): 71–83.

McGuinness, C., Sproule, L., Walsh, G. and Trew, K. (2009) *Inside EC Classrooms and Schools: Children, Teachers and School Principals*. Belfast: CCEA. http://ccea.org.uk/sites/default/files/docs/research_statistics/early_years/2_Inside_Classrooms.pdf (accessed 30 August 2016).

McInnes, K., Howard, J., Miles, G. and Crowley, K. (2011) 'Differences in practitioners' understanding of play and how this influences pedagogy and children's perceptions of play', *Early Years: An International Journal of Research and Development* 31 (2): 121–33.

NAEYC (National Association for the Education of Young Children) (2009) *Developmentally Appropriate Practice in Early Childhood Programs Serving Children from Birth through Age 8. Position Statement*. Washington, DC: National Association for the Education of Young Children. www.naeyc.org/files/naeyc/file/positions/position%20statement%20Web.pdf (accessed 30 August 2016).

Siraj-Blatchford, I. and Sylva, K. (2004) 'Researching pedagogy in English pre-schools', *British Educational Research Journal* 30 (5): 713–30.

Verenikina, I. (2004) 'From theory to practice: What does the metaphor of scaffolding mean to educators today?' *Outlines: Critical Social Studies* 6 (2): 5–16.

Walsh, G., Sproule, L., McGuinness, C., Trew, K., Rafferty, H. and Sheehy, N. (2006) 'An appropriate curriculum for the 4–5 year old child in Northern Ireland: Comparing play-based and formal approaches', *Early Years: An International Journal of Research and Development* 26 (2): 201–21.

Walsh, G., Sproule, L., McGuinness, C., Trew, K. and Ingram, G. (2010) *Developmentally Appropriate Practice and Play-Based Pedagogy in Early Years Education: A Literature Review of Research and Practice*. Belfast: CCEA. www.nicurriculum.org.uk/docs/foundation_stage/eye_curric_project/evaluation/Literature_Review.pdf (accessed 30 August 2016).

Walsh, G., Sproule, L., McGuinness, C. and Trew, K. (2011) 'Playful structure: A novel image of early years pedagogy for primary school classrooms', *Early Years: An International Journal of Research and Development* 31 (2): 107–19.

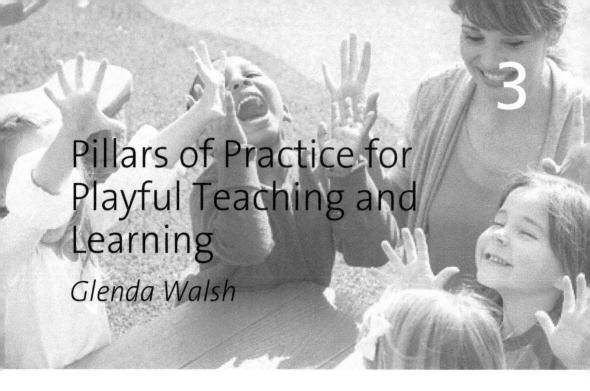

Pillars of Practice for Playful Teaching and Learning

Glenda Walsh

Chapter Overview

In the opening chapter of this book, the concept of 'Playful Teaching and Learning' (PTL) was introduced as a fruitful way forward for teachers, enabling them to blur boundaries between play and learning, and play and work. In this chapter I intend to go further and I begin to unpick the fundamentals of playful teaching and learning which I have termed 'pillars of practice'. I have used the term 'pillar' as it implies the idea of a support, and we anticipate providing early years practitioners with the supporting structure of PTL, which will enable them to fully synchronise playing, teaching and learning in the context of the early years setting or classroom. The pillars identified within this chapter draw on and develop the initial thinking of Walsh et al. (2010) in their handbook: *Playful Structure: Six Pillars of Developmentally Appropriate Practice.*

The Role of Teaching in Play

As a teacher educator, I am often confronted with challenging questions from undergraduate students. Sharon posed the question:

As a student teacher, why would I need to take a module on play? It is all about being child-centred, is it not? All teachers are expected to do is to sit back and watch and there's nothing very challenging about that ... I came to university to learn how to teach children and advance their knowledge and understanding of different aspects of the curriculum – not to wait for children to discover by themselves. You really wouldn't need too many qualifications to do that.

Sharon's experience or lack of experience up to this point had led her to believe that play was all about being child-centred and, for her, being child-centred was associated with everything other than teaching. From her perspective, child-centred theories advocated a teacher who is almost invisible, who acts as little more than a provider of resources, who simply follows the lead of the child. Subsequently, Sharon did sign up for the module and has since become an outstanding early years teacher. Yet, her narrow-minded reflection on early years education, although personal to her, mirrors that of many others in society as a whole. In our efforts to ensure a shift away from formal education for our youngest children and to provide them with a pedagogical approach that is more developmentally appropriate, Early Years Education, it seems, has distanced itself from anything that is associated with 'teaching'. As a result, the role of the teacher in children's learning has almost been relegated to the sidelines (Langford, 2010).

The central thesis of this book is that the concept of Playful Teaching and Learning (PTL) revitalises the role of teaching and learning within children's playful experiences but *not* at the expense of neglecting the children's interest, their enjoyment and sheer fun. Drawing on evidence from different strands of the Enriched Curriculum research (McGuinness et al., 2010), the growing evidence base calling for a more balanced pedagogical approach in the early years (Wood, 2010), together with a more explicit role on the part of the early years teacher (Fleer, 2015), I propose that the concept of PTL requires the early years teacher to create certain conditions in the early years setting or 'pillars of practice'. Although these pillars, in some cases, may at first sight appear slightly contradictory, they are, like any supporting pillar, each needed for a specific purpose and goal in creating the necessary conditions for a successful and fully blended PTL approach. I turn now to discussing each of these pillars.

Pillar 1: Establish Caring Yet Nurturing Relationships

Establishing secure relationships is foundational for enhancing children's social and emotional wellbeing (Bergin and Bergin, 2009) and for transforming the principle of PTL into practice. If we want children to feel confident to express their own ideas, make mistakes without fear of failure, take risks on a daily basis and think outside the box, it goes without saying that the ethos of the school or setting must be warm and encouraging. As Bergin and Bergin (2009: 150) argue, to be truly effective, "teachers must connect with and care for children with warmth, respect and trust". The benefits of such healthy relationships with teaching staff for later academic outcomes have also been well documented (e.g., Mashburn and Pianta, 2006). Such thinking is reinforced in a recent study by Hamre et al. (2014), which involved approximately 1,400 preschool children and 325 early childhood teachers from across the USA. Not only did they study how children developed socially and academically, they also investigated the ways teachers taught. Hamre and her team found that it was not just the quality of the instructional interactions that mattered for children's academic progress, but also what they termed 'responsive teaching' which involved teachers' sensitivity in responding to children, the ability to foster positive relationships and respect for children's autonomy.

Of course most early years settings/classrooms are already warm and welcoming places; the challenge is to ensure that every child is secure in their relationship with the teacher and that children are secure with one another. Children arrive in early years classrooms with their own unique history of family relationships and attachments (Walsh et al., 2010). However, evidence from Buyse et al. (2009) suggests that even children who are less securely attached to their mothers can form quite positive relationships with their teachers, provided that teachers are sensitive enough to the children's specific needs.

The role of the practitioner in securing a positive relationship with young children is therefore paramount. Nevertheless, Hayes (2008) cautions against an overly narrow definition of the caring role of the adult, perceived principally as 'mothering', in a setting-based context. Such an image, she points out, obscures the critical educational value of early years education and the complex intellectual challenge of working with young children. Instead she argues for the need to reconceptualise the word 'care' as 'nurture', not in an effort to undermine the importance that should be placed on developing a sound rapport with young children, but rather to move beyond the "gentle smiles" and "warm hugs" (p. 437) image where the adult has a more educative role in nurturing the affective and dispositional aspects of learning. In her opinion, the word nurture or, more specifically, "nurturing pedagogy" places greater emphasis on engaged levels of interaction between children and adults, requiring the adult to "actively nourish, rear, foster, train and educate the child through his or her practice" (Hayes, 2008: 437).

In this way the role of the nurturing teacher supports young children in their efforts to develop the toolkit which will enable them to build what

Claxton et al. (2011) refer to as "learning power". Here the emphasis is placed not only on ensuring that children are happy, safe and secure in their learning environment but that the care of the mind is addressed in its fullest sense, where children's confidence, self-esteem, tolerance, resilience and social awareness are nurtured and their abilities to concentrate, persevere, reason, predict, analyse and question are appropriately fostered.

Sheridan and Pramling-Samuelsson (2013: 219) remind us of the bi-dimensional nature of the young child, perceived as both "beings and becomings". In their opinion young children can be competent and capable, but also vulnerable and dependent on support and care. In an effort to respond effectively to their complex nature, it is imperative that a sensitive and delicate pedagogy is embraced where caring for children's needs and nurturing their dispositions become fully intertwined to ensure effective learning takes place. Consider the following case study in a composite class where children are aged 4–6 years.

Case Study 3.1: The Café Society

The teacher, Mrs Davis, takes her snack with the children. She calls it her Café Society and sees it as an opportunity to further develop oral language work with a class of children many of whom have come to school with poor language skills. The children fetch their own break and take it back to their seats. One girl, Jemima, immediately claims to have a healthy break. She does not put up her hand before she speaks. Mrs Davis asks Jemima to say what she has to eat and drink. Jemima names flavoured water, an apple and a cheese portion. Another boy chimes in that he has a healthy break too and names the contents of his box. Children now vie with each other to claim healthy eating habits. One boy, George, is accused of having a fizzy drink, against school rules. Mrs Davis asks him in a conversational tone whether that is true and makes a joke about it. When George acknowledges it, she remonstrates but more in the manner of a peer than a teacher. Meanwhile three boys at another table are talking about football and ignoring this conversation entirely. The main conversation changes direction when one girl says her mummy is expecting a baby next week. Mrs Davis says that she knows that and takes a genuine interest in the expected event, asking a number of pertinent questions. Then she turns to another girl and says, "Your sister is going to have a baby too, isn't she?" The two girls launch into excited comparisons of preparations.

Pause for Thought

Think about the cameo above and consider what strategies the teacher is using to build up a caring relationship with the group of children involved.

How, in your opinion, is the practitioner nurturing the young children's confidence to participate in this relaxed situation?

Hayes advises us that too much emphasis can be placed on the custodial side of care, yet Sheridan and Pramling-Samuelsson caution that we must be mindful that young children are still vulnerable and dependent to some extent. What challenges might arise in practice from attempting to blend care and education in an early years context?

Pillar 2: Enjoy Playful Yet Skilful Interactions

The concept of PTL invites the early years teacher to actively participate in the young child's learning experiences, based on the notion that adults' participation in children's playful experiences is "an essential part of a teacher's job" (Hakkarainen et al., 2013: 223) as it is vital for provoking higher order learning, including learning content knowledge (Hedges, 2014). However, evidence suggests that teachers' interactions, particularly in children's play, have been conceptualised principally as a simple binary, that is, as either being involved or not involved (Fleer, 2015). When involved, teachers' interactions tend to be classified in terms of passive roles such as facilitator, observer, mediator and when involved they can sometimes be accused of "smuggling curriculum content" (Hedges, 2014: 198) into the learning experience or what Davis and Peters refer to as "hijacking the direction of learning" (2011: 5). In these latter cases, the interactions tend to comprise artificial questioning such as "what shape is this?", "what colour is that?", and "how many are there?", interrupting in some cases the flow of children's learning rather than actually accentuating it (Hunter and Walsh, 2014).

Howard and McInness (2013) argue that the role of the educator as 'play partner' has been greatly underplayed in practice and it is this construct of 'playfulness' that is an essential ingredient of the interactions in the concept of PTL. Evidence from the Enriched Curriculum classes highlighted that in high-quality settings, teachers were able to adopt a playful approach with young children with relative ease (Walsh et al., 2011). From Wood's (2010) perspective, playful ways of interacting with others comprise humour, teasing, jokes, mimicry, riddles, rhymes, singing, etc.; whilst playful approaches refers to the creative, imaginative and flexible ways in which materials and resources can be used. For Wood, playful moods can range from wild and boisterous to moments of focused contemplation. Howard and McInness (2013) emphasise that children need playful adults to engage with them in meaningful ways to make the experience more stimulating, enjoyable and entertaining. In essence, the characteristics of playful interactions between adults and children, can be summarised as:

- being intrinsically motivating, engaging and enjoyable;
- being light-hearted in tone in the sense of being free from stress for both parties; and
- leaving some room for spontaneity.

(Walsh et al., 2010: 14)

Yet if interactions on the part of the early years teacher were deemed solely to be playful, the experience could be categorised simply as mere frivolity or indeed silliness. Therefore it is essential that such interactions are appropriately skilful in an effort to deepen and extend the learning potential. Hakkarainen et al. (2013) clarify how such playful interactions can also become skilful in nature. They argue that adults need to:

- observe and try to catch children's play ideas – their initiatives;
- step into children's play and expand upon the initial idea of the child;
- get involved in joint play with a child or children;
- reach togetherness with a flow of mutual experience – this is the highest level of play involvement; and
- ensure genuine participation in joint play activities develops all participants – both children and adults.

(Hakkarainen et al., 2013: 224)

Through the use of stories and a narrative form of role play, Hakkarainen et al. (2013) illustrate how playful, yet skilful, interactions on the part of the children and practitioner can become intertwined. They indicate that at first a motivating theme should be captured for the purposes of the role play scenario, characterised as spontaneous, improvisational and creative. Then a coherent storyline through dialogic interactions with children must be constructed by the adults involved, taking into account the children's ideas at all times. Emotional involvement of all participants – adults and children – is, in their opinion, a key feature of the interaction. A dramatic tension then should be introduced into the role play scenario and the resultant experience should be highly challenging and motivating, where according to Hakkarainen and Bredikyte (2014: 249) "the joint play of adults and children creates collective higher mental functions".

Likewise, Van Oers and Duijkers (2013) provide guidance on how to deepen and extend the playful experience through adult interaction. Although they are referring to role play situations specifically, such skilful pedagogical strategies could be used in a variety of playful situations. They refer to five key 'impulses' which they believe should be part of the 'expert teachers' repertoire'. These are:

- Orienting – teachers explore the situation and related activities with the children and focus the children's attention on specific aspects or actions.
- Structuring and deepening – the teacher tries to set the scene with the children by introducing a problem and discussing what is to be done – in this way adding more detail, structure and depth to the activity.
- Broadening – connecting the role play activity with other activities and capacities for children. For example, in the doctor's play, children can be encouraged to think about the waiting room and how to decorate it, including leaflets, posters, etc., drawing the children into writing and drawing texts.
- Contributing – introducing new resources into the play scenario that respond to the children's specific interests and requests.
- Reflecting – encouraging the children to get involved in discussion about the on-going playful experience which have important evaluative functions but also provide opportunities for new ideas and developments to emerge.

(Van Oers and Duijkers, 2013: 518–19)

Case Study 3.2: The Presence of Mr Wonka

A class of 6–7 year old children has been working extremely hard with their teacher over the past number of weeks learning about Willy Wonka and his Chocolate Factory. This morning, they have been advised that a special visitor will be coming into their classroom at some point in the day. Unknown to the children the visitor is actually the famous Mr Wonka himself. After lunch, the teacher enters the classroom dressed as Willy Wonka and thanks the children for all the superb work they have been doing on the theme of chocolate. Then Mr Wonka explains that he has a major problem. Unfortunately his design team have all gone down with the flu and he has no one to design the wrappers for his new chocolate bars. He has chosen this class at Primrose Gardens School to take up the challenge.

The children were ecstatic. Their brains went into advanced power where they started to offer suggestions and possibilities. Mr Wonka then produced chefs' hats, aprons and tablecloths, along with boxes of unwrapped chocolate bars. The children chose which chocolate station they wanted to work at, where there was an array of materials to enable them to make their designs. During this time, Mr Wonka visited each of the chocolate wrapper stations, consulting on designs and offering his advice when needed. He reminded them to think of the target audience, to consider the colours they were using and to come up with an original and exciting name for their bar that would entice other children to buy it. Jessica was very busy at her design and had come up with the word 'delicious' for her bar. She explained to Mr Wonka that she wanted her wrapper to look nice but also to smell nicely, but she could not think of how she might create that 'chocolatey' smell. Mr Wonka thought for a minute and then came up with the idea of rolling her wrapper when finished in chocolate powder or maybe even painting the design using melted chocolate. Deciding upon the latter, immediately they both set to task, melting chocolate in the nearby microwave. Soon other children decided that this might be a good idea too. After one hour's work of intense labour where all children were completely engrossed and on task, Mr Wonka congratulated the children on their hard work and stressed that he would bring the wrappers back with him to his factory and ensure that all of their designs would be put to good use.

Pause for Thought

Consider the 'teacher in role' strategy. Reflect on the opportunities and challenges such an experience might afford in the early years classroom/setting.

In light of what you have read above, consider the playful strategies that are being used in this more structured task to deepen young children's learning and reflect on how you might use some of them in practice.

Reflect on Van Oers' key impulses. In what ways does the teacher in the above scenario make use of any of these in an effort to foster deeper learning?

Pillar 3: Create Enjoyable Yet Challenging Opportunities

PTL also embraces the notion that experiences offered to young children should be interesting and enjoyable, yet appropriately purposeful and challenging, in line with Barrett's thinking (2005: 162) when he talks about "hard fun". Drawing on ideas from Papert (1996) within the field of computer technology, Barrett argues that learning is fun because it is appropriately challenging and actually stretches the young mind. Such thinking resonates with the earlier work of Laevers (2000), which stresses the need for children to be fully involved for quality learning to take place. In this way Barrett (2005: 174) argues that the fun in "hard fun" should not be perceived as superficial, but rather a fun that is rigorous and demanding. For him, "fun without hardness is frivolity – hardness without fun is drudgery".

But the difficult question is: how can we ensure such "hard fun" experiences in practice? Whilst play has been perceived as the medium through which young children learn best, evidence articulated in Chapter 1 suggests that in practice it can be low-level, immature and sometimes even boring. In many cases the experiences offered to children are subordinated to policy directives and are aligned too closely with levels of progression and an assessment-led agenda. It would seem that complex and high-level opportunities and experiences to develop and enhance young children's cognitive powers of thinking and creativity are not always put into practice (Hunter and Walsh, 2014). Recent research, however, has been trying to identify what these rich opportunities look like which, on the one hand, allow for fun and enjoyment, but likewise are purposeful, meaningful and enrich young children's learning. For example, Wood (2010) emphasises that a degree of choice, control and imagination should be allowed for in an effort to retain the joy of childhood but, in so doing, the competent teacher should also make connections between children's own interests and goals and between educational goals and those of the curriculum. In this way a more meaningful experience for children and adults will take place.

In a similar vein, Hedges (2014) advocates the use of inquiry-based experiences in the early years setting which build upon children's interests and already acquired "funds of knowledge" – for example, their everyday knowledge of experiences such as economics, household maintenance, literacy and the arts – as a means of allowing enjoyment and challenge to thrive. In this way, teachers grasp a deeper and richer understanding of what is intriguing for the child and afford them opportunities to respond in meaningful ways. Using a "funds of knowledge" approach, according to Hedges (2014), opens up possibilities of reconciling playful experiences with prior knowledge that is relevant to the content of the curriculum and, in so doing, enables children to address aspects of the curriculum in a more meaningful, individualised and engaging manner. Taking children's interest in food preparation as an example, Hedges (2014: 193) illustrates how, by tuning into how children pretend to go shopping, prepare food and then share the food with others, teachers can make authentic links with early content knowledge across a range of subject areas:

- writing shopping lists and reading recipes (Literacy);
- weighing and measuring items and pricing and paying for goods and services (Mathematics);
- cooking and preparing food (Science);
- choosing goods and services according to the budget (Economics);
- learning to negotiate roles, solve problems and deal with conflict (Social Sciences).

Following this line of reasoning, it can be seen that enriching children's interest-based experiences with content learning possibilities provides a genuine foundation for enabling enjoyable yet challenging experiences to be fully realised in practice.

The work of Broadhead and Burt (2012) helps us to clarify how experiences can retain their enjoyment but yet afford opportunities for depth and challenge. All too often we see play experiences in an early years context which are restricting and narrow in approach. Let's take, for example, the grocer's shop area, where shopkeepers have been assigned to play for the morning and where a few used food containers are on display, alongside a tiny, plastic cash register. Initially some customers pass by and voice their requests but before very long the shopkeepers find themselves with very little to do and hence either move on to a new activity or become bored and frustrated in the process, without ever engaging in purposeful and meaningful playful learning. Instead, Broadhead and Burt promote use of authentic resources that are rich in possibilities and adventure, where milk crates, barrels, cable reels, ropes, tubing, netting, etc., transform into 'whatever you want it to be places' – where children get a real opportunity to be highly imaginative and creative, where a spirit of investigation and enquiry is promoted and a sense of agency established with the support of highly competent teachers. In a similar context, Bodrova (2008), who was involved in pioneering an early years programme based on Vygotskian principles called 'Tools of the Mind', suggests that modern children have become over-used to complex, prescriptive toys, to the extent that they find it difficult to engage in imaginative role-playing unless they have the right toy. The Tools of the Mind programme draws on Vygotskian ideas and thus considers complex socio-dramatic play with minimal props to be crucial at this early stage of a young child's development. Consequently, the classroom environment and materials should be flexible and to the child's eye open-ended, with materials able to play versatile roles and children able to easily draw connections between different areas in the classroom, and move materials from one area to another. Such affordances provided by differing materials are discussed more fully by Jacqueline Fallon in Chapter 11 of this book.

When early years educators work in this way, it is also important not to overlook the 'behind the scenes' activity that Siraj-Blatchford and her team describe as "pedagogical framing" or a form of structure. Establishing the environment in a way to allow for such enriching enquiry-based experiences to occur is a complex task requiring much thinking on the part of the early years teacher in advance of the implementation process. According to Siraj-Blatchford et al. (2002), pedagogical framing requires planning, assessment, consideration of resources, the establishment of routines and the arrangement of space. Ensuring that such activity takes place in an implicit and covert way cannot be over-emphasised in an effort to allow for spontaneity, flexibility and enjoyment, yet enabling meaningful learning to take place.

Case Study 3.3: The Special Egg

During outdoor play in Orchard nursery school with 3–4 year old children, Hannah discovered a large egg hidden beneath a pile of autumn leaves just next to Meg, the wooden dinosaur climbing structure. Filled with excitement, she ran immediately to Mrs Chess, the nursery teacher, who appeared intrigued by Hannah's discovery. She advised Hannah to carry it carefully inside and put it in a safe place until outdoor playtime was over. Hannah, accompanied by Miss Brown, the nursery assistant, chose a basket to keep the egg safe and suggested that it would be good to have a blanket to keep it warm as her new baby brother Sam had a nice comfy blanket for his pram. On returning from the outdoors Mrs Chess encouraged the children to go into the quiet room because Hannah had something very important to show them. When Hannah revealed her discovery, the children were ecstatic.

They all wanted to know what it was – some said a dragon's egg, others suggested a baby monster but when Hannah explained that she found it under Dino – Bobbie shouted "Meg has had a baby – it is a dinosaur egg, of course". Then Sophie thought it might be a good idea to Google it to see if other dinosaur eggs look like theirs and then Mollie added; "Is it really alive?". Mrs Chess asked the children what they might do to find out and after several suggestions they thought a stethoscope could be a helpful device. On deciding that they could hear a heartbeat, Mrs Chess suggested that they would keep it in the basket beside the radiator with Hannah's little blanket on top and that they would keep watch over it until the end of school and then Miss Brown would take it home with her for the weekend. The children seemed content with this, so long as she would look after it very carefully.

To the children's delight on Monday morning, the egg had hatched in Miss Brown's kitchen over the weekend. All that remained was its shell. The children were so excited when Miss Brown came into the nursery holding a big box with a blanket over it. Oh, what can it be? There in the box was a big moving 'something'. How were they going to find out what it was? They felt it, they stroked it, they talked to it but they could not work out what it was. Then entered Dr Kirkpatrick, dressed in a white coat, with glasses and a stethoscope around his neck from London Zoo (the local biology teacher, really) who advised the children that it was a baby gecko. After much discussion about what he ate, where he slept and whether it was a boy or a girl, the children decided that he could be called Greg. They agreed it was probably best if he went back to London Zoo as they could look after him very well and Dr Kirkpatrick added that he would send them emails from time to time to let them know how Greg was doing. Bye bye special egg!

Pause for Thought

In what ways does this snapshot of practice provide a fun but challenging experience for the children?

How does the teacher make use of children's own interests or funds of knowledge to inspire learning?

Key Messages

In this chapter we have learned that:

- The role of the teacher is of paramount importance to the quality of the PTL experience.
- The fundamentals of the PTL experience have been described as pillars of practice.
- Each pillar brings its own unique contribution to the overarching framework.
- Pillar 1 requires the early years practitioner to balance caring for children's needs and interests alongside nurturing children's dispositions and affective strategies to enable them to be successful learners.
- Pillar 2 showcases how teacher interactions require a degree of playfulness to initiate interest on the part of the child and to ensure full acceptance by them. Likewise such interactions must also be appropriately skilful to ensure that learning is drip-fed into the situation in a natural and what appears to be a spontaneous manner.
- In Pillar 3, we learn that the teacher's role in the PTL experience is also about creating experiences that are enjoyable yet effectively challenging to maintain interest and guarantee stretch, extension and progression within children's learning at all times.
- Although each pillar is of separate importance, when combined in any early years setting or classroom, they form an effective framework to guarantee an effective learning experience for the 3–8 year old children involved.

Further Reading

Wood, E. (2013) *Play, Learning and the Early Childhood Curriculum* (third edition). London: Sage.

References

Barrett, T. (2005) 'Who said learning couldn't be enjoyable, playful and fun?', in E. Poikela and S. Poikela (eds), *PBL in Context: Bridging Work and Education.* Tampere: Tampere University Press. pp. 159–77.

Bergin, C. and Bergin, D. (2009) 'Attachment in the classroom', *Educational Psychological Review* 21: 141–70.

Bodrova, E. (2008) 'Make-believe play versus academic skills: A Vygotskian approach to today's dilemma of early childhood education', *European Early Childhood Education Research Journal* 16 (3): 357–69.

Broadhead, P. and Burt, A. (2012) *Understanding Young Children's Learning through Play: Playful Pedagogies.* Abingdon: Routledge

Buyse, E., Verschueren, K. and Doumen, S. (2009) 'Preschoolers' attachment to mother and risk for adjustment problems in kindergarten: Can teachers make a difference?', *Social Development* 20 (1): 33–50.

Claxton, G., Chambers, M., Powell, G. and Lucas, B. (2011) *The Learning Powered School: Pioneering 21st Century Education.* Bristol: TLO Ltd.

Davis, K. and Peters, S. (2011) 'Moments of wonder, everyday events: Children's working theories in action'. *Teaching and Learning Research Initiative.* www. tlri.org.nz/sites/default/files/projects/9266_%20davis-summaryreport.pdf (accessed 13 September 2016).

Fleer, M. (2015) 'Pedagogical positioning in play – teachers being inside and out-side of children's imaginary play', *Early Child Development and Care* 185 (11–12): 1801–14.

Hakkarainen, P. and Bredikyte, M. (2014) 'Understanding narrative as a key aspect of play', in L. Brooker, M. Blaise and S. Edwards (eds), *The Sage Handbook of Play and Learning in Early Childhood.* London: Sage. pp. 240–51.

Hakkarainen, P., Bredikyte, M., Jakkula, K. and Munter, H. (2013) 'Adult play guid-ance and children's play development in a narrative play-world', *European Early Childhood Education Research Journal* 21 (2): 213–25.

Hamre, B., Hatfield, B., Pianta, R. and Jamil, F. (2014) 'Evidence for general and domain specific elements of teacher–child interactions: Associations with pre-school children's development', *Child Development* 85 (3): 1257–74.

Hayes, N. (2008) 'Teaching matters in early practice: The case for a nurturing peda-gogy', *Early Education and Development* 19 (3): 430–40.

Hedges, H. (2014) 'Children's content learning in play provision: Competing tensions and future possibilities'. In L. Brooker, M. Blaise and S. Edwards (eds), *The Sage Handbook of Play and Learning in Early Childhood.* London: Sage. pp. 192–203.

Howard, J. and McInness, K. (2013) *The Essence of Play.* Abingdon: Routledge.

Hunter, T. and Walsh, G. (2014) 'From policy to practice?: The reality of play in primary school classes in Northern Ireland', *International Journal of Early Years Education* 22 (1): 19–36.

Laevers, F. (2000) 'Forward to basics! Deep-level learning and the experiential approach', *Early Education* 20: 20–9.

Langford, R. (2010) 'Critiquing child-centred pedagogy to bring children and early childhood education into the centre of democratic pedagogy', *Contemporary Issues in Early Childhood* 11 (1): 113–27.

Mashburn, A. and Pianta, R. (2006) 'Social relationships and school readiness', *Early Education and Development* 17 (1): 151–76.

McGuinness, C., Sproule, L., Walsh, G. and Trew, K. (2010) *EYECEP: Report 2. Inside EC Classrooms and Schools: Children, Teachers and School Principals.* Belfast: CCEA.

Papert, S. (1996) *The Connected Family: Bridging the Digital Generation Gap.* Atlanta, Georgia: Longstreet Press.

Sheridan, S. and Pramling-Samuelsson, I. (2013) 'Preschool a source for young children's learning and well-being', *International Journal of Early Years Education* 21 (2): 207–22.

Siraj-Blatchford, I., Sylva, K., Muttock, S., Gilden, R. and Bell, D. (2002) 'Researching effective pedagogy in the early years', *Research Report Number 356.* London: HMSO. www.327matters.org/Docs/RR356.pdf (accessed 13 September 2016).

Van Oers, B. and Duijkers, D. (2013) 'Teaching in a play-based curriculum: Theory, practice and evidence of developmental education for young children', *Journal of Curriculum Studies* 45 (4): 511–34.

Walsh, G., Sproule, L., McGuinness, C. and Trew, K. (2010) 'Playful structure: Six pillars of developmentally appropriate practice'. *Research Report.* http://www.nicurriculum.org.uk/docs/foundation_stage/eye_curric_project/evaluation/Playful_Structure_Handbook.pdf (accessed 30 August 2016).

Walsh, G., Sproule, L., McGuinness, C. and Trew, K. (2011) 'Playful structure: A novel image of early years pedagogy for primary school classrooms', *Early Years* 31 (2): 107–19.

Wood, E. (2010) 'Developing integrated pedagogical approaches to play and learning', in P. Broadhead, J. Howard and E. Wood (eds), *Play and Learning in the Early Years.* London: Sage. pp. 9–26.

Section 2
Playful Teaching and Learning across the Curriculum

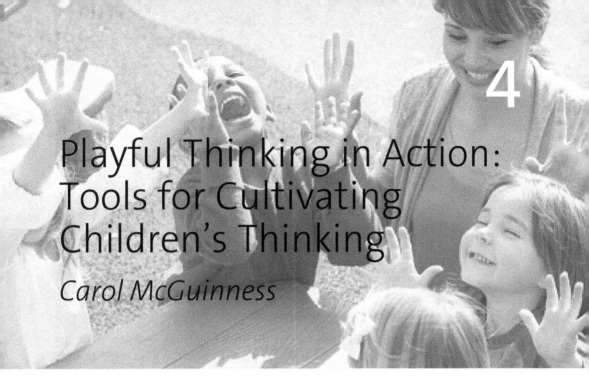

Playful Thinking in Action: Tools for Cultivating Children's Thinking

Carol McGuinness

4

Chapter Overview

By the end of the chapter, I hope you can:

- Recognise the importance of explicitly cultivating children's thinking in playful settings;
- Understand that cultivating children's thinking involves paying attention both to their ability to think as well as to their desire and inclination to do 'good thinking' – their thinking dispositions;
- Appreciate the value of using tools to help children to think better;
- Capitalise on the idea of playfulness for supporting children's thinking.

Cultivating Children's Thinking: Key Ideas

Cultivating something requires attention to detail, an understanding of what is being cultivated and of the actions that will promote growth, as well as some degree of patience.

When I mention the possibility of adopting a more explicit approach to cultivating thinking to early years practitioners, they often reply that it is not necessary, that young children are natural thinkers and that learning to think does not need special attention unlike, perhaps, learning to read.

Robson and Hargreaves' (2005) interview study with early years practitioners who work with 3–5 year olds tends to confirm this view. While they all considered the development of thinking in young children was an important part of their role, they reported that it often remained an implicit rather than an explicit part of their planning. Also, in terms of their definitions of what kinds of thinking were important for young children, all agreed that 'thinking' could be contrasted with rote learning and 'telling' but beyond that, their meaning of thinking was not specific. They tended to group it with active learning strategies and play, although the importance of 'talking about thinking' was well recognised. In addition as children transition through the early stages of primary school, pedagogy can become very didactic and target-driven with little specific attention to cultivating thinking. The purpose of this chapter, then, is to demonstrate how early years practitioners can be more explicit in helping children learn how to think better and that playfulness and playful experiences present unique opportunities for doing so. This is highly consistent with the Playful Teaching and Learning principles that underpin this book.

What Does It Mean to Think Well?

A distinction is often drawn between remembering and thinking. We generally consider that thinking goes beyond retrieving information from our memories and that it involves some transformation of what we know that leads to a new understanding or action. For example, it can include:

- breaking information into parts to find a new combination or pattern (analysing);
- putting information into groups based on similarities and differences (categorising, classifying);
- comparing two different things and seeing the significance of the similarities and differences (comparing and contrasting);
- making predictions and imagining situations that we have not directly experienced: what would happen if ... (possibility thinking);
- linking causes and effects and creating chains of reasoning (causal reasoning);
- producing new solutions to problems that we could not previously solve (problem solving);
- identifying and clarifying problems to solve (problem finding);
- making choices and weighing up pros and cons (decision making);
- synthesising ideas or materials into novel and creative combinations (creative thinking);

- designing new products based on novel ideas (innovating);
- planning, setting goals, monitoring and adjusting thinking (metacognitive thinking);
- reflecting on and evaluating thinking in order to improve it for future situations (metacognitive thinking).

But of course thinking can be done well or done in relatively haphazard or impulsive ways. For example, making a prediction can be just a wild guess or it can be based on reasons and evidence; decision making can be an impulsive reaction and just mean doing the first thing that comes into your head, or it can be based on a careful consideration of options and consequences (see Swartz and McGuinness, 2014). So, as educators, cultivating thinking demands that we not only afford opportunities to children to think in these different ways but that we feed their growth by creating models of what it means to think more skilfully and then make the models more visible for learners. The following sections on creating tools for thinking go some way to prompting practitioners in this direction.

But cultivating thinking goes beyond the ability to think skilfully – important though that is. For example, Tishman et al. (1993: 148) point out that, as well as being able to think well, children need to be motivated and eager to think and be willing to expend the time and effort that thinking sometimes demands. They point to several examples of thinking dispositions: being broad and adventurous; being curious and oriented towards problem finding; seeking understanding and building explanations; being planful and strategic; being careful and accurate; seeking and evaluating reasons; and being metacognitive. Costa and Kallick (2014: Chapter 5) refer to these kinds of personal attributes as habits of mind, and they extend the list to include perseverance, flexibility, and managing impulsiveness, among others.

The idea of thinking dispositions opens thinking out beyond the world of the intellect to the wider world of children's emotions, motivations and personal tendencies. Lucas and Claxton (2010) have recently named these broader kinds of learning "new kinds of smart" and argue that they should be at the heart of all education, including during the early years.

What Is the Role of the Adult in Cultivating Children's Thinking?

Historically, play has had a central role in developmental theories of children's thinking. For example, for Piaget (1962), pretence play was important in developing children's symbolic thinking and their ability to mentally represent the world. Vygotsky expanded on this viewpoint and pointed to the importance of socio-dramatic role play in the development of children's social cognition, especially perspective-taking, and, as children play out more elaborate roles in context, they develop greater self-regulatory skills. Compared to Piaget, Vygotsky (1978) proposed an alternative pathway for children's cognitive development, arguing that what children experience in social interactions gradually becomes internalised as mental representations.

This basic insight shifted the focus for cognitive development away from children's direct interaction with objects and physical environments towards a more social theory of cognitive development, mediated by more experienced adults. Thus, ideas grew about the role of mediated learning – that learning is supported and scaffolded by more knowledgeable adults such as teachers and carers. From the point of view of pedagogy, tools for learning became prominent as aids to learning – communication tools such as language and other forms of communication like diagrams, number systems and models. The idea of tools for thinking will be developed in this chapter – what Vygotsky (1978) called "psychological tools".

What Is Mind-reading and Why Is It Important for Playful Pedagogies?

Another important idea with relevance for early years pedagogy comes from research on children's theories of mind (Flavell, 2004). Theory of mind refers to our understanding that people have mental states, such as thoughts, wants, motives and feelings that are often different from our own. Ashington (1998) explains that, as adults, we use this theory of mind to explain our own behaviour to others, by telling them what we think and want ("I am considering it", "I disagree", "I prefer to") and we interpret other people's talk and behaviour by responding to what we understand their thoughts and wants to be. This capacity to interpret other people's mental states and to act accordingly is often summarised as mind-reading (though not of the magical kind!). Doing it successfully allows us, both as children and as adults, to enter into a whole new world of meaning, interpretation and action; for example:

- playing with roles, rules, games and other forms of make believe;
- interpreting jokes and guessing games;
- appreciating humour and surprises;
- understanding misleading information, tricks and lies;
- following writers' intentions and their use of other literacy twists.

Understanding these mental states and being able to respond accordingly underpins many forms of play and playfulness.

Theories of mind are acquired by degrees, from infancy through childhood to adolescence and into adulthood. While younger children can talk about what they feel, want and like and can talk about what other people think and know, a crucial change in children's theory of mind occurs between four and five years of age when children realise that people talk and act on the basis of the way they think the world is, *even if their thoughts do not reflect the real situation.* Children who have made this step in development recognise what are called false beliefs, thus distinguishing between the mental state (the belief) and what is the case in the real world (the reality). Children then begin to understand a whole range of different things: that people think differently and act on what they believe is going to happen *even if it is not true.* This step in development greatly enhances their capacity to engage in more extended role play scenarios where they act out the mind states of role characters, behave accordingly, and then respond appropriately to other children who are also in-role. There is a lot of complicated mind-reading required, with children often switching between in-role and out-of-role behaviour and talk in quick succession.

The transition to nursery, kindergarten and school settings presents additional challenges for children with regard to interpreting and responding to adults' intentions about teaching and learning. Wang (2015) argues that reciprocal mind-reading – teachers and children reading one-another's minds – is at the heart of any successful pedagogy, remembering that mental states include desires and feelings as well as thoughts about the world. For responsive and playful pedagogies, successful mind-reading takes on a new significance, as the adult depends on so many mind-reading devices to enhance the playful experience of the child, such as humour, surprises, ambiguity, deliberate mistakes, guessing games, dramatic roles and so on, to say nothing of the importance of mind-reading for story interpretation and more advanced socio-dramatic role play and rule-games.

Pause for Thought

What are your views on putting the idea of cultivating 'thinking' at the heart of teaching and learning in the early years? Could there be risks as well as benefits?

What key ideas outlined in this section particularly caught your attention? Why? How are they relevant to your work with young children?

Tools for Thinking: Thinking Vocabulary

Vygotsky drew attention to the importance of tools as mediators in children's learning, especially the role of language in the development of thinking. In this section, links will be made between children's emerging theories of mind and their use of mental verbs such as 'think', 'know', 'guess', 'remember', 'explain', as well as more precise mental words like 'sort', 'decide', 'solve', 'predict', 'plan'. What this might mean for early years practitioners will be illustrated through a case study.

About the relevance of theory of mind and children's language, Ashington explains,

> At school entry, children's theory of mind is intuitive, embedded in everyday social interaction. Teachers can encourage children to make their understanding explicit by talking about it. Mental activities are not directly observable, but they become objects of reflection through language. (1998: 48)

Thus, teachers can build on children's capacity to talk about their thinking by deliberately expanding their thinking vocabulary just as they might expand vocabulary for any new topic. Here is an example of how some teachers introduced thinking vocabulary into their classes in a playful way.

Case Study 4.1: The Thinking Word Wall

The specific example comes from a large urban primary classroom with 8–9 year olds (McGuinness et al., 2006)

At the beginning of the school year just before the project began, Mrs Murphy played a thinking game with the class. She wanted to find out what words they knew that referred to 'thinking' of some kind. The plan was to create a Thinking Word Wall and to add new Thinking Words as the children encountered them. The panels in Figure 4.1 show how the Thinking Word Wall developed.

Notice that the first words the children suggested are more like everyday conversational words, with the exception of the word 'estimate' which the children knew from their maths classes. Then, as the Thinking Word Wall grows, the words become more precise and related to the thinking work that the children were experiencing – using the words 'similarities and differences' from their experience of making comparisons, and the words 'pros and cons' during decision making.

The first words on the Thinking Word Wall	The Thinking Word Wall grows	The Thinking Word Wall at the end of the year
Ideas	Ideas	Ideas
Use your memory	Use your memory	Use your memory
Put in order	Put in order	Put in order
Guess	Guess	Guess
Estimate	Estimate	Estimate
Sort it out	Sort it out	Sort it out
	Similarities and differences	Similarities and differences
	Discuss	Discuss
	Decide	Decide
	Pros and cons	Pros and cons
		Solve
		Solutions
		Predict
		Make a plan
		Conclude

Figure 4.1 The Thinking Word Wall

Words were only written on the Thinking Word Wall when the class was confident that they understood what they meant and had been discussing and practising them during their classwork – a tougher test than mere word comprehension. In the final panel in Figure 4.1, notice that the additional words are about making predictions, planning, problem solving and drawing conclusions.

Teachers' comments about using the Thinking Word Wall

At the start, the class were lost with words like 'options', 'pros and cons'. Now they are familiar with those words through repetition and familiarity.

Children are beginning to use the language to discuss types of thinking - but we still have a long way to go in this area of vocabulary.

The children learned quite difficult vocabulary because of its context and began to talk about thinking quite effectively toward the end of the year.

(Continued)

(Continued)

Children are using the vocabulary freely during class and group discussion.

Children are more likely to say things like, "I think that" or "I don't agree".

Figure 4.2 makes suggestions for thinking words that might be suitable to help younger children become aware of different mental states and intentions related to learning, and then examples more suitable for children as they move through the primary grades.

Building thinking vocabulary for younger children	Advancing thinking vocabulary to the next stage	Advancing thinking vocabulary even further
Pretend		Compare and contrast
Think	Explore	Look for evidence
Remember	Suggest	Consider possibilities
Guess	Observe	Speculate
Notice	Wonder	Suppose
See	Explain	Predict
Describe	Sort	Reflect
Respond	Connect	Classify
	Solve	Sequence
	Choose/decide	Conclude
	Ideas	Options
	Reasons	Pros and cons
		Analyse
		Create
		Point of view

Figure 4.2   Progressing children's thinking vocabulary

Tools for Thinking: Thinking Together

Although thinking is normally considered to happen 'inside the head', it is increasingly recognised that thinking is often more than a solo activity. Vygotsky specifically proposed that, developmentally, learning involves internalising activities originally witnessed and practised in co-operative settings. So cultivating thinking demands that children 'talk together' so that they can 'think together' and eventually 'think independently' – other-regulation to self-regulation. Littleton and Mercer (2013) use the term 'interthink', pointing out that talking not only enables us to interact with one another but also allows us to think together. A similar meaning is captured in the term 'sustained shared thinking', defined as "an episode in which two or more individuals 'work together' in an intellectual way to solve a problem, clarify a concept, evaluate activities, extend a narrative. Both parties must contribute to the thinking and it must develop and extend the understanding" (Siraj-Blatchford et al., 2002: 8). The case study examples below show classroom interactions demonstrating some of these points.

Case Study 4.2: Thinking Together

This case study consists of excerpts of classroom dialogue between a teacher and a small group of children. In both cases the focus of dialogue is on the activity of thinking itself – sorting and classifying in the first example, and decision making in the second example.

Example 1: Sorting and classifying with 4–5 year olds (from Walsh et al., 2007)

The children have been working in small groups for some time on a sorting activity with different materials. Towards the end, the teacher asks:

Teacher: What have you done with your elephants this morning?
Jessica: I made a set of elephants.

Teacher prompts Jessica to explain what a set means.

Jessica: Sets are a collection.
Teacher: Ryan (who was holding up a set of uniblocks): What do we call this?
Ryan: A pattern.
Teacher: What is special about your blocks?
Ryan: It's a tower.
Teacher: Is it a tall or short tower?
Ryan: It's a long tower.

Teacher then turns to Paul: What did you do with your dogs?

Paul: I put them in yellow, pink and white. (child pointing to the groupings in front) Can you sort them a different way for me, teacher?

(Continued)

(Continued)

Teacher: Well Paul, let me see. Can you give me some help? (pause)
Paul: I have a good idea. Let's make a set of big dogs and small dogs.
Teacher: Well done, Paul. What a good idea!

Note:

- The teacher builds on the thinking language of sorting, grouping and classification and the children are beginning to use thinking words spontaneously in the classroom conversations.
- While the theme of sorting is sustained through the interaction, each child initiates a slightly different version of the conversation, and is confident in making suggestions and ideas.
- The teacher resists the temptation to make a suggestion about an alternative way of sorting, turning the question back to the child.
- These children are capable of explaining their reasons and the basis for their thinking.

This teacher drew attention to the importance of thinking in other ways as well, using phrases like "let's think", "this is very good thinking", "I am going to give you some 'thinking' time", "I am looking for the best thinkers today". To complement the language, she also used a range of gestures to make the thinking more explicit in the setting: pointing to her head while referring to thinking, asking children to put on their thinking caps and to tie them tightly.

Example 2: With 8–9 year olds (from McGuinness et al. 2006)

The class are reading a story about the Irish Famine where the main character (the mother) is faced with an important decision about the future of the family. So the children are exploring the question, "What can she do"? This group of five 8-9 year olds are examining one of her possible options and have recorded four pros and four cons related to the option. The teacher, Mr Smith, spots this opportunity to intervene.

The children are considering an important aspect of decision making: the relative weight that is given to various consequences. Do they all weigh the same, or could one be so important that it would outweigh all the rest?

Teacher: ah ... four cons and four pros; did it work out like that or did you try to get four pros and four cons?

John: ... it just worked out.

Teacher: Is it important that it just works out like that?

Peter: Unless you get one pro ... there is no point in doing it.

Teacher: There'd be nothing positive ... do you have to get four cons?

Children together (chorus): No ...

Teacher: Why not?

Martin (who hadn't spoken before): One ...

Teacher: What do you mean ... one?

Martin :   You could have one con and lots of pros.

Teacher: Yes, and the pros would win then?

Martin: No ...

Jamie (who hadn't spoken before): ... it could be so bad, like getting evicted or you could die ...

Teacher: It could be so bad that ten pros wouldn't be good enough ... (teacher gets distracted by something else in the room) Are we nearly finished ...?

Billy: ... even a thousand pros would not be good enough.

Note:

- The children's use of the words 'pros and cons'. They have a precise language to talk about their thinking.
- The teacher's intervention slows down their thinking and provokes them into new judgements.
- There is a sustained dialogue on the issue.
- It is an illustration of joint thinking – each child speaks and the understanding emerges and is co-constructed, sometimes by just a single word.

Several thinking programmes are available for both younger and older children that show how promoting classroom conversations and dialogue can positively impact on children's cognitive growth; for example, Thinking Together programmes for primary schools based on Interthinking (Littleton and Mercer, 2013), Children's Articulating Thinking (ChAT) for the early years (Whitebread et al., 2015), as well as Philosophy for Children (Lipman et al., 1980).

Pause for Thought

From reading Case Study 4.2, what points did you note about the role of the adult in the dialogic interaction? How will it affect your class-room practice in the future?

Tools for Thinking: Using Thinking Organisers

Because thinking goes on 'inside the head', it is largely hidden from learners who are trying to figure out how to do it when confronted by challenging tasks, or who are being asked by teachers or parents 'to think harder'. That is why so many of the pedagogical suggestions in this chapter are about making thinking more visible. Early years practitioners can make the steps in thinking more transparent through the use of guiding questions, thinking routines or through outlining visually a plan for thinking. These techniques are called thinking organisers and can be used in subtle ways both to prompt children's thinking and also to document the results of their thinking. Thinking organisers can be used to scaffold adult/children interactions during whole class teaching (see Case Study 4.3) as well as to support children working independently in groups. Thinking organisers are central to 'Thinking-Based Learning' (TBL) (Swartz et al., 2007) as well as to 'Visible Thinking' (Ritchhart et al., 2011). See also Salmon (2010) for thinking routines work specifically with younger children.

Case Study 4.3: Horton's Dilemma

This case study has been adapted with permission from Swartz and Parks' (1994) compilation of thinking lessons. It shows how thinking can be explicitly cultivated as a natural part of children's storytelling.

Dr Seuss's *Horton Hatches the Egg* tells the story of a faithful elephant who is tricked by his irresponsible friend Mayzie the bird into sitting on her egg, while Mayzie goes off on a holiday and decides to not return. Horton's loyalty is challenged several times in the story as he encounters various hardships such as facing stormy weather, being laughed at by his friends and being captured by hunters. Dr Seuss's books present many opportunities for exploring thinking and are very engaging because of the rhyme and repetition in the language as well as the comical pictures. Horton's refrain in this story is

I meant what I said

And I said what I meant

An elephant's faithful

One hundred percent

The teacher wants to provoke the children's imagination with the narrative, while at the same time drawing their attention to the options that might be available to Horton and to the consequences of each choice. The teacher uses the following questions to prompt the children's thinking.

Deciding What to Do

- What are some things Horton can do? (exploring options)
- What will happen if he does that? (making predictions and exploring consequences)
- Would that be a good thing to happen or a bad thing? (examining pros and cons)
- Is this a good choice for Horton to make? (evaluating the options based on the pros and cons)

So at the beginning of the lesson she first explores Horton's decision to sit on the egg, prompting the children to think why he might do that (e.g., to take care of the egg, because he is a loyal friend) and asking them what that tells them about Horton as a person, compared to Mayzie.

She continues reading with the children discussing Horton's adventures, then pauses where he is faced with the nasty hunters, and asks, "What should Horton do now?". Children come up with lots of ideas: run away with the egg, run away without the egg, fight the hunters, talk to the hunters and explain what he is doing, and so on. At this point, the teacher begins to record the children's ideas at the top of a big visual organiser (see Figure 4.3) which she has displayed in front of the class. This allows her to record all their ideas and then follow the children's direction on which one or two ideas to explore in more detail, asking, for example, what might happen if Horton did try to run away with the egg, or if he did fight the hunters. She then goes on to guide the

(Continued)

(Continued)

children in their exploration of several of the other options, inviting them to propose what might be a good thing for Horton to do.

Notice the teacher's use of the questions to prompt the thinking as well as the role of the visual organiser in making the steps in the thinking more visible. These devices act as thinking organisers and allow the children to see more clearly what might be going on in Horton's mind as he figures out what to do, and by implication in anybody's mind in such circumstances. It also presents a 'model of good thinking' for future use.

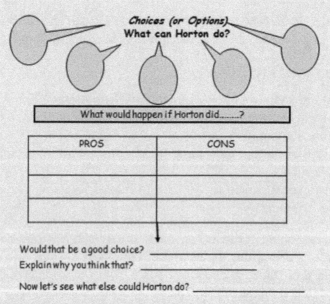

Figure 4.3   Example of a thinking organiser for 'deciding what to do'? Adapted with permission from Swartz and Parks 'Graphic Organiser for Choosing' (1994: 46) with help from Carol Weatherall

Pause for Thought and Action

Look through the story *Horton Hatches the Egg*, and find other points in the story where the teacher could have paused and asked: "What are some things Horton can do?"

Find some other stories suitable for your children that you could use to prompt decision making, using the thinking organiser.

The Importance of Metacognitive Thinking

Finally, I want to stress the central role of metacognition for cultivating children's thinking. The term metacognition, meaning 'going beyond' cognition, was introduced by Flavell (1979) and is often used interchangeably with 'thinking about thinking'. It certainly does involve an act of reflection but it means more than that. Metacognition generally refers to two complementary strands:

- knowledge about cognition – about cognition in general and one's own cognition – involving some degree of awareness;
- self-regulation or the ability to plan, monitor and adjust one's thinking in relation to task demands and to evaluate thinking outcomes.

Thus, in order to be able to plan and adjust their thinking, children need to be aware of their own thinking processes, and the pedagogical approaches to make thinking more visible are a necessary first step in helping thinking become more metacognitive.

Metacognition occupies a privileged position in the development of children's thinking as it orchestrates a wide range of other thinking and self-regulatory processes, even for young children. Recent observation studies with younger children (3–5 year olds) reveal that they can exercise a considerable degree of self-regulation during play tasks – planning, self-correcting, evaluating outcomes – which implies some degree of metacognitive competence (Whitebread et al., 2015; Robson, 2016).

While appreciating the added importance of metacognitive thinking, the approaches for cultivating this form of thinking are surprisingly similar to those tools for thinking that have been discussed so far:

- Observing and listening to children's actions and talk for evidence of emerging metacognitive competence, as in Case Studies 4.1 and 4.2.
- Putting conversations about thinking at the heart of adult–child interactions, focusing not just on what children are thinking about but also on the process of thinking itself, as in Case Study 4.2.
- Using tools for thinking, such as building thinking vocabulary, creating space and time for a dialogue about thinking, as illustrated in all three case studies.
- Using more explicit prompts and thinking organisers to scaffold metacognitive thinking, as in Case Study 4.3. For example, Swartz's ladder of metacognition (Swartz et al., 2007) invites children to become more competent metacognitive thinkers by answering increasingly more advanced questions about their thinking: What kind of thinking are you doing? How are you doing it? Is this a good way to do this thinking? How will you do it next time?

Key Messages

- While children are natural thinkers, early years professionals can develop their thinking further by adopting a more intentional pedagogy that focuses on the idea of cultivating thinking.
- Cultivating thinking is not only about developing the child's intellect; it also embraces thinking dispositions such as curiosity, persistence, managing impulsivity, being planful and careful, building understanding and seeking reasons.
- Developing and using 'tools for thinking' can build children's thinking competence, can make their thinking more visible, and can document the results of their thinking.
- Talking about thinking plays a significant role in cultivating thinking, particularly children talking and thinking together.
- Adopting a bird's-eye view on thinking – 'going meta' – is particularly important for cultivating thinking.
- Playful teaching and learning can benefit from a deeper understanding of the characteristics of children's theories of mind so that the reciprocal mind-reading opportunities between adults and children in any playful teaching relationship can be more fully explored.

Further Reading and Resources

Further teaching resources are available from the University of Cambridge Thinking Together website. https://thinkingtogether. educ.cam.ac.uk/resources/ (accessed 1 September 2016).

Further information on using thinking routines with young children is available from the National Association for Educating Young Children's website www.naeyc.org/tyc/files/tyc/file/V4N5/Tools%20 to%20Enhance%20Young%20CHildren's%20Thinking.pdf (accessed 1 September 2016).

More information on Robert Swartz's *Thinking-Based Learning* (TBL) approach is available from the Centre for Teaching Thinking website http://teach-think.org/resources/lessons-and-articles/ (accessed 1 September 2016).

Resources related to supporting the Thinking Skills and Personal Capabilities Framework are available from the Northern Ireland Curriculum website www.nicurriculum.org.uk/curriculum_microsite/ TSPC/the_think_pack/index.asp (accessed 1 September 2016).

References

Ashington, J.W. (1998) 'Theory of mind goes to school', *Educational Leadership* 56 (3): 46–8.

Costa, A.L. and Kallick, B. (2014) *Dispositions: Reframing Teaching and Learning*. Thousand Oaks, CA: Corwin.

Flavell, J.H. (1979) 'Metacognition and cognitive monitoring: A new area of cognitive-developmental inquiry', *American Psychologist* 34 (10): 906–11.

Flavell, J.H. (2004) 'Theory-of-mind development: Retrospect and prospect', *Merrill-Palmer Quarterly* 50 (3): 274–90.

Lipman, M., Sharp, A.M. and Oscanyan, F.S. (1980) *Philosophy in the Classroom*. Philadelphia, PA: Temple University Press.

Littleton, K. and Mercer, N. (2013) *Interthinking: Putting Talk to Work*. Abingdon, Oxon: Routledge.

Lucas, B. and Claxton, G. (2010) *New Kinds of Smart: How the Science of Learnable Intelligence is Changing Education*. Maidenhead: McGraw-Hill International.

McGuinness, C., Sheehy, N., Curry, C., Eakin, A., Evans, C. and Forbes, P. (2006) *Building Thinking Skills in Thinking Classrooms: ACTS [Activating Children's Thinking Skills] in Northern Ireland*. London: ESRC's TLRP, Research Briefing No 18.

Piaget, J. (1962) *Play, Dreams and Imitation in Childhood*. New York: Norton.

Ritchhart, R., Church, M. and Morrison, K. (2011) *Making Thinking Visible: How to Promote Engagement, Understanding, and Independence for All Learners*. San Francisco, CA: Wiley.

Robson, S. (2016) 'Self-regulation, metacognition and child- and adult-initiated activity: Does it matter who initiates the task?' *Early Childhood Development and Care* 186 (5): 764–84.

Robson, S. and Hargreaves, D.J. (2005) 'What do early childhood practitioners think about young children's thinking?' *European Early Childhood Education Research Journal* 13 (1): 81–96.

Salmon, A.K. (2010) 'Engaging young children in thinking routines', *Childhood Education* 86 (3): 132–7.

Siraj-Blatchford, I., Sylva, K., Muttock, S., Gilden, R. and Bell, D. (2002) 'Researching Effective Pedagogy in Early Years (REPEY)', DfES Research Report 365. London: HMSO. www.327matters.org/Docs/RR356.pdf (accessed 13 September 2016)

Swartz, R. and McGuinness, C. (2014) *Developing and Assessing Thinking Skills: The International Baccalaureate Project. Final Report Part 1: Literature Review and Evaluation Framework*. The Hague: International Baccalaureate Organisation. www.ibo.org/globalassets/publications/ib-research/continuum/student-thinking-skills-report-part-1.pdf (accessed 1 September 2016).

Swartz, R.J. and Parks, D. (1994) *Infusing the Teaching of Critical and Creative Thinking in Elementary Instruction*. Pacific Grove, CA: Critical Thinking Books & Software.

Swartz, R.J., Costa, A., Kallick, B., Beyer, B. and Reagan, R. (2007) *Thinking-Based Learning: Activating Students' Potential*. Norwood, MA: Christopher-Gordon.

Tishman, S., Jay, E. and Perkins, D.N. (1993) 'Teaching thinking dispositions: From transmission to enculturation', *Theory into Practice* 32 (3): 147–53.

Vygotsky, L.S. (1978) *Mind in Society: The Development of Higher Psychological Processes*. Cambridge, MA: Harvard University Press.

Walsh, G., Murphy, P. and Dunbar, C. in collaboration with the EYECEP team (2007) *Thinking Skills in the Early Years: A Guide for Practitioners*. Belfast: Stranmillis University College.

Wang, Z. (2015) 'Theory of mind and children's understanding of teaching and learning during early childhood', *Cogent Education* 2 (1): 1011973. https://doi.org/10.1080/2331186X.2015.1011973

Whitebread, D., Pino-Pasternak, D. and Colman, P. (2015) 'Making learning visible: The role of language in the development of metacognition and self-regulation in young children', in S. Robson and S.F. Flannery Quinn (eds), *The Routledge International Handbook of Young Children's Thinking and Understanding*. Abingdon: Routledge. pp. 199–214.

Playful Pedagogies in Early Childhood Mathematics

Ross Ó Corráin and Liz Dunphy

Chapter Overview

By the end of this chapter you will be able to:

- Identify playful approaches for supporting children's emerging abilities to communicate mathematically;
- Judge which playful pedagogies might best suit your children;
- Integrate playful pedagogies into early mathematics provision.

Children's disposition towards engaging in mathematical ways of thinking and knowing is influenced by how they feel about mathematically-related activities. Playful pedagogies, including playful contexts and playful interactions, are important in engaging children (Gifford, 2004; Moyles, 2010). Playfulness with worthwhile, meaningful and enjoyable mathematics is essential in promoting positive dispositions and increases children's proficiency with mathematics (Dooley et al., 2014). This chapter focuses on playful strategies that support 4–6 year old children's engagement in mathematical thinking and communicating.

Playful Mathematical Learning

A variety of playful mathematical learning is essential in engaging young children in early education settings in the range of mathematical content and processes, and in helping them to develop strong learning dispositions. These experiences should involve opportunities to explore and to solve problems; to acquire and use mathematical vocabulary; to reason; and to communicate mathematically. Dispositions such as trying things out, taking risks and persevering are developed as children engage in playful ways with a range of materials including everyday materials (such as shells, pine cones, leaves) and structured materials (such as unit blocks or linking chains). Playful learning in early mathematics will see children engaged in block play to develop their spatial awareness and problem solving; pretend play such as a shoe shop where children develop curiosity, skills of comparison and work with real money; or discussing picture books rich in mathematical language (such as *The Washing Line* by Jez Alborough).

Playful Strategies

Gifford (2005) suggests that playful mathematical interactions might include a range of strategies. These are summarised by Montague-Smith and Price (2012), and in Table 5.1 below we exemplify each of these strategies with our own examples drawn from practice.

Table 5.1 Playful strategies in practice

Strategy	Possible learning example
Deliberately misunderstanding a child's instructions in order to draw out a teaching point	When measuring how tall a child's block tower is with links, the teacher measures from halfway up the tower in order to provoke a response from the child, perhaps indicating the correct measuring procedure for this task, to measure the full tower from the bottom to the top
Using playful challenges such as "I bet you can't count this many"	When creating snakes in art for our pretend pet-shop, the teacher says, "There are too many spots on your snake. There is no way we could count how many there are"
Using puppets to model misconceptions and to promote risk taking	When counting on a number-line, Frederico the Frog sometimes gets the order of numbers mixed up: Frederico says, "One, two, three, four, five, seven, eight, nine, six, ten." The children correct Frederico's mistake.
'Tricking' the children by doing the unexpected, for example suddenly changing the direction of counting	Using counting-based echo clapping (teacher claps, children echo), the teacher changes the regular pattern from *1 clap / 2 claps / 1 clap / 2 claps* to *1 clap / 3 claps / 1 clap / 3 claps*
Using humour such as greatly over or under estimating	When comparing the sizes of animal figures in the small world zoo, the teacher comments: "I think the polar bear is taller than the giraffe. Yes, the polar bear is the tallest animal in our zoo".

Montague-Smith and Price (2012) suggest that the power of such strategies is that they can be individually interpreted by children, are enjoyable for all and allow for a high level of risk without the pressure of getting the 'right' answer. Strategies such as these should be considered as part of a continuum of playful mathematical learning experiences that children will experience in the early years. These provide contexts in which the teacher can develop and use a suitably coherent range of playful ways of teaching.

Conceptual Framework

Mathematical proficiency

Mathematical proficiency has been identified as a key aim of mathematics education. The term mathematical proficiency is used to describe key aspects (conceptual understanding, procedural fluency, strategic competence, adaptive reasoning, and productive disposition) that should be developed as children engage with mathematics, and proficiency has been identified as a key aim of mathematics education (National Research Council (NRC), 2001: 116–33). As a result of their enriching mathematical experiences, children become increasingly mathematically proficient over time. While this chapter concentrates on adaptive reasoning, the interwoven nature of the strands means that all are addressed to some extent, albeit implicitly.

Proficiency through mathematisation

Mathematical proficiency is developed through engagement with mathematical processes such as communicating, reasoning, argumentation, justification, generalisation, representing, problem solving, connecting, and communicating. These processes are included in the overarching concept of mathematisation (NRC, 2009). If we want to develop young children's proficiency in mathematics we must focus on mathematisation in the early childhood classroom. Supporting children in mathematising means "helping them to interpret their experiences in explicitly mathematical form and understand the relations between the two" (Ginsburg, 2009: 415). Supporting children also means enabling them to use a range of processes that are necessary for interpreting and understanding.

> Together, the general mathematical processes of reasoning, representing, problem solving, connecting, and communicating are mechanisms by which children can go back and forth between abstract mathematics and real situations in the world around them. In other words, they are a means of both making sense of abstract mathematics and for formulating real situations in mathematical terms – that is, for mathematizing the situations they encounter. (NRC, 2009: 43)

Focusing on adaptive reasoning

High-quality mathematics education for children aged 3–8 years relies on opportunities for rich and engaging interactions with knowledgeable educators who challenge children to think and communicate mathematically (Dooley et al., 2014). Educators offer support for children's mathematising. While the interdependence and interconnection among the proficiency strands is recognised, this chapter illustrates how one aspect of proficiency, *adaptive reasoning,* can be promoted with young children. "One manifestation of adaptive reasoning is the ability to justify one's work" (NRC, 2001: 130). This justification can be both formal and informal. Children clarify their reasoning by talking about concepts and procedures and giving good reasons for the strategies that they are employing. This is supported by collaboration with others and by the use of physical and mental representations of problems. In this chapter we illustrate how educators can support children's adaptive reasoning by engaging them in this high-level activity utilising a range of playful pedagogical strategies (contexts and interactions).

In this chapter we focus on the playful teaching and learning of mathematics with an emphasis on adaptive reasoning. We suggest that the key to successfully developing adaptive reasoning with young children is to develop interesting and playful approaches to engaging children in mathematical processes, supporting adaptive reasoning and promoting their mathematical proficiency. In the sections which follow we present classroom-based evidence which illustrates a range of playful pedagogical approaches. We provide details of how these approaches were developed, examples of their application and evidence of children's responses.

Playful Contexts

In our experience being playful does not come naturally to all teachers. Being silly, becoming the customer in the pretend shop or giving characterisation to a puppet can be challenging for some, making it harder to infuse playfulness into structured mathematics lessons. Playfulness is increasingly recommended as an important aspect of pedagogy in early years classrooms (Walsh et al., 2011) and we know that it is a powerful motivator for young children (Moyles, 2010). It also gives children a context for a mathematical activity and a reason to communicate their experience of it. Giving children a meaningful, communicative purpose behind writing, drawing or thinking and talking mathematics has been found to be a strong motivator for children (Dijk et al., 2004). In the following case study we illustrate how to provide such motivation.

Case Study 5.1: Talking Tom

In Ross's classroom children are often set mathematical problems by Talking Tom (an animated cat). This iPad application allows the user to dictate 45 seconds of dialogue which Tom then repeats. Below is one example of a problem Tom set the children to explore the properties of the number 4.

Tom: Oh, hello boys and girls. Today I am a little bit sad. I got four new frogs for my birthday but they keep hiding. I never know how many frogs are hiding and how many frogs I have. By drawing some pictures for me, maybe you could help me figure how many are hiding and how many frogs I have?

Following this guideline from Talking Tom the children set about exploring the different ways four frogs could be arranged under and on top of a leaf, drawing pictures for Tom as they work.

An analysis of video recordings, taken from research into the efficacy of Talking Tom as a support, shows the children repeatedly express their interest in helping Tom and a positive response to his comments (Ó Corráin, 2014). The children appear proud when Tom praises them for their work. When Tom thanks Mick for his help on a frog problem, Mick sits up straight in his chair and begins to smile. In other sessions Tom sends the children replies to their videos and Gerry giggles when Tom says his name. Nicholas asks, "Are we helping Tom today? I told my Mum about Tom". When asked if they liked helping Tom all four children say "Yes". They explain why. Mick: "Because he always needs help"; Lizzy: "Because ... I like it because it's kind of like a game doing what we are doing"; Nicholas: "Yes, we help him writing numbers ... number lines and it is fun. Is it his birthday again?" (Ó Corráin, 2014: 60-1).

The children draw their mathematical workings around their picture of Tom with his birthday hat on. Mal and two other children do not include Tom in their representations. When asked at the end of the session why it was important to draw that mathematical work Mal replies, "So Tom can learn", indicating he is linking his work to the playful motivation for the mathematical activity (Ó Corráin, 2014).

Further evidence of the children's engagement with Talking Tom appears in their representations of Tom's missing frogs. While talking to

(Continued)

(Continued)

him about his representations, Mick tells Ross, "I writted [sic] all the numbers in their own box so Tom knows which one they are hiding in". When asked about an image in his representation he explains, "That's his hand taking it back" (Ó Corráin, 2014). Here Mick makes reference to Tom in his explanations. He is linking together the context (Tom) and the problem Tom has set his group. He uses that link to motivate his communication of his work through his drawing. These findings support the work of Dijk et al. (2004) who advocated meaningful and stimulating contexts to provide children with a reason to communicate their mathematics.

With young children it is important to give them a reason to complete mathematical tasks or problems, and in particular a reason that makes sense to children. In this case study, the reason for exploring where the frogs are going is to help Tom keep track of his pet frogs. Tom is a colourful, attractive character; this gains the children's interest. Helping him is fun, which motivates these children. By recording their answers in drawings or representations the children begin to pictorially present their mathematical workings, an early form of more abstract mathematical notation. The children in the case study linked Tom (a playful context) to the mathematical activities he set them. While Tom was included in their responses in the lessons, the children remained focused on the mathematical problem he had set them. The goal in contextualising mathematical activities was to find a balance in creating a playful context, Talking Tom, that was compelling, relevant and interesting for the children but did not distract from the mathematical task under discussion (English and Watters, 2004).

In this context it is Tom and not the teacher who is pretending not to know what to do and looking for the children's help. The children answer him with confidence and he responds as the less able other. Applications such as Talking Tom have the potential to allow teachers who are less comfortable with puppets to introduce elements of playfulness into their mathematics lessons.

Pause for Thought

Think of a three year old child you know. What playful character, problem or story might you use to give that child a reason to engage in a counting activity?

Think of the last time you saw a child engaged in mathematical play. What materials could you offer to encourage the child to draw or record the mathematics involved?

Reflect on the reasons you currently give children to participate in mathematical activities. How could you make them more playful?

Digital Tools

Children learn from hands-on, playful and meaningful mathematical exploration and discovery (Montague-Smith and Price, 2012). Most teachers are convinced of the importance of working in this way with the youngest children, but in practice they often rely on worksheets or textbooks to complete their lessons (Dunphy, 2009). But what if you could continue the playful exploratory work children engage in into how they *record* their mathematical working? In our experience, digital tools such as a camera linked to an Interactive Whiteboard (IWB) provide a way of doing this. We explore this further in the case study which follows.

In Ross's classroom, photographs taken by the children provide a useful tool for mathematisation as well as providing a means to record and discuss playful learning. By allowing the children to record their mathematical experiences as they worked more time was available for playful learning without being inhibited by prescriptive textbook activities. We argue that this process provided a strong stimulus for the children to talk about their learning as they had ownership over how they were recording their mathematics.

Case Study 5.2: The Tallest Tower

Gerry is working on a tower problem for Talking Tom. He is building towers of different heights with three cuboidal boxes in order to explain the words 'taller' and 'shorter'. Gerry uses an iPad to take photographs of his work. Now Ross displays these on an IWB as Gerry explains his work to his peers and to Tom. Gerry uses the photograph on the IWB to describe and illustrate with his hands how he made a short tower. Pointing to the bottom box in the tower, he uses his hands to indicate that he has laid the box along its long side.

(Continued)

(Continued)

Gerry points at the box and moves his hands horizontally from left to right as he describes his work, "We made the box long ... and all of another boxes ... *pointing to the boxes laid flat on the top* ... and then they make the tower shorter" (Ó Corráin, 2014: 58). The opportunity the IWB brings is the large format of the image, allowing all the children to see it clearly and Gerry to interact with the picture.

Figure 5.1   Gerry's towers

As the image changes to a taller tower, Gerry continues describing his work:

Gerry: And when you put all of the boxes on top of each other [lifting his hand up high into the air] ... then it's getting higher and higher ... [uses hands to gesture higher and higher. Ross moves on to the next picture of the taller tower].

Teacher: Tell me what is different here.

Gerry: They are all standing on each other.

Teacher: [returning to first picture] But look here, they are all standing on each other, aren't they?

Gerry: It looks like they are lying on each other … [gestures with finger from left to right].
Teacher: Oh that is a good description. What changed here to make it taller?
Gerry: They are standing on their heads … [gestures up].
Nicholas: I think they are standing on their tippy toes.

As discussed, young children need lots of hands-on experiences with various mathematical materials in order to practise and refine their competence across all areas of mathematics. By playing with the boxes in this case study, the children are exploring the different heights the towers can be in a real context, making changes, trying new combinations, making mistakes and solving a problem for themselves. Taking the photographs allows this work to continue uninterrupted, while still providing evidence of the learning that took place.

This case study highlights the potential of capturing playful learning in a child-friendly way. Quickly moving from one image to another allowed Ross to playfully challenge Gerry on his assertion that the second tower was taller because the boxes were "standing" on each other. Through the use of photographs the discussion moved from one image to another in seconds. This allowed Gerry the opportunity to compare the towers. He explained that they were no longer lying on each other, but instead "standing on their heads" (Ó Corráin, 2014). This use of digital images also allowed for Nicholas and Ross to engage in math-talk with Gerry.

Whether as a means of recalling playful activities or as a stimulus for engaging in mathematical talk, the potential of putting children's work onto the IWB is clear. Bourbour et al. (2014) found that teachers are mainly using the IWB to explain or present textbooks to children in large format. We argue that the simplicity of IWB use illustrated here is accessible to all teachers, irrespective of their competence level in digital technologies.

The children in this classroom used the camera to record and represent their mathematics and as a way of communicating their work to their peers. The digital representation of real life objects such as the box towers served as a new way for the children to explore the visual language of mathematics. This suggests that the use of the IWB to show children's representations can lead seamlessly to engaging them playfully in mathematisation and in discussion of their mathematics.

Pause for Thought

Think of some other household materials you could use to engage children in playful mathematics (such as creating patterns with bottle lids, matching coloured socks).

Imagine giving a group of four year old children a digital camera to take pictures while going for a walk around the local environment. What mathematical concepts might you encounter on the journey (patterns, shapes, numbers)? What questions will you ask about those pictures to encourage the children to use mathematical language?

Eliciting Talk about Mathematics through Playful Interactions

Mathematics is a way for children to understand the world around them and one way they can communicate that understanding. For children to express their mathematical understanding and learning they have to be able to use the language of mathematics confidently. Our experience suggests that a fear of getting a 'wrong' answer can sometimes hold young children back from responding during mathematics activities. So how can we provide an environment that takes that fear away and supports the development of mathematical language?

We suggest creating a learning environment where everyone, teacher and children, are talking about their mathematical ideas, concepts and experiences. This is known as a 'math-talk' environment (Hufferd-Ackles et al., 2004; NRC, 2009). The teacher and children build a partnership where everyone is responsible for sharing their knowledge, understanding and learning in all mathematical interactions. A math-talk environment can provide opportunities for children to think mathematically and to reflect their thinking in their talk. Through this they begin to connect their world to mathematics and mathematics to their world. With this environment in place, we suggest that a playful approach to mathematical language can provide a safe space for children to explore the world of mathematics without the fear of wrong answers.

Supporting Math-talk

The teacher plays a vital role in providing opportunities for math-talk to take place and in extending learning through leading, modelling and scaffolding math-talk. When teachers engage in math-talk they can support children in connecting the concepts and language that constitute mathematics (NRC, 2009). Many factors can impact on the quantity and quality of children's math-talk, including social context, cultural attitudes to mathematics and the needs of children with English as an additional language (Sarama and Clements, 2009). It is the teacher's role to ensure that all children have the time, resources and adult input to support their mathematical learning and consequently their math-talk (Clements et al., 2004).

It is also the teacher's role to ensure the mathematics learning environment is a safe one for children where risk is rewarded and where all responses, methods and ideas are respected and examined (Hufferd-Ackles et al., 2004). We have found that playfully challenging children's mathematical language is a powerful tool for encouraging math-talk. Putting children in a position of power where the teacher appears not to understand a word or phrase used is one such strategy. In the following case study Ross playfully challenges the children's use of certain language.

Case Study 5.3: Egg Box Problem

Katie (five years) is working to find as many ways as possible to place two eggs in an egg box with six spaces. She records her findings by drawing each way on a blank page (see Figure 5.2). She is free to represent her results in any way that makes sense to her. As Katie works on the problem and draws, Ross questions her about her work:

Teacher: Katie, tell me about what you have done.
Katie: [moving two eggs into position in the egg box] Over here ...
Teacher: Now remember I am silly, I don't remember what the words 'here' and 'there' mean.
Katie: This one is at the back and this one at the left.
Teacher: Just check now. This is your left hand and this is your right hand.
Katie: So this one is at the back and this at the right.

Later in the lesson, Katie uses her drawing to explain her findings to her teacher and to five other children (five and six years old) who have also been working on the egg box problem:

(Continued)

(Continued)

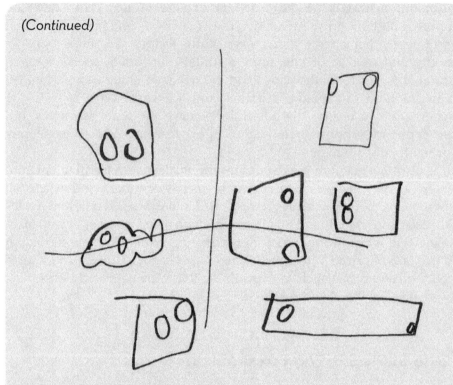

Figure 5.2 Katie's egg representation

Katie: Those are together.
Teacher: What about this pair?
Katie: They are not together. They're separate.
Teacher: Separate! That's a great word.
Nicholas: What's separate?
Lizzy: I know. Separate means that they're … that they're … It's like my dogs at home. My big dog Hercules has to stay in the kitchen while our little dog has to stay in the front room.
Teacher: So they are separate. You have to separate your dogs.
Mal: They can't be next to each other. Another way means they can't be with each other anymore.
Teacher: … That word separate was a fantastic word to teach us. Thank you, Katie.
Fergie: These are together … [she moves her two eggs together] These are together too but a different side … [moving both eggs to the opposite side].

The involvement of the teacher as questioner and deliberately-confused other supported the children in their use of math-talk. The playful and targeted misunderstanding of the words 'here' and 'there' naturally led Katie to think about her use of mathematical language and to become more specific in its use. The co-learner/co-planner environment created is one where Nicholas feels comfortable asking what the word 'separate' means. This led on to a mathematical discussion where the children explained the meaning of 'separate' for him.

Pressure is taken out of the lesson by careful use of teacher statements rather than questions. The teacher says "Tell me about" and "Separate, that's a great word" rather than "What is your answer?" or "What does that word separate mean?" which allowed the conversation to flow from the children rather than be led by the adult. Rather than correcting the incorrect use of 'left' but scaffolding the language with her hands as a reference point the teacher supported Katie in correcting her own mistake and taking ownership of her work.

Encouraging young children to talk about their mathematics and to use correct mathematical language is an essential but challenging role of the early years teacher. Where children lack confidence, it can be built by encouraging them to take the 'risk' of talking about their mathematics through the teacher being 'silly', playfully challenging their use of words or pretending not to understand, but to need help. We do this to take the pressure off the young child and to show that it is ok not to understand; even teacher does not understand everything.

Through the use of these strategies teachers can encourage children to use more specific mathematical language as they engage in mathematics lessons. These strategies give children the confidence to experience uncertainty, to question and find out together, to develop their own methods and solutions to mathematical problems. Targeted input from teachers is needed to make children's experiential knowledge and mathematical thinking explicit (Clements et al., 2004). Creating this playful environment that encourages and supports math-talk must include a move from the traditional teacher–child model building towards child–child talk (Fuson et al., 2005). By challenging children's use of certain language we can provide a model for them to challenge each other. These peer-to-peer challenges leading to peer-to-peer math-talk demonstrate the beginnings of a math-talk environment where the children will rely less on the teacher (Diezmann et al., 2002).

Pause for Thought

Think of a three, four or five year old child you know. What kind of mathematical vocabulary does that child have? Do they use correct mathematical terms? How can you support the child's mathematical language development (using stories, pretending not to understand, challenging language use)?

Reflect on the role the teacher took in order to encourage math-talk. Was it successful/unsuccessful in your opinion? What would you do in the teacher's position?

Suggest an engaging scenario for extending children's spatial aware-ness in your setting. What strategies could you use to increase their understanding of spatial awareness and use of positional language (per-haps related to the location of resources in your setting)? How can these strategies be adapted for promoting other mathematical language use?

Key Messages

- In this chapter we have presented a range of case studies demon-strating playful strategies for early mathematics learning and for the playful engagement of young children in mathematical thinking and communicating in the early years classroom.
- We have discussed how the aim of developing key aspects of math-ematics proficiency from the early years influenced the choice of pedagogical strategies and framed the work reported here.
- Our concerns with developing positive dispositions led us to con-struct the learning in playful ways (Walsh et al., 2011).
- The pedagogy demonstrated in this chapter is both proactive and intentional and the playfulness, learning and teaching are fully intertwined (Wood, 2013; Walsh et al., 2011).

Further Reading and Resources

Bourbour, M., Vigmo, S. and Pramling Samuelsson, I. (2014) 'Integration of interactive whiteboard in Swedish preschool practices', *Early Childhood Development and Care* 185 (1): 100–20.

Cook, G., Jones, L., Murphy, C. and Thumpston, G. (1997) *Enriching Early Mathematical Learning*. Buckingham: Open University Press.

www.talkingtom.com Talking Tom is the playful digital tool used in the case studies above.

Tucker, K. (2014) *Mathematics through Play in the Early Years* (third edition). London: Sage.

References

Bourbour, M., Vigmo, S. and Pramling Samuelsson, I. (2014) 'Integration of interactive whiteboard in Swedish preschool practices', *Early Childhood Development and Care* 185 (1): 100–20.

Clements, D., Sarama, J. and DiBiase, A. (eds) (2004) *Engaging Young Children in Mathematics: Standards for Early Childhood Mathematics Education*. Mahwah, NJ: Lawrence Erlbaum.

Diezmann, C.M., Watters, J.J. and English, L.D. (2002) 'Teacher behaviours that influence young children's reasoning', in A.D. Cockburn and E. Nardi (eds) *Proceedings of the 27th Annual Conference of the International Group for the Psychology of Mathematics Education 2:* Norwich. pp. 289–96.

Dijk, E.F., Van Oers, B. and Terwel, J. (2004) 'Schematising in early childhood mathematics education: Why, when and how?', *European Early Childhood Education Research Journal* 12 (1): 71–83.

Dooley, T., Dunphy, E. and Sheil, G. (2014) *Mathematics in Early Childhood and Primary Education (3–8 Years): Teaching and Learning. Research Report No. 18.* Dublin, Ireland: NCCA.

Dunphy, E. (2009) 'Early childhood mathematics teaching: Challenges, difficulties and priorities of teachers of young children in primary schools in Ireland', *International Journal of Early Years Education* 17 (1): 3–16.

English, L. and Watters, J. (2004) 'Mathematical modelling in the early school years', *Mathematics Education Research Journal* 16 (3): 59–80.

Fuson, K.C., Kalchman, M. and Bransford, J.D. (2005) 'Mathematical understanding: An introduction', in M.S. Donovan and J.D. Bransford (eds) *How Students Learn Mathematics in the Classroom*. Washington D.C.: The National Academies Press. pp. 217–56.

Gifford, S. (2004) 'Between the secret garden and the hothouse: Children's responses to number focused activities in the nursery', *European Early Childhood Education Research Journal* 12 (2): 87–102.

Gifford, S. (2005) *Mathematics with Children 3–5*. Maidenhead: Open University Press.

Ginsburg, H. (2009) 'Early mathematical education and how to do it', in O. Barbarin and B. Wasik (eds) *Handbook of Child Development and Early Education: Research to Practice*. New York: The Guilford Press. pp. 403–28.

Hufferd-Ackles, K., Fuson, K.C. and Gamoran Sherin, M. (2004) 'Describing levels and components of a math-talk learning community', *Journal for Research in Mathematics Education* 35 (2): 81–116.

Montague-Smith, A. and Price, A.J. (2012) *Mathematics in Early Years Education* (third edition). Abingdon: Fulton.

Moyles, J. (ed.) (2010) *The Excellence of Play* (third edition). Maidenhead: Open University Press.

National Research Council (NRC) (2001) *Adding It Up: Helping Children to Learn Mathematics*, J. Kilpatrick, J. Swafford and B. Findell (eds), Mathematics Learning Study Committee, Center for Education, Division of Behavioral and Social Sciences and Education. Washington, DC: The National Academies Press.

National Research Council (NRC) (2009) *Mathematics Learning in Early Childhood: Paths Towards Excellence and Equity*. C. Cross, T. Woods and H. Schweingruber (eds), Committee on Early Childhood Mathematics, Center for Education, Division of Behavioural and Social Sciences and Education. Washington, DC: The National Academies Press.

Ó Corráin, R. (2014) 'Enabling young children to communicate their mathematical thinking and understanding'. MEd dissertation, St Patrick's College, Dublin City University, Dublin.

Sarama, L. and Clements, D. (2009) *Early Childhood Mathematics Research: Learning Trajectories for Young Children*. New York: Routledge.

Walsh, G., Sproule, L., McGuinness, C. and Trew, K. (2011) 'Playful structure: A novel image of early years pedagogy for primary school classrooms', *Early Years* 31 (2): 107–19.

Wood, E. (2013) *Play, Learning and the Early Childhood Curriculum* (third edition). London: Sage.

6

Playful Approaches to Literacy

Catherine Gilliland

Chapter Overview

This chapter focuses on the playful approaches that we as teachers can use to help children become not only literate but addicted to Literacy. The chapter addresses three interconnecting themes. Firstly, rich storytelling is at the epicentre of all effective learning environments and this skill will be explored in relation to picture books and the ancient craft of oral storytelling within a localised context. Secondly, there are close connections in the brain between the processes of music and language (Limb, 2006); children can benefit by being immersed in rhyme, rhythm and repetition to stimulate and enrich their Literacy development. The ways in which we as practitioners can help the children's bodies come together as a self-conducting orchestra will be illustrated through a case study set in a nursery environment. Thirdly, we will delve into the world of puppetry and the magical ability of puppets to ignite language, creativity and a motivation to learn. In the opening chapter of this book, Glenda Walsh highlights the importance of play needing "richness, challenge and adventure" and a skilful, well-informed Literacy practitioner will be able to use the media of story, puppets and rhyme to achieve this. Figure 6.1 illustrates how the three themes interconnect and how they can be used in a playful way both individually and collectively to support holistic development of these essential early Literacy skills.

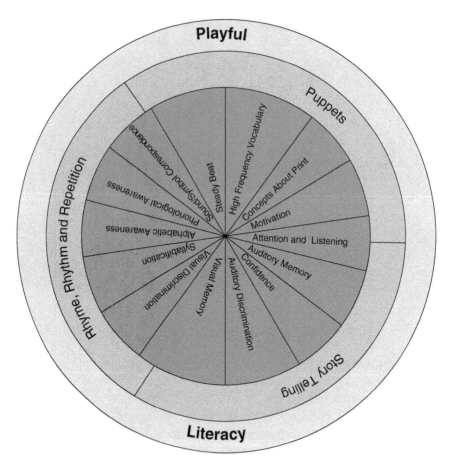

Figure 6.1 Playful Literacy themes

Rich Storytelling

As a teacher educator specialising in Literacy, my main intention is to make teachers fall in love with children's literature, as it is a most powerful learning tool in the development of language. Kennedy et al. (2012) point out the significant potential of book reading with young children for fostering the type of quality language development that is linked to Literacy. In a single reading children can travel from identifying with a villainous role such as a wicked stepmother to the heroic role of a prince in shining armour. Total immersion in the character world through playful pedagogy ensures that children develop the real narrative as they have a central role within it. Literature therefore needs to be visible within a variety of play areas so that children can engage with the language as they play. As children are most likely to learn when it stems from their personal interests

(Hedges, 2014), we must make the world of children's literature a central cog in the addiction process. The playfulness of the teacher as a storyteller is pivotal. The story must make the children enter the world with doe eyes, dribbling lip and an urgency to hear what happens next.

The case study below looks at how playful practitioners can take children's fondness for a particular story and use it to create another story, rich in natural language and localised to their learning context. Children of all ages are easily engaged when the story revolves around where they live, a person they know and the adventures that happen within. They love to hear stories of the antics of a new puppy, a silly thing that happened, or a real life story. Julia Donaldson's acclaimed story *The Gruffalo* brings children into an imaginary world, rich in rhyme, rhythm and repetition. The storyteller must make each of the characters real in voice, movement and anticipation. As Mallet (2012) states, picture books for the very youngest children reflect this age group's need for the repetition that they also find in songs and rhymes, thus demonstrating the interconnectedness of the themes of this chapter.

Case Study 6.1: The Gruffalo and the Mouse

Playful teachers, through their liveliness, spontaneity, imagination, humour and down-to-earth silliness, will be empowered to exploit and develop the children's addiction to the story of *The Gruffalo* by exploring where the mouse lived before he went to live in the forest with the Gruffalo.

Teacher: Children – do you want to know something that no one else knows about the mouse?

This needs to be in a near-whisper, as if you don't want anyone else to know. These children are the only ones who are going to hear this breaking news. This question and the way it is presented to the children sets up mystery and adventure and hooks the developing mind. Children will be spellbound by hearing that he lived in an odd numbered house in a street close to their school with the Murphy family, whose favourite food was pizza. Mr and Mrs Murphy had gone to Rome for their honeymoon and that was the first time they ever ate pizza and after that they just adored it. Such was their love of this Italian-inspired

(Continued)

(Continued)

dish that all their children were called after varieties of pizza. The eldest was Margherita, the youngest was Pepperoni and the middle child's name was Romana. Malcolm Mouse had been living there for five years and not one of the Murphy family knew he was a resident in their odd numbered house. Malcolm only came out of his cosy spot in the laundry cupboard when he could hear snoring from all the bedrooms and then he knew he was safe to go and search for some left over pizza crusts, but he always remembered to return to his cosy spot before anyone got up and before Mrs Matilda Murphy came back from nightshift in the local hospital. It was a fateful Tuesday night in February that was to be Malcolm Mouse's last night in the house. It was 'buy one get one free' at the local pizza house so, instead of the normal four 12 inch pizzas, eight pizzas arrived. They ate all the pizzas but left all the crusts and Malcolm could think of nothing as tasty. He ate all the crusts from the eight pizzas and the sheer volume of the food made him very, very sleepy. Disaster was to strike. He forgot to go to his usual hiding place in the laundry cupboard. Matilda came back from nightshift in the local hospital, looking forward to climbing into her warm bed and having a very well-deserved rest after cleaning all the wards on the seventh floor of the local hospital. As she walked into the living room she was horrified to find Malcolm, with the remote control in his paw, watching his favourite cartoon - Tom and Jerry. Matilda Murphy jumped on the sofa screaming, "There's a mouse in the house!". Malcolm knew it was time to find alternative accommodation when he saw the pest extermination van arrive outside the odd numbered house in the local street ...

Pause for Thought and Action

Now it's your turn! Have a go at creating your own secret backstory for a book the children love. For example, *Tabby McTat*, also by Julia Donaldson, is a story about a busker and a cat. Create your own story around the busker and how he came to meet Tabby and earn his living on the street. Who was he? What was his name? Did he have any family? Where did he live? Why did he become a busker? Use the story map template in Figure 6.2 to help you with your story creation.

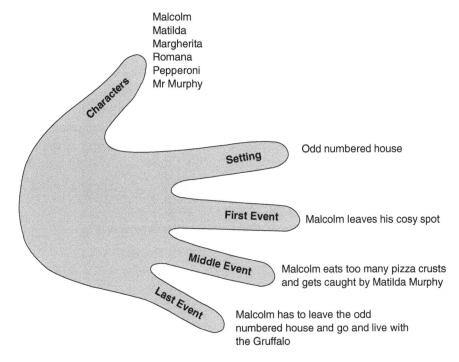

Malcolm
Matilda
Margherita
Romana
Pepperoni
Mr Murphy

Characters

Setting — Odd numbered house

First Event — Malcolm leaves his cosy spot

Middle Event — Malcolm eats too many pizza crusts and gets caught by Matilda Murphy

Last Event — Malcolm has to leave the odd numbered house and go and live with the Gruffalo

Figure 6.2 Story map template

Teachers who play with children's favourite stories and embellish them with local information and targeted vocabulary will cement the development of Literacy concepts in the most covert way. This approach enables practitioners to recycle and upcycle both the children's and the author's language and is highly effective in increasing children's listening and memory skills.

PH (University of Teacher Education) Zürich hosted a conference in September 2013 entitled *Tell me a story, show me the world*. The image chosen for the conference publicity appropriately showed two children looking at a map of the world contained within a huge speech bubble. The conference aimed to "celebrate storytelling and reading as a window on the world". This reminds us that as educators we must become immersed in this story world, and develop our ability to use literary texts and storytelling to stimulate thinking, engagement and discussion amongst the children with whom we work. Effective teachers will realise that stories in their many forms should not be confined to Literacy activities but should be used as a playful teaching and learning medium across all curricular areas.

It seems clear that there is a close connection between children being exposed frequently to both storytelling and picture books and their ability to formulate their own narrative writing. Britton (1983) famously notes that "reading and writing float on a sea of talk" (1983: 83). Stories are the waves in this sea and provide children with the necessary repertoire of language to unlock the reading and writing process. As the children hear new and fascinating stories again and again they will want to put on their storytelling coats, and there we have the beginning of the apprentice writer. Due to the fact that older children, in general, tend to receive a school diet of lengthy novels, they may not often have the experience of the beginning, middle and end in one session of reading, and this can have a negative impact on their development of narrative writing skills (Miller and Pennycuff, 2008). As children get older, we must avoid the temptation of limiting their repertoire of literary texts to the world of black and white print. *The Day the Crayons Quit* by Drew Dewalt is one prime example of a piece of literature that naturally brings a smile to the reader and reminds us of the need to use picture books with all ages (Gilliland et al., 2016).

We must always remember that children have a sense of humour and this can be widely exploited in a classroom context. Children who play with ideas and make jokes demonstrate the highest level of understanding. Our best days are the days that we laugh, and children love being 'silly'. I remember a four year old claiming that the wind must have been to the gym as it's very strong today. Also the same fun character chuckled as he was looking at a toy catalogue and asked: "Do cats make catalogues?". On another occasion the teacher explained 'octo' to a child and how it revolved around the number eight. Later a spider scuttled from under the skirting board and the child duly asked why a spider was called 'spider' and not 'octoider'. The use of humour in the classroom should be an important factor when selecting literature, reading poems or stories, singing and in all interactions with pupils.

Pause for Thought

Watch the series of Booktrust clips on sharing picture books with young children: www.youtube.com/playlist?list=PL44E4D068CBE9A197

What have you learnt about their effectiveness for developing children's understanding of mood, setting, narrative and character?

Mallet (2012) refers to the use of the word 'faction' to describe books that are a mix of fact and fiction. How do you make use of 'faction' for developing children's understanding and concepts across the curriculum?

Rhyme, Rhythm and Repetition

Many researchers and early years professionals point to the Literacy benefits of daily sessions involving rhyme, rhythm and repetition. Bower and Barrett (2014) express the advantage of using this approach: "Most children and adults find it easier to learn and remember songs and rhymes than straight prose because of the regular rhythm and predictable rhyme" (2014: 13). The simple lines of a rhyme or song can help develop children's memory, imagination and logical thinking. Bruce and Spratt (2011), similarly, recommend repeated readings and clapping of rhymes, games and associated actions in order to promote children's awareness of steady beat, phonological awareness, auditory memory and discrimination.

Playful Literacy is closely aligned to the world of music. By tuning into our inner metronome we naturally experience a sense of joy. A catchy tune makes the mind and body want to naturally move. The world of action, finger and nursery rhymes ensures this happens. The body comes together like a self-conducting orchestra and develops the reading brain in the most natural of ways. Rhyme naturally charms and delights the listener, and a child's ability to keep a steady beat is, according to Bayley and Broadbent (2004), one of the best indicators of later academic success. It is essential that we, as teachers of Literacy, provide children with activities that help them feel the strong pulse or beat in speech and music. Greenland (2010) describes the "felt sense of self" (2010: 83) that children feel in the movements of their body. This can be exhibited through the use of finger rhymes and action songs which help children to co-ordinate the upper and lower body as well as establish links between gross and fine motor skills. Goddard Blythe (2004) notes that both rhythm and sound are created as a result of movement, hence the importance of encouraging children to move when they are singing. Phonemic awareness, say Ziegler and Goswami (2006), is best developed through singing, rhymes and repetitive phrases in stories. A study by MacLean et al. (1987) found that, regardless of class background, general intelligence or memory ability, the better children are at detecting rhymes, the quicker and more successful they will be at learning to read. This provides support for the view of many experienced teachers that "good rhymers make good readers".

Not only are rhymes essential for language but their contribution to the cognitive, physical, and social and emotional areas of development should never be underestimated. Cognitive development is central to rhyme as children have to memorise and recognise patterns and sequence. These are essential for acquiring competence across all areas of the curriculum. The vestibular system is the earliest of the developing senses and is soothed by rocking, swinging and swaying movements. The different movements of action rhymes exercise the vestibular system and this is essential in the early years. Like stories and jokes, rhymes encourage children's sense of humour and children love to see playful practitioners fully enjoying the shared experience. A bond is created and this is central to their emotional diet.

Case Study 6.2 demonstrates the commitment of an experienced early years teacher to making rhyme central to the development of all children's milestones.

Case Study 6.2: Nursery Rhymes

With the new school year barely underway, my nursery class is already reciting rhymes with great confidence and in unison. They have been made aware of the stories related to the rhymes and are able to name the main characters. As the rhymes are easy to repeat, some children are experiencing the art of speaking in full sentences for the first time. They are able to answer questions related to the rhyme and have acquired a 'feel' for the structure and pattern in language. Because nursery rhymes follow the pattern of a steady beat, our inclination to move to the rhythm flows naturally. This in turn helps to make language real and alive, as well as being an enjoyable experience for the children. There is a wonderful sense of achievement in seeing Ben as he marches along singing the *Grand Old Duke of York*, watching Leah as she masters the intricate finger movements that accompany *Incey Wincey Spider*, or observing Katie Louise in the home corner singing *Rock a Bye Baby*, while rhythmically nursing a baby doll. To think that, two months ago, this group of children had no experience of togetherness and are now participating with such enthusiasm and concentration in these classroom activities. What remarkable achievements for these children! Already, they are making predictions, thinking logically, pronouncing words and speaking more confidently. This is mostly as a result of being exposed daily to nursery rhymes. These skills are all very necessary for four year olds setting out on their learning journeys.

Pause for Thought

How are the children in this class being developed physically, emotionally and cognitively through their engagement with rhyme?

How do you think your setting could improve the understanding of parents regarding daily engagement with rhyme?

Research the vestibular system and note how this links with your setting's provision for action songs and lullabies.

Familiarise yourself with the various stages of finger and action rhymes (Bruce and Spratt, 2011) and ensure this is integral to your planning and delivery.

Puppet World

The world of puppetry can also play an important part in making the teaching of Language and Literacy playful. As the teacher decides the narrative, it can go beyond the set script and, when successfully used by playful educators, puppets are pivotal to the Literacy addiction process.

In my work with puppets, Barney the Brown Bear is introduced to the children using the whisper technique – the teacher listens to a whisper from the bear – and they are always eager to know what Barney is going to reveal to them today. He tells a story each week from a bad accident at the zoo to the six-monthly checkup at the dentist. The stories are filled to the brim with high-quality vocabulary and narrative, drawing children into both the imaginative and the real worlds they live in. As there is no set text, the language can take the necessary pathway to ensure engagement, acquisition and development of story that will be the springboard for skill development. Saracho (2012) describes storytelling as being a form of Literacy communication that has a direct appeal to children's imagination. This link between a child's imagination and their language development is vitally important and can be achieved through skilful use of puppets.

In our classrooms we see children arriving with what Moat (2001) describes as "word poverty". In his book, *The Matthew Effect*, Rigney (2010) points out the stark reality of this concept by noting that "the word-rich will get richer while the word-poor will get poorer" (2010: 76). This is reiterated by Wolf (2010), who notes the stark statistic that children being brought up with word poverty have 32 million fewer words spoken to them than the average middle-class child. The playful use of puppets allows teachers to target very specific language that children need for their language development across all areas of the curriculum. This approach can be a central key to addressing the problems caused by word poverty and help to negate the Matthew Effect of the word-poor getting poorer.

The case study below describes the experiences of six-year-old pupils being introduced to a puppet for the first time. The student has prepared a lesson based around a session modelled during lectures. The comments of the student, the tutor and the children indicate the breadth of language development that results from the children's interactions with Barney.

Case Study 6.3: Barney the Bear

As a teacher trainer, having modelled a lesson on the introduction of a puppet with Foundation Stage children (aged 4-5 years), I was over-joyed to witness a student (Eimear) using this skill to bring children to this imaginative land. Barney was in a hinged, wooden box and the children were given clues as to what friend she had brought in to meet them. Several clues later and with much discussion the pupils guessed he was a bear. By introducing Barney as being shy, Eimear immediately brought out the children's caring side. One child told the other children not to shout out answers as this might scare Barney. In order to develop the children's musicality, they were asked to sing along to a jingle to help him come out of the box. This will be used weekly to signal the beginning of the session. The whisper technique, where Barney whispered into Eimear's ear, was used effectively and pro-moted conversation as they had to listen intently. Eimear had prepared an introductory session based on a local forest park. The scene was set as all the children had been there and their interest was high. The pupils expressed horrified faces when they heard about Barney's acci-dent and empathised with him as, having been to the same place, they knew the 'big hill' that he fell down and could imagine the scale of the accident. The oral story was listened to intently and Barney's interjec-tions ensured the 'authenticity' of the event. This was then reinforced through a simple PowerPoint with real life photographs of Barney receiving medical help in the ambulance and pictures of signs in the park.

Faye had been at the top of the hill and her daddy had lifted her on top of the big stone so she could relate to how steep the hill was. James had just returned to school after having his tonsils out and stood beside Barney and talked about his experience in hospital. Brian, who loved Barney and his adventure, was eager to tell about the time that he had a bandage around his head. Ronan's dad is a fireman so he was making a connection with the emergency services and was very aware of the environmental print and called out the visual vocabulary he was seeing. An email message from his doctor told the children what games they needed to play to help Barney get better. This provided the impetus for memory games, songs and rhymes and this was central in developing the children's auditory memory and discrimination.

On the final day the children were shown PowerPoint photographs of Barney's day in the park and the language generated was wide and varied. The focus on visual discrimination and memory as key reading skills was very evident and the pupils were surrounded by lots of high frequency words vitally important to their reading fluency. The children had talked about Barney informally during playtime and were anxious to know when he would visit again. The school made Barney part of their oral homework each week and the children brought home their picture of his adventure to share the story with their family. Parents have noted how much joy and excitement he has brought to the class. It was magical to see 30 children in a class with a high boy/girl ratio so absolutely enthralled in the life of Barney. The richness, challenge and adventure which, according to Glenda Walsh, characterises playful pedagogy (as described in the opening chapters of this book) was well and truly evident in this session.

Pause for Thought and Action

Create an oral story around Barney going to the optician. Then prompt the children's retelling by the creation of a PowerPoint including key features of the sequence of the story, such as Barney's appointment card, a photograph of Barney at the optician, a sample eye chart. What alphabet games can you play using the eye chart? What other visual prompts might you include?

As you create your story plot and prescription for Barney, how are you building both auditory/visual memory and discrimination as explored in the case study above? How many high frequency words have you included in the PowerPoint about Barney's adventure? What other scenarios do you think could be created around Barney?

Key Messages

- Playful approaches to Literacy are a journey of adventure where new experiences are encountered, previous events are revisited and there is infinite potential.
- There are many ways to make Literacy playful and this chapter has focused on the role of rich storytelling, rhyme, rhythm and repetition as part of a musical environment and the use of puppets to develop language.
- There are many aspects to the wonderful world of playful Literacy, but a key theme running through this chapter is the key role of the practitioner. They must be joyful, playful and show true commitment to the process.
- Teachers have a very privileged role to play in fuelling children's Literacy addiction. Informed, playful practitioners who personalise their teaching can inspire children, create a spirit of enquiry and develop the skills and confidence that ensure success in learning. Such teachers can make Literacy truly magical.

Further Reading

Bayley, R. (2007) *Action Raps*. Birmingham: Lawrence Educational.

Mallock, S. and Trevarthen, C. (2010) *Communicative Musicality: Exploring the Basics of Human Companionship*. London: Puffin.

Palmer, S. and Bayley, R. (2013) *Foundations of Literacy: A Balanced Approach to Language, Listening and Literacy Skills in the Early Years* (fourth edition). London: Featherstone.

Roche, M. (2015) *Developing Children's Critical Thinking through Picturebooks*. Oxon: Routledge.

References

Bayley, R. and Broadbent, L. (2004) *Helping Children with Special Beat*. Birmingham: Lawrence Educational.

Bower, V. and Barrett, S. (2014) 'Rhythm, rhyme and repetition', in V. Bower (ed.), *Developing Early Literacy 0–8: From Theory to Practice*. London: Sage. pp. 118–33.

Britton, J. (1983) *Language and Learning*. London: Allen Lane.

Bruce, T. and Spratt, J. (2011) *Essentials of Literacy from 0–7* (second edition). London: Sage.

Clarke, M. (2013) 'High frequency words: A neglected resource for young literacy learners', *Reading News* Summer 2013: 15–17.

Gilliland, C., Cash, T. and McElhinney, E. (2016) 'The case for picture books for all', *Literacy News,* Autumn, 7–9.

Goddard Blythe, S. (2004) *The Well Balanced Child*. Gloucestershire: Hawthorn Press.

Greenland, P. (2010) *Hopping Home Backwards: Body Intelligence and Movement Play* (second edition). Leeds: Jabado/Reading.

Hedges, H. (2014) 'Young children's "working theories": Building and connecting understandings', *Journal of Early Childhood Research* 12 (1): 35–49.

Kennedy, E., Dunphy, E., Dwyer, B., Hayes, G., McPhillips, T., Marsh, J., O'Connor, M. and Shiel, G. (2012) *Literacy in Early Childhood and Primary Education (3–8 years)*. Commissioned Research. Dublin: NCCA.

Limb, C.J. (2006) 'Structural and functional neural correlates of music perception', *The Anatomical Record Part A: Discoveries in Molecular, Cellular, and Evolutionary Biology* 288(4): 435–46.

MacLean, M., Bryant, P.E. and Bradley, L. (1987) 'Rhymes, nursery rhymes and reading in childhood', *Merrill-Palmer Quarterly* 33: 255–82.

Mallett, M. (2012) *The Primary English Encyclopaedia: The Heart of the Curriculum* (fourth edition). Abingdon: Routledge.

Miller, S. and Pennycuff, L. (2008) 'The power of story: Using storytelling to improve literacy learning,' *Journal of Cross-Disciplinary Perspectives in Education* 1(1), 36–43.

Moat, L. (2001) 'Overcoming the language gap', *American Educator* 25 (5): 8–9.

Rigney, D. (2010) *The Matthew Effect: How Advantage Begets Further Adventure*. New York: Columbia University Press.

Saracho, O. (2012) *An Integrated Play-based Curriculum for Young Children*. New York: Routledge.

Wolf, M. (2010) *Proust and the Squid: The Story and the Science of the Reading Brain*. Cambridge: Icon Books.

Ziegler, J.C. and Goswami, U. (2006) 'Becoming literate in different languages: "Similar problems, different solutions"', *Developmental Science* 9 (5): 429–36.

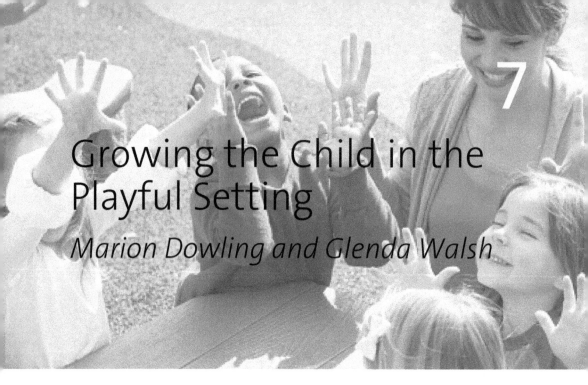

7

Growing the Child in the Playful Setting

Marion Dowling and Glenda Walsh

Chapter Overview

By the end of this chapter you will be familiar with:

- The importance of children growing socially, emotionally and dispositionally to ensure a positive educational journey;
- The role of the playful teacher and the playful environment in nurturing appropriate social, emotional and dispositional growth in the early years of a young child's education.

What Do We Mean by Growing the Child?

The type of person we become colours all else we experience and do in life. A wise head teacher once said that the aim in her school was "to follow the child with love and help grow an adequate person". Most of us would recognise an adequate person: we appreciate and admire those who have good interpersonal skills, live their lives by a clear moral code and are able to manage their feelings and empathise with the feelings of others. These people deal with the decisions they must take in life and bravely face up to difficult situations. Regardless of their intellectual capabilities, such individuals are optimistic and seem equipped to get the most out of life. These are rough and ready definitions of 'adequacy' but surely it is these qualities that we want to respect, demonstrate, encourage and promote in young children. All of these refer to aspects of young children's personal development and are embedded in many Early Years Frameworks across the world, including the UK (e.g., those published by CCEA Northern Ireland (2007) and the Department for Education England (2014).

This chapter emphasises the benefits of playful teaching and learning approaches to promote children's social, emotional and dispositional growth in the early years of their educational journey.

The Role of the Early Years Setting in Growing the Child

As young children embark upon their educational journey, they have to negotiate a number of different transitions in the process. Fabian (2007: 7) defines a transition as a "change of culture and status … leaving the 'comfort zone' and encountering the unknown: a new culture, place, people, roles, rules and identity". Niesel and Griebel (2005: 8) suggest that "How well the child passes through the gate [of the transition to preschool] has implications for lifelong learning". Consequently, it is not only the early years setting's or school's responsibility to ensure that children make adequate cognitive progress; children themselves have to be equipped with an appropriate learning toolkit (Claxton, 2000), that is, to be prepared socially, emotionally and dispositionally to deal effectively with the discontinuities that they will face throughout their educational journey. Leaving the development of such an essential toolkit to chance is futile; therefore it is the early years practitioner's responsibility to help foster and nurture such skills in the early years of schooling as advocated in Pillar One of Chapter 3.

Pause for Thought

Consider the views of this early years teacher:

I firmly believe that the early years of schooling are about developing young children's emotional resilience, social competence and positive attitudes towards learning. That is not to say that the academic aspect of children's learning should be undermined, but in my opinion it should not be prioritised at this early stage of a child's educational journey. If, by 7–8 children are confident, competent

(Continued)

(Continued)

learners who want to keep on learning, I'm quite sure no Primary teacher should or would be complaining.

What, in your opinion, are the most essential ingredients of a young child's early learning toolkit? To what extent do you agree or disagree with this early years practitioner?

The Importance of the Playful Adult to Help Grow the Playful Child

The importance of playful experiences for young children's holistic growth and development has been well documented over the years (e.g., Whitebread, 2012). As Atkin explained as early as 1991, in play children are not learning to fail and seek right answers with little thought, but rather they are developing their "self-esteem, task-orientation, attitudes to learning, persistence, flexibility and creativity" (1991: 34). A playful experience allows children to have some degree of control over their learning, to make mistakes without fear of failure, to take risks and try out new things, to learn in the company of others, and to experience a sense of joy, fun and satisfaction in the process. Yet we know that providing a playful environment for young children is in itself insufficient to foster the appropriate affective and dispositional skills young children require to enable them to become successful lifelong learners. Dowling (2014) has argued that, in an effort to move beyond the hard-line of prescriptive teaching and formal approaches, some settings have wrongly assumed that being friendly, encouraging and loving is all that is required of the early years practitioner. Yet as Dowling (2014: 133) articulates, if this "benign environment" is all that children are exposed to and they are praised incessantly and regarded as intrinsically clever, how will they ever cope with the challenges that a successful educational journey may bring? In this way a purposeful playful experience must be supported by playful teachers, those who are willing to be sensitive to young children's needs and interests, to let down their guard and to interact playfully with them, while simultaneously drip feeding learning into the process, as clearly detailed by Glenda Walsh in Chapter 3. In this way inappropriate pressure on young children is avoided, yet high levels of engagement and challenge are fostered (Walsh et al., 2011).

Pause for Thought

Reflect upon the views of another early years teacher:

> Getting it right in the early years is not just about making everything easy and cosy for young children. Sometimes I think that is where the whole play thing has gone wrong. I perceive my role as being caring and light-hearted to ensure children feel at ease in my company, but likewise to support, nurture and challenge young children's learning and development in all areas – cognitive, physical, linguistic, dispositional, social and emotional. I don't believe all of this nonsense that it will all just happen naturally when children are ready.

Based on your own experience, to what extent do you agree with the comments expressed above?

What, in your opinion, is the main role of the early years practitioner in nurturing young children's learning and development?

It is the intention of the rest of this chapter to showcase why emotional, social and dispositional skill development is essential for a successful educational journey and then to identify the role of the playful practitioner in the process.

Learning to Feel Secure in the Playful Setting

To begin this section, we are drawing on a number of statements made by young children aged 3–6 years about what makes them feel a little insecure in their setting:

Outside can be a bit scary

There are naughty boys in the playground and you could get hurt

Maybe if I get an answer wrong, the teacher might not help me

My friend told me that when you move into Year 3, the teachers don't even smile anymore

(Continued)

(Continued)

You get a test every Friday and it makes my tummy go all funny inside. If you don't get it all right, you can't even get out at break time

I would like to go back to nursery because you play more and the teacher doesn't shout

Common sense and our own experiences tell us that we cannot function properly if we are unhappy, upset or angry. Our thoughts and behaviour are heavily influenced by our feelings. Emotional competence is important both in its own right and for its contribution to social competence, academic success and mental health (Denham, 2007). As Eaude (2006: 63) states "unless children's emotional needs are met, all learning is impaired".

Fabian (2003: 106) agrees, arguing that the more confident children feel and the higher their self-esteem, the more likely they are to deal with new situations, to experiment, to explore, interact with others and to stay committed to learning through transfer. Children who have high levels of emotional well-being have been described by Laevers et al. (1997: 15) as feeling "like fish in water". To achieve this emotional state, Laevers et al. argue that children's physical needs, the need for affection, warmth and tenderness, the need for safety, clarity and continuity, the need for recognition, the need to consider themselves as competent and the need to give meaning to life, must be satisfied – a huge responsibility for the early years professional.

Young children's emotional development is rapid and profound. A three year old is full of raw emotion and they feel acutely. This is heightened as, at this age, feelings are not tempered by past experiences and most things are happening to this child for the first time. In consequence they may be desolate in distress, pent up with fury or over-brimming with excitement or joy. Young children respond to all experiences they encounter and, for those who live turbulent home lives, the effect of this responsiveness means that they may live their lives on an emotional roller coaster (Dowling, 2014).

As a coping mechanism, Denham (2007) advises that young children must learn to avoid the disorganisation of a tantrum and to begin to build up the skills to become competent at regulating their own emotions. In order to do so, Denham (2007: 4–5) highlights that preschool and school-aged children become emotionally competent in several ways:

- awareness of emotional experiences, including multiple emotions;
- discernment of own and others' emotional states;
- emotion language usage;
- empathic involvement in others' emotions;
- regulation of own aversive or distressing emotions;
- realisation that inner and emotional states may differ; and
- awareness that social relationships are in part defined by communication of emotions.

So how can the playful practitioner support the young child in building up such an emotional repertoire?

Case Study 7.1: The New Baby

Irma had a new baby brother a few weeks ago and Irma's father described his daughter as being delighted with and extremely proud of the tiny baby. Irma's daddy recounted how she helps in the home to wash and dress her new baby brother and is extremely protective of him at all times when anyone enters the house. One morning in the preschool setting, soon after the teacher's conversation with Irma's dad, Irma was observed in the domestic play area initially cuddling a doll. However, despite all of the positive revelations recounted by her father, she soon stopped and hurled the doll to the ground, shouting "we don't want you, go away you nasty thing. I don't like you".

Comment: Whilst Irma had responded to adult expectations that she would love her new brother, she was able to release her mixed feelings in the play situation.

On hearing this, how, in your opinion, should an early years practitioner support Irma regarding this release of emotion?

The Playful Adult's Role in Fostering Emotional Competence

Denham et al. (2012: 140–1) have identified the important role that the teacher plays in nurturing children's emotional competence, but highlight that early childhood teachers' roles in young children's emotional development have not been examined in the same way as the role of parents. Drawing on the evidence base pertaining to parents, they identify possible teacher roles in the development of young children's emotional competence:

- **Teacher Emotional Ability:** the way that teachers deal with their own emotional lives will contribute significantly to how they nurture the emotional ability of others.
- **Modelling Emotions:** being able to display positive emotionality in the setting/classroom will enable children to become aware of which emotions are acceptable and how to express and regulate them.
- **Teaching about Emotions:** participating in discussions about emotions provides children with tools for expressing or regulating their emotions and in turn their emotion knowledge can be enhanced.
- **Reactions:** the importance of the teacher reacting in a supportive and sensitive manner is paramount. Encouraging responses from teachers will help children to tolerate and regulate their emotions, highlighting that emotions are manageable and even useful.

Of course it is essential that all of the above takes place in an ethos of warmth, openness and respect, where teachers have developed a positive rapport with the children, have made a purposeful attempt to get to know the child and their families and provide a variety of playful opportunities to enable children to feel relaxed and at ease in their environment. Some practical suggestions for early years practitioners have been highlighted below:

- Organise a programme of home visits to get to know the young child in their home setting.
- Make time to interact with parents when they bring their child into the setting and when they pick them up.
- Engage in frequent purposeful observations of children and what they do on a daily basis.
- Create time to listen to children on a daily basis, e.g., through circle time, through the use of digital cameras, or by using puppets.
- Choose a child's interest derived from your 'conversations' with the children and take it forward in your planning for your setting.
- Consider ways in which you might react to a child when they are excited/happy/upset/frightened/angry. Write a plan showing how you could respond to a child who is experiencing positive/negative emotions. For example, if the emotion expressed is positive, how might you encourage the child, and share in their excitement? If the emotion expressed is negative, how might you acknowledge the child's emotions, showing the child warmth and understanding?
- Create a plan to help children recognise and deal with difficult emotions appropriately. Choose one of the following – circle time, storytelling, pictures, other activities – and use these to enhance children's emotional competence.

(Adapted from Walsh et al., 2010)

Learning with and about Others through Playful Experiences

The earliest social link for a child is through an attachment with a close adult. Within a secure attachment, a child feels able to rely on that adult or adults for safety and comfort. This critical and intimate bond provides the basis for the child to move out into the world and explore relationships.

Attunement is a natural extension of attachment and means being on the same wavelength as the young child; it is sometimes described as a "dance of dialogue" and the most important aspect of this 'dance' is that it is tailor-made or bespoke to that particular child (Read, 2014). This of course involves being deeply knowledgeable of each individual, through observing, listening to them and contributing to their playful experience. Trevarthen highlights the child's need for companionship:

> Children do need affection and support and protection and so on but they need a lot more than that. They need company which is interested and curious and affectionate ... Children are very good at private research. They can do it very well, but they don't do it if they are discouraged, if they feel unwanted or lonely, then they don't explore. (Trevarthen, 1998; cited in Elfer et al., 2003: 11)

Strong initial attachments with close adults pave the way for children to widen their world, branch out and grow to trust and enjoy the company of others.

Through playful interactions children:

- practise both verbal and non-verbal communication skills by accessing and participating in ongoing play, negotiating roles and appreciating the roles of others (Creasey et al., 1998);
- learn to participate in a group through waiting for their turn, and sharing materials and experiences (Devereux and Sabates-Wheeler, 2004);
- dip into, and try out, the roles of people in their home, the nursery and in the community by coming into contact with others (Creasey et al., 1998).

Pause for Thought

Note the patterns of young children's friendships: identify the most popular children and those who have difficulty forming relationships or participating in play.

(Continued)

(Continued)

Support individuals in the latter group, encourage them to gain access to a play activity by joining in and copying what the others are doing, e.g., building a wall of bricks or creating an obstacle race track using found materials.

By 3–4 years most children's passion for playing with other children really takes off. Practitioners recognise continuous questions from children seeking affirmation of friendship: "You're my friend, aren't you?", or a heart-rending cry of "Suki won't play with me".

Friendships developed in play really help children to rub along with others. Broadhead (2004) notes that the more co-operative the children's play theme, the more likely they are to recognise and appreciate the thought and perspectives of their friends. Dunn (2004) suggests that in new social relationships children learn a great deal about others and think about how to play with them. This includes learning how to give and take, conciliate, and negotiate in order to maintain the play. In their play children fall in and out of friendships. Until they learn to see another's viewpoint and to express their feelings and thoughts in words, they resort to physical actions to protect their rights. Although learning to apologise is a necessary social convention, requiring young children to say sorry will not always improve matters; the sentiment is often meaningless to a young child.

McTavish (2007: 10) stresses that learning simple techniques of conflict resolution can help:

- asking each child to describe or show what happened and to listen carefully to the other's point of view;
- helping them to recognise and reflect back what has caused the anger to erupt for each child;
- encouraging the children to suggest what they could do now to make things better;
- discussing options with them in order to decide on the best suggestion.

Implications for Children's Social Learning in Playful Contexts

Studies indicate that the best predictor of adapting to adult life is not to do with cognitive achievements but rather with how successful children are in getting along with other children. As Woolfson (1999: 14) states:

Although many parents think that success in joining the infant class depends heavily on children's ability to learn, evidence suggests that personal rather than intellectual characteristics have the biggest influence on their chance of having a good start to school.

Those who are able to sustain a close relationship with their peers are seen to be extremely advantaged (Ladd, 2003). Fortunately, most children between six and seven years are increasingly considerate towards one another and much of their activity and thinking relate to belonging to a group. At this age, children are usually positive about this way of working. In Italian schools in Reggio Emilia, children were clear about the benefits which they suggested included: the fun of doing things together; enabling your brain to work better; and sharing ideas to make a big one (Guidici et al., 2001).

Case Study 7.2: Friendships

Read the comments made by young children aged 3–6 about friendships and consider their implications for the early years setting/classroom:

I really love playing with Alice and Tom. They are my friends. They make school special

When I am sad, my friends make me laugh again

I wouldn't want my friends to go away. I love playing with them

I would be so lonely in school if I didn't have my friends

If I have to sit at a different table next year, maybe James and Sam will not be my friends anymore

Once a friendship begins to develop there are markedly more opportunities for the children involved to learn about what this other person feels and thinks.
In order to strengthen friendships practitioners may:

- provide a new child with a friend who can help to explain routines and show the new entrant resources to play with;
- encourage a more mature child to explain/show a less mature child how to do something;
- include many daily opportunities for turn-taking and sharing;
- support children to share interests by providing those who share a common schema or interest to play together;
- allow children initially to resolve conflicts in their own way.

Learning How to Become a Playful Learner: Why Dispositions Matter

Mastering new skills is gruelling work for most children and they have to be powerfully inclined to do so. We can become motivated when we feel that we are doing something interesting and succeeding at it, and so it is with children. Indeed a strong evidence base has highlighted the importance of initiating a desire to want to learn in children (see, e.g., Dweck, 1986) in an effort to ensure overall school success. As Stephenson and Parsons (2007: 143) indicate, school is the context in which children's growth as a learner begins and it is only when dispositions for learning are continued to be strengthened across the entire school career that "children will emerge as effective learners for life". Katz (1995) points out that children may have acquired skills but not be disposed to use them. She later describes this as "damaged disposition hypotheses" (Katz, 2011: 125). For example, some educators in their attempt to teach reading skills, damage children's dispositions to read, resulting in "aliterate children" (Da Ros-Voseles and Fowler-Haughey, 2007: 7). Knowledge and skills and the dispositions to use them are therefore closely inter-connected. Claxton and Carr (2004: 87) emphasise that education for the twenty-first century must move beyond a mere focus on curriculum content, by directly attending to children's attitudes towards learning (i.e., fostering in children a desire to be ready, willing and able to engage profitably with learning) to ensure overall success. We want to be encouraging children to display lively, playful minds which are "challenge-seeking, persist in the face of difficulty and enjoy exerting pressure in the face of task mastery" (Dweck, 1986: 1040). Therefore, a major component of early years education, according to Katz (2015), must be to provide young children with a wide range of experiences, opportunities, resources and contexts that will provoke, stimulate and nurture young children's intellectual dispositions: reasoning, predicting, solving problems, questioning, persisting, co-operating and being curious, to name but a few.

Pause for Thought

Read the following statements made by young children (3–6 years of age) about their early school experiences:

I love Year 3. You learn really important stuff there. It is still fun and it is better!

In Year 1 you still get to play but it's not baby play. You know you have to be big to play there

I can't wait for the big hard questions

For you, what are the underpinning messages that they are telling us?
   In light of these messages, what kind of early years experience do you consider most appropriate?

Nurturing Dispositions through Playful Learning and Teaching Experiences

It is now well known that young children learn more effectively when they are active, having fun and having regular and frequent access to adults. Children will play with what they know but there comes a time when they seek new experiences; the observant teacher recognises this need and provides nuggets of inspiration. Claxton and Carr (2004) talk about the need to develop a "potentiating" rather than a "prohibiting" learning experience for young children. They describe prohibiting environments as those which are highly structured and prevent young children from expressing a particular kind of learning response. In contrast, potentiating environments invite children not only to express certain learning dispositions but actively challenge them in the process. Katz (2015: 3) supports this thinking, highlighting that excessive and premature formal experiences may weaken or even damage children's dispositions for learning but, in addition, she argues that practices which she describes as "mindless, trivial if not banal" can do likewise, where children's playful minds are not fully stretched. Consequently, early years educators must focus on providing young children with "enjoyable yet challenging opportunities" as suggested in Chapter 3 as being a key pillar of the playful teaching and learning philosophy. These can be described as rich learning opportunities which are firmly based on children's own interests and their own funds of knowledge and ways in which these can be cultivated are identified below:

- Ensure that children have access to a rich range of continuous provision and are encouraged to become involved in experiences that are of particular interest to each individual.
- Ask parents about their child's home interests and build on these.

- Be alert to the power of screen-based media and popular culture when children will consider and replay the characters they have viewed.
- Support superhero play: become familiar with the characters; help to build contexts around them; provide open-ended resources to use with small world superhero figures.
- Plan for children to have time in play to allow their ideas to simmer and crystallise.

Case Study 7.3: TV-based Play

Visiting a primary classroom, I chatted to five year old Isabel about her view of school life. She appeared only moderately enthusiastic about the daily programme but said that she loved playtimes best. I innocently asked her if she played skipping games outside, and in return received a withering response.

"No, of course not, we play *Casualty* and I'm Chloe [a central character in the TV series]".

Isabel continued, showing real animation, "Do you know, I love it, playing Chloe I mean. When I go to bed at night, I start to think about all the things that Chloe might do next day".

Isabel's teacher, Maria, listened to the conversation, smiling: "So perhaps in class discussion time later, we could hear what the *Casualty* staff have been up to today, Isabel".

Comment: Maria described Isabel as a very sociable child with a vivid imagination but who found it difficult to listen and concentrate in adult-led activities. She quickly realised that Isabel's energies and enthusiasms were most evident in fantasy play derived from watching the popular TV series. Maria admitted that initially she had ignored this but had recently shown an interest in the play and had encouraged the players to reflect on the play themes and consider alternative scenarios to the ones depicted in the programme. She found that children in this cohesive social group recalled the familiar content in detail, but also ingeniously suggested new sub-plots and introduced new characters. Isabel and her friend had started to draw some of the characters and write captions to describe their roles.

Pause for Thought

Children's freely chosen play at break times often reveals their abiding interests.

How far do you observe and tune into these play themes, capitalising on children's background knowledge and motivation to promote positive dispositions towards learning?

Key Messages

- In this chapter we set out to highlight how playful teaching and learning experiences can help support the development of young children emotionally, socially and dispositionally.
- In doing so we stressed how young children's emotional, social and dispositional competence is best developed through the provision of playful experiences with the support of a playful adult.
- In addition we emphasised how friendship skills developed in play help children to recognise and appreciate the thoughts and actions of others.
- In playful encounters, we argued that young children release their feelings and learn to manage them safely.
- Finally we claimed that children are motivated to learn when they are engaged in interesting and challenging playful experiences.

Further Reading

Dowling, M. (2014) *Young Children's Personal, Social and Emotional Development* (fourth edition). London: Sage.

References

Atkin, J. (1991) 'Thinking about play', in N. Hall, and L. Abbott (eds) *Play in the Primary Curriculum*. London: Hodder and Stoughton. pp. 29–36.
Broadhead, P. (2004) *Early Years, Play and Learning*. Oxford: Routledge.

CCEA (2007) The Northern Ireland Curriculum Primary. CCEA: Belfast http://ccea. org.uk/sites/default/files/docs/curriculum/area_of_learning/fs_northern_ ireland_curriculum_primary.pdf (accessed 13 September 2016).

Claxton, G. (2000) 'A sure start for an uncertain future', *Early Education* 30: 7–10.

Claxton, G. and Carr, M. (2004) 'A framework for teaching learning: The dynamics of disposition', *Early Years* 24 (1): 87–97.

Creasey, G.L., Jarvis, P.A. and Berk, L. (1998) 'Play and competence', in O.N. Saracho and B. Spodek (eds), *Multiple Perspectives on Play In Early Childhood Education*. Albany, NY: State University of New York Press. pp. 116–43.

Da Ros-Voseles, D. and Fowler-Haughey, S. (2007) 'Why children's dispositions should matter to all teachers', *Young Children on the Web*, www.naeyc.org/files/ yc/file/200709/DaRos-Voseles.pdf (accessed 6 September 2016).

Denham, S.A. (2007) 'Dealing with feelings: How children negotiate the worlds of emotion and social relationships', *Cognition, Brain Behaviour* X1 (1): 1–48.

Denham, S.A., Bassett, H.H. and Zinsser, K. (2012) 'Early childhood teachers as socialisers of young children's emotional competence', *Early Childhood Education Journal* 40: 137–43.

Department for Education (DfE) (2014) *Statutory Framework for the Early Years Foundation Stage* www.foundationyears.org.uk/files/2014/07/EYFS_ framework_from_1_September_2014__with_clarification_note.pdf (accessed 13 September 2016).

Devereux, S. and Sabates-Wheeler, R. (2004) 'Transformative Social Protection', IDS Working Paper 232, Brighton: Institute of Development Studies, University of Sussex. www.unicef.org/socialpolicy/files/Transformative_Social_Protection.pdf (accessed 13 September 2016).

Dowling, M. (2014) *Young Children's Personal, Social and Emotional Development* (fourth edition). London: Sage.

Dunn, J. (2004) *Children's Friendships*. Oxford: Blackwell.

Dweck, C.S. (1986) 'Motivational process affecting learning', *American Psychologist* 41 (10): 1040–8.

Eaude, T. (2006) *Children's Spiritual, Moral, Social and Cultural Development: Primary and Early Years*. Exeter: Learning Matters.

Elfer, P., Goldschmied, E. and Selleck, D. (eds) (2003) *Key Persons in the Nursery*. London: David Fulton.

Fabian, H. (2003) 'Young children changing schools: Disruption or opportunity', *European Early Childhood Research Journal,* Monograph Series No 1: 99–107.

Fabian, H. (2007) 'Informing transitions', in A.W. Dunlop and H. Fabian (2007) (eds), *Informing the Transitions in the Early Years: Research, Policy and Practice*. pp. 3–17.

Guidici, C., Rinaldi, C. and Krechevsky, M. (2001) *Making Learning Visible: Children as Individuals and Group Learners*. Reggio Emilia: Reggio Children.

Katz, L. (1995) *Talks with Teachers of Young Children*. Norwood, NJ: Ablex.

Katz, L. (2011) 'Current perspectives on the early childhood curriculum', in R. House (ed.), *Too Much, Too Soon*. Stroud: Hawthorne Press.

Katz, L. (2015) *Lively Minds: Distinctions between Academic versus Intellectual Goals for Young Children*. University of Illinois: Clearinghouse on Early Education and Parenting.

Ladd, G. (2003) 'School transitions/school readiness: An outcome of early childhood development', PhD Thesis, Arizona: Arizona State University.

Laevers, F., Vandenbussche, E., Kog, M. and Depondt, L. (1997) *A Process-Oriented Child Monitoring System for Young Children*. Leuven: Centre for Experiential Education.

McTavish, A. (2007) *Feelings and Behaviour: A Creative Approach*. London: Early Education.

Niesel, R. and Griebel, W. (2005) 'Enhancing the competence of transition systems through co-construction', in A.W. Dunlop and H. Fabian (2007) (eds), *Informing Transitions in the Early Years: Research, Policy and Practice*. Buckingham: Open University Press. pp. 21–32.

Read, V. (2014) *Developing Attachments in Early Years Settings*. Abingdon: Routledge.

Saracho, O. and Spodek, B. (eds) (1998) *Multiple Perspectives on Play in Early Childhood Education*. Albany: State University of New York.

Stephenson, M. and Parsons, M. (2007) 'Expectations: Effects of curriculum change as viewed by children, parents and practitioners', in A.W. Dunlop and H. Fabian (2007) (eds) *Informing Transitions in the Early Years: Research, Policy and Practice*. Buckingham: Open University Press. pp. 137–48.

Walsh, G., Gray, C., McMillan, D., Hanna, K., Carville, S. and McCracken, O. (2010) *Examining Pedagogy in Early Childhood: Professional Development Model*. Dublin: Department of Education and Science.

Walsh, G., Sproule, L., McGuinness, C. and Trew, K. (2011) 'Playful structure: A novel image of early years pedagogy for primary school classrooms', *Early Years* 31 (2): 107–19.

Whitebread, D. (2012) 'The importance of play', Belgium: Toy Industries of Europe (TIE). www.importanceofplay.eu/IMG/pdf/dr_david_whitebread_-_the_importance_of_play.pdf (accessed 5 September 2016).

Woolfson, R. (1999) 'From nursery to infant class', *Nursery World* 93 (3369): 14–15.

8

Playful Learning in Natural Outdoor Environments

Richard Greenwood

Chapter Overview

For a number of reasons, many children today have fewer opportunities than children in previous generations to play and learn in natural outdoor environments. Teachers and early years professionals are in a position to provide memorable and enjoyable natural outdoor learning experiences, and the benefits as well as the possible barriers to doing this are discussed in this chapter. What does a 'playful' approach to learning outdoors in natural environments involve for teachers? What is their role and to what extent should children be given choice in what happens during these sessions?

Children's Distance from Nature and Educationalists' Responses

Many children growing up in the twenty-first century are detached from the natural world. The reasons for this are complex but well documented and include what could be termed both 'push' and 'pull' factors. Encroaching urbanisation, increased traffic and greater publicity surrounding 'stranger danger' have meant that many parents are reluctant to allow children the degree of outdoor freedom which their own generation enjoyed, while modern technology offers an exciting alternative to outdoor play as the number of devices and absorbing games proliferate (McClintic and Petty, 2015; Waller, 2007). In his seminal book *Last Child in the Woods*, Louv (2005) coined the phrase "nature deficit disorder", arguing that children's lack of positive experiences in outdoor natural environments can lead to a lack of affinity for the natural world.

Given these constraints and pressures, many professionals in early years and primary school settings have realised the importance of providing the children in their care with first-hand opportunities to play and learn outside in what Robertson (2014: 12) called "nature-rich outdoor spaces", engaging with natural materials and living things. They see it as vital that they metaphorically remove the walls between outdoor and indoor spaces to challenge the view that the enclosed classroom is the only place where important learning occurs. For some children this may be their only opportunity to play safely and freely outside.

Many adults' most vivid memories of early life and of schooldays in particular are memories of activities which took place out of doors, whether they be holidays, day trips or residential trips, or just playtimes (Waite, 2007). If memories are an important aspect of children's learning, it stands to reason that as education professionals we should provide as many memorable experiences as possible (Waite and Rea, 2007).

'Outdoor learning' is an umbrella term which includes all types of learning experiences that happen outside. It may be helpful to view different types of outdoor learning as situated along an activity continuum which ranges from whole class, directed activities, focusing on a particular investigation, to an individual child's self-chosen activity – free play. All experiences along this continuum should make the most of the unique and special nature of being outdoors, taking advantage of the variety, dynamism and unpredictability provided by changing weather conditions and changing seasons, the space and freedom which the world outside the classroom can afford, and the natural and sometimes living elements which are found there (Robertson, 2014).

As many teachers of young children will attest, children seem to be almost 'programmed' from birth to be active explorers of their environment rather than to sit in the same place for long periods. Bilton (2010) suggested that young children seem to know instinctively that the outdoors is a natural learning environment. She described how those who spend time observing young children are aware that in most cases they have a lack of concern for weather conditions and cannot wait to play outside. Research by Play England found that 86% of the children surveyed preferred to take part in outdoor activities rather than play on their computers indoors (Lester and Maudsley, 2007).

Pause for Thought

Thinking of your experience of working with young children, to what extent do you agree that most children today have less freedom to play outside on their own than children in previous generations? If so, are there additional reasons beyond those listed above why this might be so?

Children's development of ICT skills is obviously important for their futures, but how can parents and teachers find a balance between 'screen time' and 'fresh air time'?

Reflecting on your work, to what extent do you agree that it is one of the roles of education professionals to "provide as many memorable experiences as possible"?

Where do most of the experiences that you provide for your children lie along the 'activity continuum'?

Benefits of Learning Outdoors

Following the publication of the UK Government's 'Learning Outside the Classroom Manifesto' (DfES, 2006), which aimed to encourage more widespread use of outdoor educational opportunities, guidance materials for the Early Years Foundation Stage (EYFS) in England (DCSF, 2007) as well as local authorities listed a number of reasons why outdoor learning in early years settings is important. These included benefits for children in promoting healthy and active lifestyles, physical activity and freedom of movement, the development of children's confidence and well-being, social benefits as children play and discover together, and the opportunity for children to experience new challenges, assess risks and develop their creativity, problem-solving skills, imagination, inventiveness and resourcefulness. When playing outdoors, children grow emotionally and academically, increase their self-esteem, and develop in their participation in imaginative play, enjoying sensory experiences. In addition, children's behavioural and attendance problems may reduce (Clements, 2004; Maynard et al., 2013). Bilton (2010) outlined recent research within early years settings in which specifically boys and children of a lower social class were helped in terms of their language development, co-operative play and attention span by spending significant time playing out of doors. Expanding upon this, Woods (2013) noticed the improvement in "sustained talk" (2013: 55) amongst children playing in natural environments, particularly when the area within which the children were playing did not contain artificial, added, fixed features. Children who rarely interacted with others appeared to "work and play above themselves".

Barriers and Risk

Woods (2013) noted that the advantages and individual qualities which outdoor activities present are often the very same characteristics which challenge adults – for example temperature, rain, muddy ground, open space and lack of boundaries. The time-consuming nature and practical difficulty of getting a class of children ready to go outside is an obvious additional barrier, as is teacher confidence due to lack of experience (Nundy et al., 2009; Ofsted, 2011). Children's playfulness, especially outdoors, is a challenge to an adult's desire to control the learning environment. Other practical issues such as cost and changing educational priorities stop some schools and teachers from taking children out of doors (Rickinson et al., 2004; Waite, 2011).

As long ago as 1930, the famous nursery educator Margaret McMillan wrote that children should be allowed to play "bravely and adventurously … in a provocative environment where new chances are made possible" (1930: 78). She provided outdoor play activities involving climbing trees and exploring a wilderness area, digging channels for water and creating large constructions using real tools. One of the main dilemmas for teachers and early years practitioners who intend to take their children out of doors is how to provide activities for children which may involve climbing, balancing, jumping, swinging and sliding, all of which hold obvious risks, when we live in a risk-averse culture, especially where children are concerned (Austin, 2007). Those observing children at play out of doors sometimes report how their charges create their own risky challenges by setting up increasingly higher jumps or balancing logs. Sandseter's work on risky play (2007, 2009) has highlighted the potential which natural spaces offer for children's risk taking behaviour, viewed by Sandseter as a natural, positive and necessary aspect of children's physical, emotional and social development. Children need to be challenged in their play in order to learn about their limitations and assume responsibility for their own actions (Constable, 2012). Through these challenges children are able to establish their own boundaries and decide on the activities in which they are comfortable taking part. Constable concluded that many school playgrounds, with their carefully designed equipment and soft surfaces, dull children's perceptions of what they can safely accomplish and lack the more realistic challenges of natural spaces. It is the role of adults to keep children safe but also to teach them about the dangers around them. Removing all risks from children's lives because of health and safety concerns can restrict the development of children's wellbeing.

Children seem to benefit most when their teachers display an enjoyment in being outdoors and an interest in physical play. Stephenson (2003: 38) called for a "… sensitive and liberal approach to supervision …" that allows children to find challenges that are "… experienced as risky but do not put them in positions of hazard". No writer who discusses the importance of allowing a degree of challenging or 'risky' play out of doors advocates a careless, negligent approach; a carefully considered risk assessment should be carried out in all outdoor areas and of all new activities before they are provided. However, children need to learn that getting hurt or stung or falling over is a part of play and that the resulting cuts and bruises are a natural part of growing up (Constable, 2012; Tovey, 2015).

Pause for Thought

For you as a teacher or early years practitioner, which of the barriers listed above seem to you to be hardest to overcome?

Do you feel that pressures produced by teachers' and parents' concerns about safety, risk and the 'litigious society' have increased or decreased in recent years?

How do teachers and early years professionals find a balance between protecting children and allowing an element of 'risky play'?

A Playful Approach to Outdoor Learning

The concept of 'playfulness' as used within this book emphasises an approach to teacher interaction with children which infuses light-heartedness, fun, creativity, engagement and spontaneity into the learning environment (Goouch, 2008; Walsh et al., 2011). The practitioner's style respects, values and trusts the children's contributions to their own learning and allows for children's ownership of the activities (Moyles, 2015). It might be argued that playtime outdoors in a natural or semi-natural environment is the perfect opportunity for teachers and early years professionals to engage playfully with the children in their care.

Outdoor play can be categorised using the same typologies used to describe indoor play. For example, Moyles (2010) described 'pure play' as being within the total control of children, 'playful learning' as play which is child or adult initiated or inspired and which engages the child in playful ways of learning, and 'playful teaching', which utilises the child's natural and innate joy in play activities but can be directed by adults. Witt (2013) analysed approaches to outdoor play as suggested by Hughes (2002) which she felt were specifically relevant for geographical learning. These included 'free exploration' and 'guided exploration', 'close encounter play', 'creative play' and 'imaginative play'. This chapter aims to help teachers to imagine how a playful approach on their part might be infused into all of these kinds of activities.

Case Study 8.1: The Spooky Tree

A class of eight year old children took part in an autumn walk around the campus of the neighbouring university college. They were split into groups of around nine or ten, each accompanied by a pair of the college's teacher education students. The children took part in identifying and collecting autumn leaves and fruit from a variety of deciduous trees, and looking out for squirrels, birds and badger setts, stopping to listen for the sounds that could be heard and to simply enjoy the autumn landscape. They took photographs which would later be printed out and brought back to the campus on a second walk two months later so that the autumn and winter scenes could be compared. Something that arrested the attention of a number of the groups was an unusually-shaped Spanish chestnut tree which, unlike the trees all around it, had no leaves at all. The student group leaders encouraged a few minutes of playful imagination as they looked at this twisted tree. What had happened here? Had the tree been struck by lightning in a terrible storm or had it been cursed by a horrible witch? Were the creatures who lived in the tree sad about what had happened? What would the children feel like if they were out here on their own under the tree on a dark, moonlit night? Back in the classroom, in the freely chosen writing activity which followed the autumn walk, lots of imaginative ideas about 'The Spooky Tree' were explored.

(Continued)

(Continued)

Figure 8.1   Children imagining spooky goings-on under 'The Spooky Tree'

(Photo: Richard Greenwood)

Pause for Thought

To what extent do you agree that playtime outdoors in a natural or semi-natural environment is the perfect opportunity for teachers and early years professionals to engage playfully with the children in their care?

Looking at the list of activities in the case study above, do you think that there are preferable ages of children when some of these activities might be encouraged?

How might a teacher planning a playful outdoor learning experience achieve a balance between active play and 'slow' play?

Thinking about the children with whom you work, is it easy/possible for young children to 'switch modes' from factual to imaginative and playful in the way that the eight year old children in Case Study 8.1 were able to do?

Children's Choices

A number of authors have emphasised the importance of allowing children to have choice in outdoor play. Broadhead and Burt (2012) argued that when children lead their own play in a positive learning environment and with good adult support, they make more progress and their playful learning can be richer and more complex than the sometimes decontextualised learning outcomes determined by adults. Austin (2007) stated simply: "How much more relevant and exciting could the learning be for our children if we allowed them to take some of the decisions about spaces to be explored and activities to be undertaken?" (2007: 1). While observing den-making activities of 3–5 year old children in a variety of outdoor settings, Canning (2010) described how the children, if given a degree of choice in how they would proceed, found ways to use the environment to fulfil their own curiosity and developed in their own motivation to play. Waters and Maynard (2010) suggested that play in a natural outdoor area can provide opportunities for teachers to respond to child-initiated interaction and build on children's interests. They stated that there was evidence that simply *being outside* is not enough and the manner in which teachers and children engage while they are outside impacts upon the resulting experience and associated learning. Therefore a tokenistic approach to outdoor provision must be avoided (Harriman, 2006; Woods, 2013). A distinction needs to be made between planned outdoor play and 'playtime' or 'breaktime'. Outdoor play may often be unplanned and serendipitous, but even play involving a high degree of choice can be both planned and purposeful. Practitioners should aim at providing children with high quality experiences which will aid their development in all areas of learning, not simply provide them with a break from indoor classroom activities or be an attempt to replicate outdoors what happens inside. The temptation of simply "taking the inside out" must be avoided by practitioners (Woods, 2013: 58). Shirley (2007) suggested that "Simply moving children's learning outdoors will not magically enhance that learning, but it has the potential to foster genuine creativity and inquisitiveness" (2007: 11).

Case Study 8.2: The Tree Trunk Train

A class of nursery children (aged three or four years) were enjoying a Forest-School-type session in a neighbouring wooded area on a cold and drizzly February morning. The children, under the supervision of

(Continued)

(Continued)

Figure 8.2   Children playing on the 'Tree Trunk Train'

(Photo: Richard Greenwood)

four adults, were suitably dressed in warm coats and scarves and Wellington boots. Within a designated area the children were allowed to choose their own play activities and to take part in these individually or in groups. Some enjoyed playing chasing games or jumping off a tree trunk while others played or explored on their own, looking for interesting twigs and leaves. A favourite group activity was sitting on the 'Tree Trunk Train' – a fallen tree trunk on a slope within the play area. The children enjoyed sitting behind each other on the log, and even queueing for the privilege! They sang choo-choo songs, helped by the adults, who sometimes sat on the log with the children and joined in their play enthusiastically.

The adults seemed to be finding a useful balance between allowing children a degree of choice in their play and encouraging individual and group activities. Sometimes they held back as children took the lead, while at other times they responded to children's questions, joined in their imaginative games, suggested what a child might do next or led enthusiastic singing.

Pause for Thought

Reflect on Austin's assertion that children's learning can be much more relevant and exciting if they are allowed to take some of the decisions about spaces to be explored and activities to be undertaken.

The teachers in Case Study 8.2 seemed to achieve a balance between allowing children a high degree of choice and planning purposeful activities; how do you think they managed this?

The Adult Role in Playful Outdoor Learning

So what might be the adult role when working with children engaged in play outside in natural spaces? A number of authors make the point that the attitude of the adults, as perceived by the children, is crucial. Bilton (2010) stressed that it is only when all of the staff support and enjoy outdoor play that it will work, but that being part of children's play is one of the most difficult jobs that early years practitioners and teachers have to do because getting it right requires a lot of effort. Constable (2014) suggested that because children learn so much by watching others around them, the attitudes of the adults who are supervising their outdoor play are crucial; if the adults are complaining about the cold or wet conditions it is likely that the children will begin to react in similar ways. In contrast, if the supervising adults get down, literally, to the children's level to smile, talk, encourage, ask questions or join in with a role play, modelling behaviour and actions, then children's enjoyment and learning should follow. It is tempting for teachers and early years professionals to see play as having few 'outcomes' or outcomes of low status, and therefore as having recreational value only; this may be even more of an issue when that play is out of doors. Woods (2013) stressed the need continually to: "... articulate the value of child-led, outdoor deep-level learning about the world, the self and others as children test out theories and experience a sense of wonder at their smallest find or discovery" (2013: 57). Guidance for the EYFS in England (DCSF, 2007) called for the provision of meaningful, engaging experiences which support children's development across the curriculum – opportunities, among others, to be: excited, energetic, adventurous, noisy and messy; to talk, listen, interact and make friends; to imagine, dream and invent; to create and construct; to investigate, explore, discover and experiment; to express ideas and feelings; to be active, run, jump, climb and dig; and to hide, relax, reflect and find calm.

However, for many professionals working with young children, facilitating all of these different kinds of activities is a difficult balancing act. Particularly difficult for some is knowing when to take a step back. Austin (2007) agreed that working collaboratively with children is a difficult skill for practitioners, quoting Bruce (2005), who suggested that only a few skilled practitioners seem to join free-flow play and develop it without destroying it. Teachers need to be in tune with the children's expressions of awe, wonder, excitement and/or questioning as they take part in outdoor play. If they are able to take opportunities to offer themselves as partners (more knowledgeable or otherwise) in the children's experiences, there is valuable learning potential in the rich, meaningful interactions which may take place (Waters and Maynard, 2010).

Witt (2013) stated that the value of playful activity outdoors was sometimes underestimated and that not all teachers and schools are comfortable with such an experiential, explorative approach, particularly given the demands of overcrowded, assessment-driven curricula in primary schools. Some of the early years teachers interviewed by Maynard and Waters (2007) said that they needed to be convinced of the learning benefits of free play in the outdoor environment. Some of these adopted exactly the same patterns of working outside as they did inside. Witt (2013) argued that the challenge for teachers as they attempted to "model a spirit of playfulness" (2013: 56) was to try to free up their planning to work with "emergent purposes" rather than detailed learning outcomes. The skill may sometimes be in judging when children want adults to be playful. Woods (2013) suggested that there are always opportunities for adults to demonstrate their willingness, ability and readiness to recognise when children want them to be playful and follow their lead, and to recognise when it would be better to withdraw. Bilton (2010) stressed that the important question which practitioners should ask themselves is – why are we joining in and how will this help the children? Woods and Hall (2013) described how when early years staff whom they observed had gained more experience in outdoor play sessions, the need that they felt to intervene and control diminished: "The staff, gradually letting go, absorbing themselves in the child-led, playful explorations, have emerged as quieter, more reflective and more natural co-constructors of new experiential understanding" (2013: 51).

Case Study 8.3: We're Going on a Bear Hunt

A teacher education student and her school placement teacher devised a series of lessons on the topic of 'Bears' for a class of five year old children. The class learned about different types of real bears but

Figure 8.3   After a successful 'Bear Hunt'!

(Photo: Richard Greenwood)

also enjoyed hearing about lots of bear characters from stories. Having read and 'performed' with the children the popular children's book *We're Going on a Bear Hunt* by Michael Rosen, the adults and the children decided that they should go on a bear hunt themselves. Adjoining the school is an area of woodland with a pond called 'Leafy Hollow', where the student set up her bear hunt trail with laminated bear paw prints and notices with the prepositions 'over', 'under', 'through', etc., pinned to trees. The children were very excited at the prospect of

(Continued)

(Continued)

meeting a bear in the forest, with one heard to say: "I'm not *really* frightened!". The children enjoyed walking through the trees, playing out some of the actions from the book and eventually finding ... a very large, but not at all fierce, cuddly bear hiding at the far end of the trail. He was carried triumphantly back to the classroom where the photos taken on the walk were uploaded to the interactive whiteboard and discussed.

The class teacher and the student teacher stayed 'in role' throughout the lesson, pretending that the bear at the end of the trail was real (or at least not saying outright that it was not!). This sense of playfulness permeated the lesson before, during and after the bear hunt itself. The children were intrigued and excited, joining in enthusiastically as they chanted "We're goin' on a bear hunt ... We're goin' to catch a big one" and as they went *over*, *under* and *through* the various obstacles in their way.

Pause for Thought

Think of a situation when you wondered if you should join in with the play of the children in your care or take a step back. What did you do? Did you end up developing the play or destroying it?

The adults in Case Study 8.3 remained 'in role' throughout the lesson; is this the best/easiest approach?

In your experience, do colleagues sometimes see outdoor play as having recreational value only?

Do you have colleagues who are unconvinced of the learning benefits of free play in the outdoor environment? What might be the best way to convince them?

Playful actions

Below is a list of activity suggestions which it is hoped will provide a good deal of 'playfulness potential' for teachers and early years practitioners.

They are listed in no particular order and the age group of the children who might take part in the activities is not stipulated.

Children, either individually or in groups, could:

- make a collection of natural materials/objects that are smooth/rough, prickly or soft, etc.
- make marks on a blank piece of paper using objects found in the environment
- gather natural materials to create seasonal pictures
- take photographs of natural shapes or colours with digital cameras, mobile phones or tablets
- tiptoe through or sit quietly in a wooded area, listening for sounds
- gather twigs and tie them with twine into bundles of five or ten
- make or gather things that can be taken out and 'flown' on a windy day
- create a habitat, either imaginary or representative of a real habitat which the children have heard about, for example a desert, a jungle or a swamp
- gather material to stick into a small piece of clay to create a beautiful bird or a scary monster and talk about it afterwards. Give it a name, decide where it lives and what it eats and record a 'wildlife documentary' about it on video
- build a den/shelter building – for themselves or for fantasy creatures such as fairies, elves or giants
- make a house from sticks for the second of the Three Little Pigs
- talk about camouflage and what you would need to hide from a Big Bad Wolf
- choose a well-known story such as *The Gruffalo* by Julia Donaldson, and get the children to find 'food' that the various animal characters would like to eat

Key Messages

- Taking groups of children out of the classroom and into natural outdoor spaces is not an easy option for teachers or early years professionals. Most will attest to the potential benefits of doing so but will also be able to list numerous barriers and difficulties. Then,

(Continued)

(Continued)

when outside, decisions are also difficult concerning the best way to use the available time and to what extent children should be allowed choice over what they do during outdoor time.

- Positive adult attitudes to the importance of play and learning outside, as well as to the sometimes adverse weather conditions, are crucial.
- Time spent outdoors in a natural or semi-natural environment is the perfect opportunity for adults to engage playfully with the children in their care. For teachers, knowing when to follow rather than lead, when to join in with children's play or withdraw is a skill which often can only be developed 'in action'.
- Ideally, throughout all of the activities which take place, adults can develop in their ability to "model a spirit of playfulness".

Further Reading and Resources

Bilton, H. and Crook, A. (2016) *Exploring Outdoors Ages 3–11: A Guide for Schools* (London: David Fulton) provides ideas on how to encourage children's learning through outdoor exploration by following one primary school's outdoor practice through an entire academic year.

Richard Louv (2005) describes a widening gap between children and the natural world, and the potential impact on our physical, mental and societal health. You can read more of his work at http://richardlouv.com/ (accessed 6 September 2016).

References

Austin, R. (ed.) (2007) *Letting the Outside In: Developing Teaching and Learning Beyond the Early Years Classroom.* Stoke-on-Trent: Trentham.

Bilton, H. (2010) *Outdoor Learning in the Early Years: Management and Innovation* (third edition). Oxford: David Fulton.

Broadhead, P. and Burt, A. (2012) *Understanding Young Children's Learning through Play.* London: Routledge.

Bruce, T. (2005) *Developing Learning in Early Childhood.* London: Paul Chapman Publishing.

Canning, N. (2010) 'The influence of the outdoor environment: Den-making in three different contexts', *European Early Childhood Education Research Journal* 18 (4): 555–66.

Clements, R. (2004) 'An investigation of the status of outdoor play', *Contemporary Issues in Early Childhood* 5 (1): 68–80.

Constable, K. (2012) *The Outdoor Classroom Ages 3–7*. Oxford: Routledge.

Constable, K. (2014) *Bringing the Forest School Approach to Your Early Years Experience*. Oxford: Routledge.

Department for Children, Schools and Families (DCSF) (2007) *Guidance for the Early Years Foundation Stage*. Available from https://web.archive.org/web/20140824070514/http://www.urbanforestschool.co.uk/PDF/3_3b_ep.pdf (accessed 6 September 2016).

Department for Education and Skills (DfES) (2006) *Manifesto for Learning Outside the Classroom*. London: HMSO. www.lotc.org.uk/wp-content/uploads/2011/03/G1.-LOtC-Manifesto.pdf (accessed 14 September 2016).

Goouch, K. (2008) 'Understanding playful pedagogies, play narratives and play spaces', *Early Years* 28 (1): 93–102.

Harriman, H. (2006) *The Outdoor Classroom*. Swindon: Corner to Learn.

Hughes, B. (2002) *A Playworker's Taxonomy of Play Types* (second edition). London: Playlink.

Lester, S. and Maudsley, M. (2007) *Play, Naturally: A Review of Children's Natural Play*. London: Play England/National Children's Bureau.

Louv, R. (2005) *Last Child in the Woods: Saving Our Children from Nature Deficit Disorder*. London: Atlantic Books.

Maynard, T. and Waters, J (2007) 'Learning in the outdoor environment: A missed opportunity?' *Early Years* 27 (3): 255–65.

Maynard, T., Waters, J. and Clement, J. (2013) 'Child-initiated learning, the outdoor environment and the "underachieving" child', *Early Years* 33 (3): 212–25.

McClintic, S. and Petty, K. (2015) 'Exploring early childhood teachers' beliefs and practices about preschool outdoor play: A qualitative study', *Journal of Early Childhood Teacher Education* 36: 24–43.

McMillan, M. (1930) *The Nursery School*. London: Dent.

Moyles, J. (ed.) (2010) *Thinking about Play: Developing a Reflective Approach*. Maidenhead: Open University Press.

Moyles, J. (ed.) (2015) *The Excellence of Play* (fourth edition). Maidenhead: Open University Press.

Nundy, S., Dillon, J. and Dowd, P. (2009) 'Improving and encouraging teacher confidence in out-of-classroom learning: The impact of the Hampshire Trailblazer project on 3–13 curriculum practitioners', *Education 3–13* 37 (1): 61–73.

Ofsted (2011) *Geography: Learning to Make a World of Difference*. Report, February 2011. www.gov.uk/government/uploads/system/uploads/attachment_data/file/413725/Geography_-_learning_to_make_a_world_of_difference_report_summary.pdf (accessed 6 September 2016).

Rickinson, M., Dillon, J., Teamey, K., Morris, M., Mee, Y.C., Sanders, D. and Benefield, P. (2004) *A Review of Research on Outdoor Learning*. London: NFER. www.field-studies-council.org/media/268859/2004_a_review_of_research_on_outdoor_learning.pdf (accessed 6 September 2016).

Robertson, J. (2014) *Dirty Teaching: A Beginner's Guide to Learning Outdoors*. Carmarthen: Independent Thinking Press.

Sandseter, E. (2007) 'Categorising risky play: How can we identify risk-taking in children's play?' *European Early Childhood Education Research Journal* 15 (2): 237–52.

Sandseter, E. (2009) 'Children's expressions of exhilaration and fear in risky play', *Contemporary Issues in Early Childhood* 10 (2): 92–106.

Shirley, I. (2007) 'Letting the outside in: Developing teaching and learning beyond the early years classroom', in R. Austin (ed.), *Letting the Outside in: Developing Teaching and Learning Beyond the Early Years Classroom*. Stoke-on-Trent: Trentham. pp. 1–12.

Stephenson, A. (2003) 'Physical risk-taking: Dangerous or endangered?' *Early Years* 23 (1): 35–43.

Swarbrick, N., Eastwood, G. and Tutton, K. (2004) 'Self-esteem and successful interaction as part of the forest school project', *Support for Learning,* 19 (3): 142–46.

Tovey, H. (2015) 'Adventurous play outdoors', in J. Moyles (ed.), *The Excellence of Play* (fourth edition). Maidenhead: Open University Press. pp. 213–24.

Waite, S. (2007) '"Memories are made of this": Some reflections on outdoor learning and recall', *Education 3-13* 35 (4): 333–47.

Waite, S. (2011) 'Teaching and learning outside the classroom: Personal values, alternative pedagogies and standards', *Education 3–13* 39 (1): 65–82.

Waite, S. and Rea, T. (2007) 'Enjoying teaching and learning outside the classroom', in D. Hayes (ed.), *Joyful Teaching and Learning in the Primary School*. Exeter: Learning Matters. pp. 52–62.

Waller, T. (2007) '"The Trampoline Tree and the Swamp Monster with 18 heads": Outdoor play in the Foundation Stage and Foundation Phase', *Education 3–13* 35 (4): 393–407.

Walsh, G., Sproule, L., McGuinness, C. and Trew, K. (2011) 'Playful structure: A novel image of early years pedagogy for primary school classrooms', *Early Years* 31 (2): 107–19.

Waters, J. and Maynard, T. (2010) 'What's so interesting outside? A study of child-initiated interaction with teachers in the natural outdoor environment', *European Early Childhood Education Research Journal* 18 (4): 473–83.

Witt, S. (2013) 'Playful approaches to learning out of doors', in S. Scoffham (ed.), *Teaching Geography Creatively*. London: Routledge. pp. 47–58.

Woods, A. (ed.) (2013) *Child-Initiated Play and Learning*. Oxford: David Fulton.

Woods, A. and Hall, V. (2013) 'Exploiting outdoor possibilities for all children', in A. Woods (ed.), *Child-Initiated Play and Learning*. Oxford: David Fulton. pp. 50–67.

ICT Made Playful

Christine Stephen

9

Chapter Overview

Digital technologies are often talked about as a new way for children to learn and to accelerate their learning. Information and Communication Technologies (ICT) offer the prospect of engaging children in playful activities that are motivating, satisfying and support playful learning. However, research suggests that the technologies alone are not enough to promote learning and that the role of educators is critical for encounters with digital resources to support learning. This chapter is about young children's encounters with ICT, the kinds of learning that technologies can facilitate and the important contribution needed from educators if digital resources are to offer opportunities for playful teaching and learning. This chapter aims to help readers:

- Understand current debates about digital play and digital learning;
- Become familiar with the kinds of learning associated with encounters with technologies;
- Learn about the kind of pedagogical interactions necessary if children are to have positive and playful learning experiences with ICT.

ICT and Young Children

Parents, policymakers and educators talk of the need for children to develop digital competencies for future economic success. This argument, along with the belief in the potential of Information and Communication Technologies (ICT) to enhance or accelerate learning, has encouraged the growing market in educational toys for use at home and led to increased provision of digital hardware and software in preschool settings and the early years of primary school. As any educator or researcher who has introduced a tablet or new digital camera into a classroom knows, such resources are highly prized by young children. Nevertheless, our understanding of the nature of playful learning and teaching with these resources is still evolving and many educators feel less confident about the use of new technologies than about more traditional resources.

There is a broad and increasingly polarised debate about the positive or negative outcomes of encounters with digital resources (see a summary of this debate in Stephen and Plowman, 2014). Some are concerned that using technologies is inappropriate for young children, citing anxieties that these resources encourage passivity, limit physical exploration, increase social isolation and are developmentally inappropriate in the early years. On the other hand, enthusiasts for digital resources argue that they extend opportunities to acquire knowledge and understanding, prompt the development of new competencies and offer new ways of collaborating and constructing knowledge. Others focus on claims that technologies are fun and motivating. This debate is unlikely to be resolved in any definitive manner. There is a lack of clear cut research findings about the risks and benefits and a growing body of evidence that what makes a difference is the way in which educators make use of ICT as well as the design features of particular technologies. In the meantime, technologies are a ubiquitous feature of the world in which children are growing up and a part of their everyday life at home, in the community and in their educational settings. The challenge for educators is to take account of the experiences of technologies which children bring to their nursery or classroom and to respond to the opportunities which they offer, just as they do with traditional playroom resources such as sand, construction equipment and props for role play (see also the discussion of 'funds of knowledge' in Chapter 3 of this book).

Pause for Thought

Research evidence suggests that the attitudes of teachers towards ICT and their own skill with technologies make a difference to the ICT experiences they offer children. To what extent do you see technologies as a threat or as an essential part of the early years setting/classroom experience?

To what extent does your familiarity with some technologies influence the experiences you offer children in your class? Try to think of some specific examples.

The Research Context

The discussion which follows will draw on the international literature and, in particular, findings from our own series of studies, carried out over the last fifteen years, about young children engaging with technologies at home and in educational settings (see, for instance, Stephen and Plowman, 2008; Plowman et al., 2010; Stephen et al., 2013). In our exploration of children's learning with new technologies we set out to consider what children were learning and how the practitioners responsible for their care and education could support this learning in preschool settings. In later studies we extended our interest to children's engagement with, and learning from, digital technologies at home. Throughout this chapter we will adopt a broad definition of digital technologies or ICT resources, encompassing desktop computers, laptops and tablets with touch screen or keyboard and mouse interfaces; mobile phones; digital cameras; interactive television and DVDs; games consoles and products like the Wii which use a television display; audio and recording devices; and educational resources such as reading devices and responsive globes and toys designed to simulate interactive equipment such as cash registers and bar scanners.

Our studies focused on children aged three to five years old, growing up in central Scotland. These children were attending local authority part-time preschool provision and came from families which mirrored the socio-economic patterns of Scotland. The settings we explored adopted the predominantly child-led, active and play-based approach to early education in line with good practice guidance in Scotland. Children chose freely from a range of activities prepared to reflect their current interests. Brief adult-led large or small group activities were offered in most settings at some point during each daily session. We worked through cycles of practitioner planning, action and data collection in the playroom. The research team and practitioners shared data gathered through observations, recordings and interviews. We researched children's activities and learning at home with digital technologies in two longitudinal studies. Both of these investigations engaged case study families in multiple rounds of data collection which included conversations with parents and children, video recordings and text diaries.

Is Digital Play Playful?

Play is often defined in terms of distinct features such as a focus on process rather than product, on mastery and spontaneity. Yet, although children's encounters with digital technologies are often described as "playing with the computer", many technological toys, computer games or programmes and apps marketed as appropriate for young children have little scope for spontaneous activity or individual choices. They typically focus on 'right answers' to closed questions, on practice of already attained concepts and prescribed ways of responding. For instance, art packages for young children involve them in drawing and colouring in just as they would with crayons and paper. Computer games and apps require children to match shapes or quantities and identify similarities and rhymes in the same way as they do with traditional card games and puzzles. Although many of these digital resources are marketed as enhancing learning to read or write or rehearse phonics skills and mathematical operations, little convincing evidence is provided about outcomes and the games often involve mundane activities, alleviated to varying extents by interactivity and entertaining features such as animation. Furthermore, we also know that when adults direct children towards particular activities in the classroom or playroom, the young learners think of this as 'work' rather than 'play' with its associated freedom and fun (Grieshaber and McArdle, 2010). In these circumstances, being invited to engage with a phonics program on a desk top computer or a maths game on a tablet will not necessarily be experienced by children as playful learning.

Pause for Thought

Recall a recent occasion when children have been using some of the technology available in an early years setting or classroom. From what you observed – did it look playful? What signs did you look for? Was the technology liberating or constraining?

Play Potential

The play potential of ICT varies with the player and the resource. While a toddler's playful exploration may be encouraged by an interactive toy which responds with lights and sounds, this is unlikely to engage the curiosity of a four year old. Digital play can foster playful competition through physical games such as using the Wii to play 'tennis' or 'bowling' or support playful collaboration between children and teachers; for example, as they work together to solve problems, negotiate roles and take risks while making an animated film (Marsh, 2010). Building on the distinction between epistemic and ludic play made by Hutt et al. (1989), Edwards and Bird (2015) identified two forms of play with digital technologies. They argue that children's play with a novel technology is initially epistemic (moving through exploration and problem solving to skill acquisition and intentional use) before moving on to ludic play where the resource can be used symbolically and innovatively. This work by Edwards and Bird suggests that playful teaching should begin by observing a child's current focus in play, whether that focus is on exploring what a technology can do or on innovative or creative uses of the digital resources, and finding ways to support and extend those interests. Deciding when a child is ready to move from exploring how a resource is used to putting the technology to purposeful, task-orientated or creative use requires careful observation and professional judgement.

There is growing evidence that children are blending digital and traditional resources in their play (as in the case study below), particularly when the technologies are portable and tangible rather than screen-based. During our observations in preschool playrooms we noted many examples of non-functioning computers and mobile phones and functioning digital cameras being employed in pretend offices, hospitals, shops and schools. Marsh (2004) found that, while watching television was a central feature of the leisure activity of 2–4 year olds, this was not a passive process. The children talked about the characters and narratives in the programmes they viewed and built on the storylines in their own pretend play. The playful teacher will find many opportunities in blended play to support learning about and through technologies.

Case Study 9.1: Olivia: Digital Play, Pretend Play and Blended Play

Olivia (almost five years old) stayed in a holiday house which contained three laptops, a BlackBerry, two Kindles, three tablets, three adult digital cameras and her own child's digital camera. She did watch some DVDs, played a game on a tablet for a few minutes and took

(Continued)

(Continued)

some photographs of animals on her digital camera, but the most enduring technology-related activity was when she decided she needed her own computer for a pretend game about going to work and set about making one with shiny card and a pen. The card was folded (shiny side out like Mummy's computer) and then she drew a screen on the upright portion and keys and a mouse pad on the horizontal. This computer was used with apparent satisfaction by Olivia in several long imaginative games during the holiday and adults were drawn in to use it too when the role they had been allocated by her required this.

Do Digital Technologies Support Learning in Educational Settings?

A review of the literature about the measurable outcomes from engaging with technological games and digital resources suggests that any expectation that there will be clear evidence of positive gains is misplaced and that a more conditional and nuanced conclusion is warranted. Indeed, the conclusion reached by Bolstad (2004: 71) that "literature about the *potential* of ICT in early childhood education is more common than research which evaluates its *role* in early childhood education" remains pertinent over ten years later. The tentative and conditional state of understanding about young children's encounters with digital resources is exemplified in studies such as that by Couse and Chen (2010) who found that, while tablet computers were a "viable tool" for 3–6 year olds to use in an educational setting, it was the way the teachers made use of the technology which made a difference.

In the typical, richly-resourced playrooms and classrooms children experience in post-industrial societies, digital technologies can extend the range of options available but offer little that is different in terms of the cognitive operations demanded by traditional resources and activities. Children match, sort, categorise and count with both traditional and digital resources. For instance, communication and language may be developed as children hear stories being told or listen to audio recordings, explore the contents pages and indexes of books or navigate the menus and icons on screen displays, and talk about pictures they have drawn or images captured by digital cameras. Indeed, most of the technological games children experience online or via apps require at least a functioning understanding of the concept being rehearsed, such as managing quantity by employing the idea of more and less, identifying rhymes or an implicit ability to add or subtract. This suggests that playful learning with playful teachers can be seen as a necessary precursor to purposeful encounters with digital technologies and positive learning experiences.

The thinking about learning which is implicit in the design of technological resources does not always match the pedagogic approach of early years educators. Playful teachers will want to establish whether the technology affords the kind of pedagogic interactions they seek to offer young learners. Many games supply the correct answer without explanation after several failed attempts, leaving children without any knowledge of the mistake they have made, unless an adult is on hand to clarify errors and offer alternative ways to understand ideas. The closed design of many technological games is especially surprising in the light of contemporary aims to promote creativity and collaborative working in the early years curriculum. Vangsnes et al. (2012) identified a further obstacle to educators' plans to use computer games to encourage higher-order thinking and problem solving. They found that the powerful gaming orientation which the program engendered in the children meant that the young learners wanted to focus on competing in the game and were reluctant to have the kind of reflective discussions which their teacher envisaged.

Pause for Thought

Think about some of the computer games or apps available in your early years setting or classroom. What do the characteristics of the game tell you about how the designers think learning happens? Do their ideas about how to facilitate learning match your own? What is missing from these games?

Three Forms of Learning

In our investigations in preschool playrooms we found three forms of learning when children engaged with digital technologies:

- operational – learning how to use technological resources;
- curricular knowledge and understanding – acquiring new knowledge, practising understandings being acquired and extending competencies to new areas;
- developing positive dispositions to learning – such as confidence, persistence, enjoyment.

Operational learning was perhaps the most widely anticipated outcome and children did learn how to use the resources available to them. For example, they learned how to access and use games they wished to play on desktop computers, how to use the zoom function on a digital camera and interact with a storyboard on a tablet. Practitioners reported examples of children who learnt to manipulate audio-playing equipment so that they could listen to stories as they chose, to manage the stages necessary to access and to use a drawing package and transfer photographs from a digital camera to a desktop computer and then review the images. They learned to use a digital microscope and how to navigate program menus to find the games they most enjoyed.

Children demonstrated their acquisition of new knowledge and understandings across a range of content areas. For instance, in one setting where children were making extensive and enthusiastic use of a digital video camera, the practitioner noted evidence of specific individuals developing a more sophisticated understanding of the conventions of interviewing. Elsewhere educators recorded changes in children's competency at linking spoken and written language as they listened to, re-told and acted out stories. There were notes about children's progress with mathematical concepts and matching and sequencing as they engaged with computer games, about fluency with phonics tasks in computer games and about the use of the language of exploration and questioning as children and adults investigated science packages, websites and the images revealed by digital microscopes.

The development of positive dispositions towards learning was an unexpected outcome of engaging with technologies but one which was welcomed by these practitioners who were keen that children should become independent learners responding to their own curiosity. The evidence showed children becoming increasingly confident and independent in their use of ICT and persisting when they encountered difficulties such as problems with printers or manipulating controls designed for adult use. There were records, too, of children overcoming initial anxieties, expressing satisfaction when they overcame doubts and enjoying activities with technologies. This enhanced pleasure in learning activities and satisfaction with the outcomes of their encounters with technology reflects the developmental power of play identified by Howard and McInness (2013).

It is worth noting that the practitioners in the nursery settings who participated in our studies made it clear that they were learning too. They talked about having to acquire specific operational skills in order to make some technological resources and activities accessible in the playroom and about the benefits of training. They extended their pedagogical knowledge as they learned how to integrate technologies across the curriculum, learned how and what to observe as children engaged with ICT and found ways of appropriately locating technological resources and integrating them in their planning. As their experience with ICT grew, so too did the practitioners' positive disposition towards digital technologies and media as educational resources. They became more confident users, more able to persist until they solved technological problems independently and more comfortable with extending the range and sophistication of the resources which they allowed children to access freely in their playrooms. Their encounters with ICT in the settings where they worked and the competencies with the resources which they were familiar with in their personal lives became, with opportunities for reflection and development, an important new part of their professional repertoire of pedagogic skills.

The Critical Role of Educators in Playful Learning with Technologies

Our early observations in preschool playrooms revealed children sometimes intensely engaged in an activity mediated by a computer program or other technology, perhaps exploring options or competing to collect points or rewards. On the other hand, we saw children spending time waiting passively for a turn or observing others playing a game. We observed children becoming bored, frustrated and disengaged and abandoning technological resources to move to another option in the playroom or outside area or to follow a group of friends. It was clear that not all activity with ICT was experienced as positive or playful by the children but, because there were other choices that children could make, their dissatisfaction was not always evident to their educators. Our research in these settings suggested that, if children are to have the kind of intense and rewarding engagement with technologies that characterise positive learning opportunities, they need proactive support in the form of particular types of pedagogic actions and interactions. We have conceptualised this support from educators as *guided interaction*, a process which scaffolds the action between the child and technology and draws on the pedagogic knowledge and practices of skilful practitioners. Our research suggested that the kinds of learning we have described above happened when children's encounters with ICT were mediated by guided interaction from adults. This can be observed in the case study examples below.

Case Study 9.2: ICT Interactions

Maggie (preschool practitioner) sat down beside Stuart (three years old) who was struggling to play a counting game. She explained how to drag objects into position on the screen and placed her hand over Stuart's so that they could rehearse this together. Maggie moved away but positioned herself so that she could still see the screen. Stuart was immediately totally absorbed. He paused occasionally to draw Maggie's attention to what he was doing and smile broadly before continuing with the game after she praised his progress.

Kirsten was walking around the playroom with the new digital video camera and recording her peers and practitioners saying hello. The nursery teacher intervened to model how to prompt children to answer questions and demonstrated how to zoom in on the speaker. Later Kirsten was delighted to show her video about 'nursery today' to her friends.

Elizabeth (preschool practitioner) noticed Sam and Paul (both four years old) exploring the listening centre. They tried on the earphones and started to listen to a story but left after just a few minutes. Elizabeth found some character puppets that were appropriate for the story the boys chose and suggested they listen again and play with the puppets as they listened. Elizabeth then invited the boys to act out the story in the puppet theatre and joined the audience while Sam and Paul played out the roles with enthusiasm and pleasure.

Guided Interaction

Our analysis, underpinned by socio-cultural understandings of the processes of learning, suggests that guided interaction takes two forms which are mutually reinforcing. *Distal guided interaction* encompasses all the pedagogic decisions and actions that educators take at a distance from the children, including their plans, the selection and positioning of resources, the deployment of staff and local expectations about curriculum and good practice. All of these distal interactions make a difference to children's experiences with ICT and the opportunity for learning that follows. *Proximal guided interaction* refers to the direct, face-to-face actions that educators take with children to ensure positive encounters with technologies. This support for learning is multimodal and includes physical help, modelling and demonstrating how to use a resource, giving instructions and explanations, prompting and providing feedback and offering emotional support. Playful learning with technologies will follow as practitioners find ways of offering playful guided interaction.

Playful teaching with ICT demands attention to playful structure through distal guided interactions, such as the careful choice of resources and activities and ensuring that educators are familiar with the use of resources so that they can be employed smoothly without obstacles in playful interactions. Playful proximal guided interaction will include invitations to explore, consider 'what if' options, share fun and pleasure, find ways to learn together and support children with aspects of encounters with technology that they find challenging or that make them anxious or disengaged. It also demands careful observation of and response to the ways in which some children's engagement with technologies is shaped by the behaviour of their peers, their social status in the peer group and the roles which they are allowed to take when sharing access to technologies (Ljung-Djärf, 2008; Arnott, 2013).

> **Pause for Thought**
>
> What opportunities for playful teaching can you see as you interact directly with children and technologies?

Learning with Technologies in Everyday Life

In our studies of children's experiences with new technologies at home, we found evidence of the same kinds of learning as we noted in their educational settings. Operational learning was evident at home, for instance, as children become proficient at using remote controls, viewing DVDs and using mobile phones to take photographs. They acquired new content knowledge and understanding too, often prompted by the interests or activities of their families, such as sport. There were also examples of encounters with digital technologies at home which encouraged positive dispositions towards learning. Parents gave accounts of children's satisfaction as they learned new operational skills, became faster and more accurate at games that involved letters and numbers, shape and colours and became able to participate independently in family technology practices. At home the children became familiar with adult uses of technologies for everyday life such as online shopping, using laptops for work and the communicative possibilities of mobile phones, emails and Skype. These technological activities with their parents and siblings were rewarding for the younger children, but it is clearly a challenge for educators to offer children the same range of authentic ICT experiences that they can have at home. On the other hand, we found that parents and older siblings were more inclined than early years practitioners to be directive in their interactions with children and technology, leaving plenty of scope for playful teachers to offer engaging and developmentally appropriate playful interactions with digital resources in their educational settings.

We have been describing playful learning with ICT as a dynamic interaction between the technologies, adults (educators or parents) and children. However, it is important to acknowledge that not all children are keen to use technologies and that growing up in a family of enthusiastic ICT users does not mean that a child will share this interest. The children in our studies (and in the case studies below) had distinct and individual preferences among traditional and digital activities and held clear views on the pleasure and potential for fun that different resources offered them. Somewhat to the surprise of their parents, who tended to see their child as a keen and capable user of any of the technologies available to them, the children were discriminating users. They were able to describe which features of games or technologies they found boring, difficult or too childish, which they could manage with ease and which computer games or technological activities they were good at.

Case Study 9.3: Kelly and Robert: ICT contrasts

Four year old Kelly's father worked for a computing firm and she was growing up in a household with several computers, a Wii and an older brother who was an enthusiastic player of computer games. However, Kelly sulked when asked to take part in a Wii game for a video diary and her mother allowed her to stop after one round. She had to be persuaded to show the researchers how she used a children's digital reading device but was enthusiastic about showing us her dolls and their clothes and accessories. During their mornings together Kelly and her mother chose to play pretend games or make use of their exten-sive supply of craft and painting materials.

Robert found technological games a great way to engage in competition. He wasn't interested in reading or writing but loved sport and action games outside or on the Wii. Robert liked to win and had a repertoire of games with which he was confident of success. When introduced to new games by other children he became distressed when he was not winning or could not understand how to gain a better score. He relied on his older sister to help with his technology activities as his grandmother thought that he should find out how the games worked by himself. His sister tolerated Robert's requests for help but had little enthusiasm for the games herself.

Family Attitudes

Children's experiences with and expectations about technologies are further shaped by the attitudes and practices of their family. We found three dimen-sions of difference between families which influenced children's experience of learning with digital technologies. Firstly, whether parents were sceptical about the educational value of technological resources and toys or enthusi-astic about the benefits shaped the extent to which children were encour-aged to engage with ICT and parents' decisions about spending on traditional and technological resources. Secondly, parents' ideas about how children learn made a difference to the level of support they offered. Some children were expected to learn through trial and error, while others were used to careful direction. Thirdly, their family's typical everyday practices and priorities influenced the opportunities children had to engage with technologies alone and with siblings. A playful educator who wants to tune her interactions to the experience a child brings to the setting will want to avoid any preconceptions about typical home experiences with ICT.

Pause for Thought

What do you know about the technologies that children in your early years setting or classroom use at home and how they use them?
   How could you find out more?

Key Messages

- Whether digital technologies offer the same opportunities for playful encounters as more traditional activities in the early years remains a matter for debate. The evidence about specific and sustained learning outcomes from engaging with particular digital technologies is not yet clear but we can conclude that some of these resources can offer satisfying opportunities for fun and opportunities for playful learning.
- Children learn how to use new technologies, extend their knowledge and understanding as they engage with these resources and develop positive dispositions towards learning. Nevertheless, children come to early years educational settings with individual preferences about engaging with ICT and expectations about these resources which have been influenced by the family context in which they are growing up.
- Educators play a crucial role in ensuring that children's encounters with technology are likely to support positive and playful learning. Playful teaching with digital resources means paying attention to the kind of cognitive and social activities that the digital resources afford and the ways in which guided interaction can be enacted in a playful pedagogy.

Further Reading

Edwards, S. and Bird, J. (2015) 'Observing and assessing young children's digital play in the early years: Using the Digital Play Framework', *Journal of Early Childhood Research*, doi: 10.1177/1476718X15579746

Plowman, L., Stephen, C. and McPake, J. (2010) *Growing Up With Technology: Young Children Learning in a Digital World*. Abingdon: Routledge.

Stephen, C., Stevenson, O. and Adey, C. (2013) 'Young children engaging with technologies at home: The influence of family context', *Journal of Early Childhood Research* 11 (2): 149–64.

References

Arnott, L. (2013) 'Are we allowed to blink? Young children's leadership and ownership while mediating interactions around technologies', *International Journal of Early Years Education* 21 (1): 97–115.

Bolstad, R. (2004) *The Role and Potential of ICT in Early Childhood Education: A Review of New Zealand and International Literature*. Wellington: New Zealand Council for Educational Research.

Couse, L.J. and Chen, D.W. (2010) 'A tablet computer for young children? Exploring its viability for early childhood education', *Journal of Research on Technology in Education* 43(1): 75–98.

Edwards, S. and Bird, J. (2015) 'Observing and assessing young children's digital play in the early years: Using the Digital Play Framework', *Journal of Early Childhood Research* doi: 10.1177/1476718X15579746

Grieshaber, S. and McArdle, F. (2010) *The Trouble With Play*. Maidenhead: Open University Press.

Howard, J. and McInness, K. (2013) *The Essence of Play*. Abingdon: Routledge.

Hutt, S., Tyler, C., Hutt, C. and Christopherson, H. (1989) *Play, Exploration and Learning: A Natural History of the Preschool*. London: Routledge.

Ljung-Djärf, A. (2008) 'The owner, the participant and the spectator: Positions and positioning in peer activity around the computer in pre-school', *Early Years: An International Journal of Research and Development* 28 (1): 61–72.

Marsh, J. (2004) 'The techno-literacy practices of young children', *Journal of Early Childhood Research* 2 (1): 51–66.

Marsh, J. (2010) 'Young children's play in online virtual worlds', *Journal of Early Childhood Research* 8(1): 23–39.

Plowman, L., Stephen, C. and McPake, J. (2010) *Growing Up with Technology: Young Children Learning in a Digital World*. Abingdon: Routledge.

Stephen, C. and Plowman, L. (2008) 'Enhancing learning with information and communication technologies in pre-school', *Early Child Development and Care* 178 (6): 637–54.

Stephen C. and Plowman L. (2014) 'Digital play', in L. Brooker, M. Blaise and S. Edwards (eds) *The Sage Handbook of Play and Learning in Early Childhood*. London: Sage. pp. 330–41.

Stephen, C., Stevenson, O. and Adey, C. (2013) 'Young children engaging with technologies at home: The influence of family context', *Journal of Early Childhood Research* 11 (2): 149–64.

Vangsnes, V., Økland, N.T.G. and Krumsvik, R. (2012) 'Computer games in pre-school settings: Didactical challenges when commercial computer games are implemented in kindergartens', *Computers and Education* 58: 1138–48.

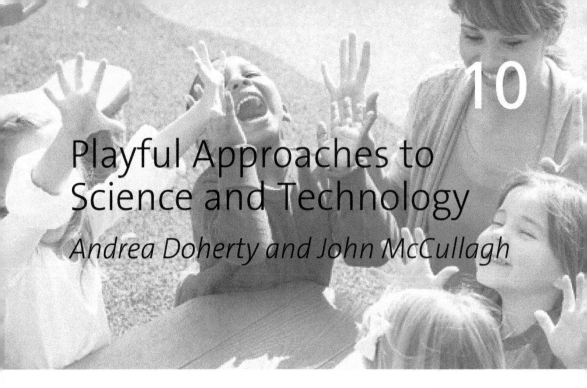

10

Playful Approaches to Science and Technology

Andrea Doherty and John McCullagh

Chapter Overview

This chapter will explore current provision in primary science and technology and how the use of playful pedagogies can reinvigorate and re-enthuse children and teachers about this curricular area. Snapshots of practice will be presented to explain what playful pedagogies are, and how they 'play out' in the primary science classroom. By the end of this chapter you will be able to:

- Critically reflect on how playful pedagogies can support science and technology teaching and learning;
- Visualise a range of playful science and technology activities;
- Incorporate playful approaches to science and technology teaching and learning in your classroom.

In the UK and many other countries around the world, schools and teachers aim to develop their practice to ensure children receive a broad and balanced curriculum that encourages high achievement and engagement. This means that the use of creative and innovative approaches that put children at the centre of their learning is required (Briggs and Hansen, 2012). Indeed, learning is no longer simply about presenting children with facts and expecting them to learn; instead it is about getting children actively involved and engaged in their learning. This is particularly relevant to the curricular area of science and technology where, for generations, scientific facts were rote-learned and over-structured experiments completed and recorded in a formal structure that drained any fun that might have existed in actually completing a practical activity. Harlen et al. (2003) claimed that this approach to science compromises children's depth of learning because the content is not relevant or meaningful to children, and is not presented in a context to which children can relate. Interestingly, Brunton and Thornton (2010) stated that the best scientific explorations are those cultivated through experiences that engage and build on children's interests. Through employing play or playful approaches teachers can use children's interests as a starting point from which to begin introducing and incorporating science concepts and skills.

The Context of Primary Science

In recent years, concerns about the decreasing profile of science within the primary curriculum have been raised at local, national and international levels. The latest report from the Confederation of British Industry (CBI, 2015) reported that science and technology have become less of a priority in many schools in England, Wales and Scotland, with many schools setting aside too little teaching time for this area of the curriculum. The research, carried out by Brunel University London, highlighted the need to engage children at the earliest stages of primary school with exciting, interesting and challenging science experiences. This would serve, not only as the crucial starting point for the "STEM (Science, Technology, Engineering and Mathematics) Pipeline", but also for developing lifelong skills and behaviours such as reasoning, analysis and curiosity (CBI, 2015: 10). With the reported percentage of schools committing two hours or less per week to science being higher in the lower primary (48%) than at Key Stage 2 (36%) there is an urgent need to develop science provision for the youngest of our children. The picture in Northern Ireland is equally, if not more, worrying. The recent Education and Training Inspectorate report *An Evaluation of the Implementation of 'The World Around Us'* (ETI, 2015) found that in 54% of schools the science and technology strand was still under-developed and "provision focused on low level factual learning with isolated topics and lacked purposeful investigative experiences for children" (2015: 37). Strategies suggested by teachers (CBI, 2015) to make children more engaged in science include "more experiments and practical content" (74% of surveyed teachers) and "linking topics to real-life situations and the world they live in" (63%).

Beeley (2012) described science, for young children, as the process of coming to understand their world through purposeful play. Moreover, Bulunuz (2013) found that "children [who had been] taught science through play had greater understanding of science concepts than children taught science through direct instruction" (2013: 226). So how and why do playful approaches support science learning?

Playful Pedagogies Supporting Quality Science Teaching and Learning

> Play and science are often thought of as dichotomous constructs, with play representing fancifulness and frivolity, and science representing serious, logical thinking. (Bulunuz, 2007: 56)

From birth children want to learn and naturally seek out problems to solve (Lind, 1999), thereby indicating that children think scientifically long before they actually enter a classroom (Zeece, 1999). The challenge for educators in primary settings is therefore to sustain this interest in science and technology, and to employ pedagogies that present science in a fun and accessible way, whilst ensuring scientific rigour and process.

Playful contexts enable the teacher to recreate real-life scenarios and narratives in a safe and secure environment, where children's imaginations are encouraged so as to aid their understanding of what can be abstract and inaccessible scientific concepts (Ward et al., 2008). Play supports scientific understanding because children can explore these difficult, but authentic, concepts through a familiar activity that they find enjoyable. The value of play is noted not just for young children, but also, as Osborne and Brady (2001) have observed, as useful for adults too. They observed undergraduate level engineers participating in playful contexts in a bid to develop their science enquiry skills. Bergen (2009) claimed that playfulness facilitates the scientific process, particularly scientific questioning, and therefore suggests that engaging in play actually *develops* proficiency in science. In contrast, Ghosh (2014) argued that a playful approach belittles the seriousness of science and claimed that children need to see science as more than play, and recognise how it contributes to driving societal, technological and economic development. We, however, refute Ghosh's ideas and have observed how very real and serious scientific issues can be taught in the early years with children recognising their value and relevance.

The case study below presents a classroom where an authentic learning experience is presented to children to learn about the topic of Electricity.

Case Study 10.1: Electricians' Academy

Miss Hill, the teacher, settles all 25 of the Primary 3 (seven year old) children on the story mat and begins the lesson with great excitement.

Miss Hill: *Good morning, apprentice electricians, welcome to a new day at the Electricians' Academy. You have been doing really well during your training so far and we have found out lots of interesting things about electricity, which we have been recording in our Electricians' Big Book and we are going to look at it now. Who can remember what were we doing during last week's task?*

The teacher displays the Big Book showing photographs, text and children's drawings of the previous lesson when the children explored the concept of a complete circuit and how they had helped fix old Mrs Brown's reading light so that she could read her favourite book in bed. On seeing the pictures, hands quickly shoot up.

Sophie: *Poor Mrs Brown's light was broken. The wires weren't together and it wouldn't light so she was sad. But me and Callum told her about our circuit and we fixed it for her. The wires were in a circle. We drew the picture of it.*
Miss Hill: *Did everyone find out why the light wouldn't work?*

This receives an enthusiastic response with almost everyone keen to explain.

As her teaching assistant switches off the lights in the classroom, Miss Hill produces from behind her back what appears to be a small witch puppet consisting of a table tennis ball-like head to which she has stuck long strands of cotton hair, and a long black dress. The children are transfixed. Lowering her voice, Miss Hill introduces their visitor.

(Continued)

(Continued)

Miss Hill: *Apprentices, I would like you to meet Wanda the Electrical Witch. She needs electricity in order to have her magical powers and to have electricity we need to have a complete circuit without any breaks in the wires. Would you like to be the wires in her circuit?*

With great excitement the children are directed to stand in a large circle all the way around the classroom and invited to hold hands with the people directly on either side of them. Miss Hill holds Wanda in one hand, ensuring that her thumb is touching the small metal strip on one side of Wanda's head and that the child on the other side of Wanda is doing the same. As soon as the circle of hands is complete, Wanda's head flashes red and a strange, intermittent buzzing sound is heard. There is a collective whoop of excitement and the sound and flashing stop as children inadvertently drop hands as they put their hands to their faces in awe.

Miss Hill: *Oh, Wanda has gone silent again. How can we get her to do her magic again?*

Jack: *Miss, we need to hold hands, everyone, and then it will work.*

Miss Hill ensures all hands are 'connected'. Before holding hands herself with the child beside her, she addresses the class.

Miss Hill: *Now, what do you think will happen when I hold hands with Katie?*

Class: *The witch will light up.*

Miss Hill: *Well, let's see!*

The children continue to explore how they can get Wanda to light up by holding hands and forming a complete chain or circuit.

Role Play

This whole-class activity, in the form of a role play scenario, illustrates how a playful approach to the topic of Electricity can result in excitement and sustained engagement, and help humanise an otherwise potentially abstract and challenging area of the science curriculum. The children's transformation into apprentices, even though this happens at the beginning of the sequence of lessons, almost serves by itself as a 'rite of passage' for the children who have previously shown Miss Hill that they are 'up to the challenge'. All children love to take on roles, so making them in essence 'learners' is always a good idea. The notion of being an apprentice at the Academy elevates the importance of this series of lessons and weekly tasks, and provides children with a purposeful identity. In Vygotsky's exploration of role play he described how a child acts 'a head taller' (1978: 102) as they adhere to the rules of their role, and engage in the appropriate discourse and behaviour. Within the 'Electricians' Academy', children ceased being 'children' and adopted a more grown-up, adult-like persona.

The Big Book provides the visual cues for consolidating and reinforcing prior learning and facilitates an inclusive group approach to the whole-class endeavour. It acts as a prompt for "sustained shared thinking" towards clarifying and solving the given problem (Siraj-Blatchford and Sylva, 2004: 718). The children's weekly mission is to investigate or explore a particular aspect of the topic and, in doing so, help solve a problem. As Beeley (2012) discussed, this sense of purpose, and helping others, is a powerful motivator for young children in play. Each group is provided with an actual tool-kit containing all the resources required to carry out the task. Each week, on successful completion of the enquiry task, each child is presented with their Electricians' Academy pay cheque, which they stick into their workbooks. In their role as apprentice electricians, the children are having a real, adult-like, life experience where they can see where and how science translates into the world. The use of a Big Book as a recording mechanism also gives the literacy learning more value as children are learning in a cross-curricular manner, and seeing synergy between science and literacy.

The excited tone of voice and enthusiastic manner of the teacher sets a playful mood from the very outset of the activity. This subtle shift in relationship from teacher–pupil to supervisor–apprentice heightens the sense of urgency and focus for learning. The colourful drawings and photographs from the previous lesson retain the attention of all and encourage children to share their accounts of how they helped old Mrs Brown. The concept of a complete circuit is consolidated by the appearance of this strange looking witch puppet. The children are truly excited and amazed at how they can control the lighting up of Wanda. They soon begin to hold hands and then drop hands in an effort to influence the outcome. The children's engagement in this 'cause and effect' activity, demonstrates Bergen's (2009) idea that playfulness facilitates the scientific process, developing their proficiency in science. The fact that all children need to be connected requires them to work together to ensure that the 'circuit' is complete. This playful hand holding acts as a precursor to the task of assembling electrical components (a battery, wires and light bulb) into a complete circuit.

The follow-up activity, where children work in smaller groups, allows each child to experience the phenomenon on a smaller scale and handle the objects more intimately. This playful experience ensures children interact physically with objects and materials, both real and imagined, and provides a relevant and stimulating context in which children will invest both emotionally and cognitively.

Pause for Thought

Explore how each of the following roles could be presented playfully to support children's learning in science and technology: builder; baker; dentist.

In what ways might children and the teacher make a record of their learning and attainment?

How could you, as the teacher, operate as both player and teacher in a scenario like this?

Play as Challenge

In addition to playful pedagogies providing meaningful and relevant learning contexts, they also provide challenge for children, and can support children in completing tasks and activities beyond their normal level. Despite play sometimes being perceived as fanciful and frivolous (Bulunuz, 2007), literature and research have shown that "a child's greatest achievements are possible in play" (Vygotsky, 1978: 100). Pearce (1999), for example, defined play as "an intense scientific study, unassigned and internally motivated" (1999: 3) and reinforced the value of play as a medium for science teaching and learning. Through playful pedagogies science becomes more child-centred, and children's enhanced level of agency and motivation becomes sufficient to sustain their focus and perseverance through what may otherwise be quite challenging concepts. In the second case study below an undergraduate student teacher, engaged in the 'Playful Technology Project', uses a story the children are reading in Literacy as the basis for the science and technology activities. This case study is a reflection on her experience of teaching science and technology through a playful approach.

Case Study 10.2: It's the Bear!

On the training day we were given a box of resources, all of which contributed to making a battery powered circuit that, when complete, would set off a buzzer, a propeller or a light. The idea was that these resources could be used across the curriculum, throughout different topics, to create a 'project' that brought the children's learning into a real-life context. I remember sitting in the training session, trying to figure out how an abundance of little fiddly resources worked, hearing buzzers going off from all sides of the room and thinking "How on earth am I going to teach this to a class of 27 Primary 2 children?".

Like everything else, though, I just had to take it one step at a time, and this was much easier to do given that the children absolutely LOVED learning about STEM (Science, Technology, Engineering and Maths). Within Literacy, I had introduced the book *It's the Bear!* by Jez Alborough, which is a children's story about a family who go into the woods for a picnic, but all their food is gradually stolen from their picnic basket by a big bear. During one lesson, whilst reading the story *It's the Bear!* again, the children received a letter from Eddy (the little boy in the story) telling them that he had heard the Primary 2 children were learning all about electric circuits and buzzers. He asked the class if they could help make a picnic basket with an alarm on it, to stop the bear from stealing their food the next time they go on a picnic. The class were very excited, asking questions like: "How did he know we were learning about circuits?"; "How did he post us that letter?"; "Did the postman bring that this morning?".

As a class we decided exactly what we could do to help Eddy: we were going to make a picnic basket with a circuit in it which had a light sensor, so that, if the bear opened the lid of the basket to steal the food, the light would shine in and an alarm would sound, scaring the bear away. In order to tell Eddy what we were doing, the children had to write a letter back to him. They used their iPads to access an app called 'Postcard' to type their writing onto a postcard, draw a picture, stamp and send the postcard back to Eddy again.

The final piece of the project involved the children making the picnic baskets. Children were able to create and decorate individual picnic baskets using junk art, into which we then placed their circuits. The children had to evaluate and test where exactly their circuit and

(Continued)

(Continued)

sensor would go, so that when the bear opened the basket the alarm would go off successfully.

I was so glad that I took part in the project because I had stepped outside my comfort zone and discovered that I really enjoyed teaching STEM in this way. A playful approach allowed for so many opportunities for cross-curricular learning, which made the learning for the children (and the teaching for me) exciting, enjoyable and REAL!

Interconnected Problem-solving

A playful approach in this scenario introduced a very definite problem, which invited children's ideas and thoughts about how the project should proceed. Children actively directed the activities and were leaders in the creation of the 'bear-safe' picnic baskets. Putting children in the driving seat meant that, through their active participation and directing of the task, children could explore and discover how the resources worked, and actively construct their own understanding. Learning involved active interaction between the child and the environment, with the teacher acting as facilitator, coach, mentor and partner in problem-solving (Kearns, 2010). The student teacher also introduced to the children a character whom they would be helping, and used their Literacy story as the source of this character. The arrival of the letter from Eddy caused excitement and surprise and children's motivation was increased instantly. The teacher was no longer in the powerful position in the classroom but became another helper in solving Eddy's picnic basket problem. Through the series of playful technology activities, the student teacher highlighted the potential for cross-curricular lessons and links, and used Literacy especially well to promote children's skills in oral and written communication. The use of the iPad provided an exciting method of recording the science and technology learning and served as a valuable planning tool through which children could envisage their project and identify what their success criteria would be. In addition, the iPad served as a means to connect reading, writing, listening and speaking, and it developed children's emerging knowledge about print within the context of science and technology (Beschorner and Hutchison, 2013).

The resources required blending specific technological devices (sensors, batteries, LEDs and buzzers) with everyday junk art. This use of junk art to make the picnic baskets presents technology as more open-ended and creative and therefore more applicable to the early years classroom. The development from simply 'junk art', to 'junk art with technology' also models how teachers can ensure continuity and progression within play, introducing challenge for children within a play area or activity with which they are already familiar. The technology aspect, which may initially seem beyond children's grasp, can be presented playfully, scaffolding the gap between what they can do alone and what they can do with the assistance of others (Bruner, 1986). In the playful scenario above, the storybook and task supported and contextualised the science and technology content, whilst the children's interactions with the resources and with their peers facilitated their achievement and therefore delivered success in the 'difficult' task. For the child, the junk art represented a real world problem they solved through the incorporation of technology. The playful approach helped to connect the physical junk art with technology and the real world, and enhanced the authenticity of the final product, which manifested the child's representation, and knowledge and understanding of science and technology.

Pause for Thought

How might you incorporate playful technology within the context of the *Three Little Pigs*, or *Fantastic Mr Fox*?

How would you access and challenge children's current thinking within these activities?

Role Play and Local Issues

Thus far we have discussed how playful contexts support science and technology within primary classrooms as teachers create and develop stories and narratives through which children can access science skills and concepts. Unlike the two previous case studies, where the construct was either imagined or a playful adaptation of a real-life scenario, the next case study demonstrates how a playful approach can extend children's thinking about a familiar physical environment. Through role play, for example, children can engage with the world around them to explore natural phenomena. In this snapshot of practice, a group of Primary 4 children (7–8 years) engage in role play, becoming scientists, to explore environmental issues regarding their local beach.

Case Study 10.3: Victor Sands and the Disappeared Beach

The teacher introduces the lesson with a video report on the disappearance of the coastline at White Rock beach. The children discuss the report and think about who uses the beach, and which animals will be affected. They then receive an email from 'Victor Sands' of the North Coast Trust, asking them to help him rebuild the beach. The children immediately start to offer ideas as to how they could help; where they could get sand; how they could make sand; and where the sand is going.

The children begin by exploring some natural materials – pebbles, shells, starfish and bones – describing what they feel like, and discussing any possible links between these materials and sand. The teacher supplies empty plastic bottles, sugar cubes, pebbles and water, and invites the children to observe what happens when this mixture is shaken. The children are going to be the motion of the ocean! They immediately begin to imitate the lateral sway of the sea in anticipation.

The classroom is awash with sounds of sugar cubes and pebbles crashing together as the children shake their bottles. Once the shaking concludes, the teacher begins recording their observations and encourages feedback, table by table. Some of the observations recognise that the sugar gets crushed, that "wet pebbles make the sugar cubes easier to crush", and "all the cubes have changed shape". At this point, the teacher observes a child smelling inside the bottle, and asks "why?". The response demonstrates curiosity and insight: "I wanted to smell it because it might've smelled different. The wet pebbles might've made the sugar smell different!". Other children note the differences in using brown and white cubes. At this point a new variable is introduced to the experiment and the class are asked to continue. This time, the motion of the ocean is stormy and rough, encouraging the children to become more physical and vigorous. Laughter sounds throughout the classroom as the children become heavily involved in the activity. The second round of feedback is once again recorded by the class teacher. This time, the observations display a higher order of thinking: "If we shake it faster, it makes it easier to make sand. If you do it faster, it makes it really quick."

Integrating Activities

This activity encouraged children to discuss and interact with an issue in their local area. The sand from a nearby beach had washed away during a period of stormy weather, almost overnight, generating news stories and reports. Whilst children might have heard about this issue at home, the opportunity to actually investigate what happened and how, may never have arisen. Through showing a video of the news, then introducing a letter from Victor Sands, the playful pedagogy brings the issue to life and gives the children a role and a purpose. The incorporation of enquiry-based approaches throughout also promotes children's thinking and they rely on their observations to make sense of the topic at hand. The combination of role play and enquiry approaches positively influences children's ease of understanding of science concepts and skills as demonstrated by the children's high level of engagement throughout the lesson (Ward et al., 2008).

The initial focus is purely on children's observations and knowledge construction, as the teacher records their ideas and comments for them. The children work in small groups and have time for discussion, highlighting the value of language to enhance understanding in science. Johnston (2010) claimed that language plays a vital role in helping children to develop scientifically. Also, providing time for children to reflect on their play and enquiry, where they can articulate the roles they adopted, the responsibilities they held, and justify the skills they utilised, correlates with Walsh et al.'s (2006) belief that effective practice involves children reflecting on their play and playful experiences. The use of a second reflection and feedback scenario, where the children were exploring the effect of vigorous shaking on the sugar cubes, results in higher-order thinking, such as making predictions and formulating hypotheses.

As a follow-up to this lesson, the children had to write an email to Victor Sands, describing what they had done and what they had found out. They developed an awareness of their local environment and had the opportunity to explore how and why certain things happen. The creation and employment of the narrative ensured that children could access these issues in a child-friendly way that encouraged their agency and developed their language and communication skills.

Pause for Thought

What local environmental issue could you refer to in your classroom?
What are the key science concepts within this?
   What strategies could you use to enhance the language climate?
   What strategies could you use to support children's observations?

Key Messages

- In this chapter we have explored the current context for science and technology, and examined its reduced profile within today's early years and primary classrooms.
- In response to this, we have highlighted the value of playful pedagogies to support quality science and technology teaching and learning with young children.
- We have presented a number of classroom scenarios to explain how and why we believe playful pedagogies support the teaching and learning of science and technology, and have provided some questions to encourage your thinking in playful terms.

Further Reading and Resources

Davies, D. (2011) *Teaching Science Creatively*. Oxon: Routledge.

Frodsham, S., McGregor, D. and Wilson, H. (2014) 'Young children's views of creativity in science: Exploring perspectives in an English primary classroom', *Journal of Emergent Science* 8: 31–41.

Gross, C.M. (2012) 'Science concepts young children learn through water play', *Dimensions of Early Childhood* 40 (2): 3–12.

McCullagh, J. (2010) *Promoting Children's Engagement in Science using Puppets, Books and Stories*, CPD unit available from https://pstt.org.uk/resources/cpd-units/promoting-engagement-using-puppets-book-and-stories (accessed 9 September 2016).

Siraj-Blatchford, J. (2001) *Emergent Science and Technology in the Early Years*, paper presented to XXIII World Congress of OMEP, Santiago Chile, July 31st–August 4th www.327matters.org/Docs/omepabs.pdf (accessed 9 September 2016).

References

Beeley, K. (2012) *Science in the Early Years: Understanding the World through Play-based Learning*. London: Featherstone Education.

Bergen, D. (2009) 'Play as the learning medium for future scientists, mathematicians and engineers', *American Journal of Play* 1 (4): 413–28.

Beschorner, B. and Hutchison, A. (2013) 'iPads as a literacy teaching tool in early childhood', *International Journal of Education in Mathematics, Science and Technology* 1 (1): 16–24.

Briggs, M. and Hansen, A. (2012) *Play-based Learning in the Primary School*. London: Sage.

Bruner, J.S. (1986) *Actual Minds, Possible Worlds*. London: Harvard University Press.

Brunton, P. and Thornton, L. (2010) *Science in the Early Years*. London: Sage.

Bulunuz, M. (2007) *Development of Interest in Science and Interest in Teaching Elementary Science: Influence of Informal, School, and Inquiry Methods Course Experiences*, unpublished EdD dissertation, Georgia State University. Available online from http://scholarworks.gsu.edu/ece_diss/3 (accessed 7 September 2016).

Bulunuz, M. (2013) 'Teaching science through play in kindergarten: Does integrated play and science instruction build understanding?' *European Early Childhood Education Research Journal* 21 (2): 226–49.

Confederation of British Industry (CBI) (2015) *Tomorrow's World: Inspiring Primary Scientists*. London: Brunel University.

Education and Training Inspectorate (ETI) (2015) *An Evaluation of the Implementation of the World around Us in Primary Schools*. Belfast: ETI.

Ghosh, P. (2014) *Neural Suitcase tells the Tales of Many Minds*. India: Partridge.

Harlen, W., Macro, C., Reed, K. and Schilling, M. (2003) *Making Progress in Primary Science*. London: Routledge Falmer.

Johnston, J. (2010) 'What emergent science is telling us about scientific development', *Primary Science* 111, Jan/Feb: 9–11.

Kearns, K. (2010) *Frameworks for Learning and Development*. Australia: Pearson.

Lind, K.K. (1999) 'Science in early childhood: Developing and acquiring fundamental concepts and skills', in American Association for the Advancement of Science (AAAS), *Dialogue on Early Childhood Science, Mathematics, and Technology Education*. Washington, DC: AAAS. pp. 73–83.

Osborne, M.D. and Brady, D.J. (2001) 'Constructing a space for developing a rich understanding of science through play', *Journal of Curriculum Studies* 33 (5): 511–24.

Pearce, C.R. (1999) *Nurturing Inquiry: Real Science for the Elementary Classroom*. Portsmouth: Heinemann.

Siraj-Blatchford, I. and Sylva, K. (2004) 'Researching pedagogy in English pre-schools', *British Educational Research Journal* 30 (5): 713–31.

Vygotsky, L. (1978) *Mind in Society: Development of Higher Psychological Processes*. Cambridge: Harvard University Press.

Walsh, G., Sproule, L., McGuinness, C., Trew, K., Rafferty, H. and Sheehy, N. (2006) 'An appropriate curriculum for 4–5 year old children in Northern Ireland: Comparing play-based and formal approaches', *Early Years* 26 (2): 201–21.

Ward, H., Roden, J., Hewlett, C. and Foreman, J. (2008) *Teaching Science in the Primary Classroom: A Practical Guide* (second edition). London: Sage.

Zeece, P.D. (1999) 'Things of nature and the nature of things: Natural science based literature for young children', *Early Childhood Education Journal* 26 (3): 161–6.

Section 3

The Role of the Playful Professional

11

Hopeful Intentions: Planning for Playful Teaching and Learning

Jacqueline Fallon

Chapter Overview

In this chapter, I discuss the relationship between planning for playful teaching and learning and the resources teachers provide for children's play. By the end of the chapter, you will be able to:

- Grasp the concept of affordance – the learning potential in the interactions the children have with the resources – and the potential for these resources to connect child-led play, teacher-led activity and Curriculum outcomes;
- Appreciate the need to have hands-on experience of the resources you provide for the children;
- Engage in observation as a way of learning about how to extend learning potential;
- Use a planning framework with long-term planning based on resources and short-term planning that reflects children's interests;
- Have an enhanced appreciation of your own professional expertise in the key pedagogical action of resource provision.

Planning for Play

Creativity in the provision of resources needs to be recognised as a sophisticated feature of professional practice, and the provision of resources as an important aspect of a teacher's expertise. The teacher's thinking about the relationship between the resources provided and the children's learning through play is a significant element of provision. Having provided multiple workshops with playdough, junk materials, large and small building blocks, small world figures and so on, I have observed how teachers and students begin to develop insights and empathy with children's experience of playful learning when they themselves play with the materials. This frequently comes as a revelation to practising teachers who often acknowledge that they have never actually played with or even handled the resources they provide. In cases where teachers have not had that opportunity, choosing resources to support learning is a theoretical activity. Familiar resources can become almost invisible and can be so taken-for-granted that they are never changed or adapted in order to continue to "provoke students' learning" (Løkken and Moser, 2012: 308).

Planning for play can take many forms, but the suggestions here are focused on using the resources provided for the children's play as the connective tissue between children's playful learning experiences and the Curriculum. Teachers who are familiar with the resources can document their potential in terms of the learning outcomes specified in the relevant Curriculum documentation. Planning in this way is consistent with the concept of pedagogical framing: "the 'behind-the-scenes' work that practitioners do with regards to provision of materials [and] arrangement of space ..." (Siraj-Blatchford et al., 2002: 7). Pedagogical framing is not about the teacher controlling the environment and the activities, but rather organising the environment and resources to facilitate the children's play (Wood, 2013), and planning the teacher-led elements of classroom practice around those resources.

Affordance

The quality of the resources selected and provided will have a considerable impact on the quality of the children's play (Moyles, 1989). The concept that best describes the quality of resources is *affordance*:

> Affordance refers to the perceived and actual properties of an object or artefact, those properties that determine just how it could possibly be used ... and how the technology facilitates or hinders learning of various kinds. (Carr, 2000: 62)

The resources and materials made available to the children for play are central to the relationship between what we plan and what the children do.

These resources and materials occupy the space between our hopeful intentions for the children's playful learning and the children's own intentionality and agency in their play. The resources chosen can carry the practitioner's plans into the children's play, as described, for example, in the case study below.

Case Study 11.1: Shoeboxes

In the first term of senior infants (5–6 year olds), Ms Clarke had provided shoeboxes for the children's construction play. Ms Clarke and the children had been together the previous year for junior infants, and the shoeboxes had been a regular part of construction play. The children had spent a considerable amount of time building the shoe boxes as high as they could, then knocking them down and starting all over again. Through observation and participation, Ms Clarke recognised that the children's play had moved on. She gave some thought to how the shoeboxes could be adapted to add challenge. Prompted by a set of stacking cups, she sorted the shoeboxes into sets of three stacked inside each other, 'Russian doll' style. She also labelled each set with a picture, with the size of the label corresponding to the size of the box, and she modelled stacking the sets during Maths time. Ms Clarke's actions illustrate the need to adapt resources to reflect, facilitate, provoke and support progression in the children's play, and the need to extend the affordance of resources to build additional challenge into the play environment.

Pause for Thought

What learning might occur when the children re-stack the shoeboxes during tidy-up time?

Connecting Curriculum and Play

Here, the teacher adapted the shoeboxes to reflect her plans for the children's learning about matching, sorting, seriation, relative size and the related language. She was also able to use the resources during teacher-led Maths time to introduce these concepts to the children. The shoeboxes carried those learning experiences (and the teacher's plans) into the children's play, actively connecting the Curriculum to the play. Using the resources in this way allows teachers to plan for play without those plans being intrusive or prescriptive.

Nonetheless, play is always structured to a greater or lesser degree by the resources and materials made available (Moyles, 1989), but I argue that a careful focus on resources provides a balance between the practitioner's plans and the children's scope for intentionality and agency in their play. An example of this is provided by the second case study below.

Case Study 11.2: Bungee Jumping Farmers

The 3–4 year olds in the pre-school setting were learning about the farm, and Sandra, the teacher, had provided a large farm set for the children to play with. The set included the Mum and Dad farmers, two children and a range of farm animals. Sandra and the children had used the farm set previously to illustrate stories and songs about the farm, and the children were familiar with the vocabulary and some activities associated with the farm. In providing the farm set for child-led play, Sandra's hopeful intention was that the children would use all their prior learning to develop their own narratives about the farm. When Sandra observed the play, she found that some of the children had used small blocks to build fields to hold groups of animals. By contrast, another small group of children had set up a bungee jump at the edge of the table using threads from the bead threading kit. The figures of the farmers were now being used as part of a play narrative based on bungee jumping! Sandra's experience demonstrates the relationship between planning for children's play and what the children choose to do. The resources Sandra provided carried her intentions into the play chosen by some children, but other children chose a different direction. The resources facilitated both outcomes.

Pause for Thought

Should Sandra respond to both groups of children – the field builders and the bungee jumpers?
    What would be an appropriate response?

Open-ended Resources

The children in that scenario were able to pursue their own ideas using the range of resources available to them. The way in which the children used the farm figures for a scenario that was quite distinct from the teacher's intention highlights the unpredictability of the processes involved in the "… negotiation of meaning in children's explorative play" (Løkken and Moser, 2012: 308). This emphasises the desirability of open-ended resources, those that do not have a specific function or end point, to enable the children's agency in play, creativity and exploration (Odegard, 2012).

Exploring a resource and its affordance in this way is important for the children, but is equally important for the playful teacher. All professional development for teachers of young children should include opportunities for hands-on activities with all kinds of materials. Of course, sharing play with the children is also a valuable way to consciously develop such experience, and reflecting on that experience enhances expertise in the provision of resources. The teacher in the first case study, who played with the shoeboxes alongside the children, began to see the possibilities beyond the initial construction activities afforded by the resources. She was able to make connections with other resources the children played with – the stacking cups – and the prior learning associated with those other resources. Reflection on experience enabled the teacher to expand the learning potential of familiar resources. This kind of sophisticated provision of resources can help practitioners to fulfil their obligations in terms of curricular outcomes without being prescriptive. This is one way of presenting subject content to children, while at the same time leaving the specifics of their engagement with that content to their own discretion in the context of child-led play. As illustrated by the case study below, in addition to content being carried into the play, the resources can also offer valuable opportunities for teaching skills in meaningful contexts.

Case Study 11.3: Junk Art

Claire (4) and Rose (5) were playing together at the junk art table. They had punched holes and used twine to connect three egg boxes to make a train; they then tried to attach a piece of cardboard tubing to the carriage on the end to turn it into a locomotive with a chimney. They made several attempts to stand the tube on the egg box and attach it with masking tape. However, they found it very difficult to get

(Continued)

(Continued)

the masking tape into the angle between the tube and box in order to keep the 'chimney' upright. Ms Wright had observed the repeated efforts, and the diminishing roll of masking tape. She asked the girls if she could be of any help. They explained the problem, and Ms Wright responded by showing the girls how to snip the end of the cardboard tube so that it could be flattened onto the egg box and securely stuck down with the tape. While the junk art materials facilitate the children's creativity, their experience illustrates the need for sensitive and respectful teacher intervention – based on observation – to enable the children to fulfil their goals and progress their play.

Pause for Thought

How can Ms Wright plan for Claire and Rose to share their new skill with the rest of the class?

Creating Connections

As well as linking content and skills to play, resources and materials can provide a link between the children's self-initiated play and contexts which are teacher-led. Resources and materials carry the children's playful experiences with them. So, for example, the bungee jumping farmers in Case Study 11.2 could provide the teacher with a playful opportunity to follow up the source of the particular narrative – in this instance, an uncle who bungee jumped off a bridge in Australia and brought back video footage of the experience. This could provide a stimulus for creative writing for older children or a lesson using the Language Experience Approach, with the teacher as scribe for the younger children. Drawing or painting from the upside-down perspective of the bungee jumpers could provide the starting point for a visual arts lesson. Such connectivity across the full range of learning contexts promotes continuity of pedagogical approach and cohesive learning experiences for the children.

The children can identify and create affordances that are not obvious, and the teacher can learn a lot by observing what the children discover

(Broadhead, 2004). Teachers have commented that they are continually surprised at the imaginative uses the children find for resources (Fallon, 2015a), and an appreciation of that range of affordance facilitates the use of resources in a variety of learning contexts. Viewing play resources as exclusively for play, and 'teaching' resources as exclusively for teacher-led activities emphasises a 'play/work' divide that is not consistent with a pedagogy of play.

Pause for Thought

What tensions can occur when children's play does not match the teacher's learning intentions, as in the case of the bungee jumping farmers?

Extending Affordance

Affordance can be identified in advance of the provision of resources, but additional affordances can be discovered as the children use the resources. Indeed, affordance varies according to the perspective of the 'perceiver' (Kernan, 2014), so an appreciation of the children's perspectives is a necessary facet of identified affordance. Through observation and reflection, the teacher can identify ways to extend the affordance of resources to enlarge the learning potential, as well as to expand the range of Curriculum outcomes a resource can carry. Extending the affordance of familiar resources is a way of progressing children's learning through play. I suggest two possible ways in which affordance can be extended:

- By adapting a resource, as in the Shoeboxes Case Study (11.1);
- By teaching the children the skills they need to fulfil their own plans for the resources, as in the Junk Art Case Study (11.3).

Adapting Resources

The example in Case Study 11.1 shows a practitioner using her knowledge of both the children she teaches and the resources she has available to creatively adapt the resources to build progression and challenge into the affordance the resources offer the children.

The standard, tried and tested resources that generally appear in early years classrooms are sometimes taken for granted (Broadhead, 2004). Consider the sand tray, for example. A combination of dry sand and disproportionately large containers generally means that sand spills out, leading over time to insufficient sand in the tray and a gritty floor. This is demotivating for children.

Now consider how different the children's experience could be if the sand tray had seven to eight centimetres' depth of damp sand. A generous quantity of damp sand in a deep tray affords a wide range of options for the children. I have observed narratives involving a pre-historic landscape with volcanoes and dinosaurs, a rough-terrain track for car racing, and a building site with cranes and earthmovers created by children with damp or wet sand. The adaptation of adding water to the sand opened up the landscaping affordance which allowed the children to develop their play narratives in those directions.

An additional consideration in the adaptation of resources is the appropriateness of the resources to the age of the children. The adaptation of the shoeboxes in the first Case Study would not necessarily be appropriate for a group of 3–4 year olds who are focused on building the shoeboxes as high as they can in order to experience the joy of knocking them down. Those children may well be exploring concepts of height and cause/effect in their play activity. The appropriate adaptation there may be to provide shoeboxes large enough to provide firm foundations for stable, tall constructions.

The point here is that all resources can be adapted and varied – indeed should be adapted and varied – and the focus should be on using them across all the teaching and learning contexts in the classroom in deliberate, considered ways. The specifics of the resources provided, the adaptations, the anticipated affordances and the content and skills they carry need to be included in planning, which will be discussed in a later section.

Pause for Thought

How could water be adapted to extend or change its affordance?
    What kind of additional resources would you provide with the adapted water for the children's play?

Skills Teaching

Observing how children are playing with the resources and discussing their play with them will provide information to the teacher about what the children need to extend and deepen the play. In Case Study 11.3, the teacher shared a skill with the children to extend the affordance of the junk materials, helping the children to extend their learning activity.

> Adults must not be afraid of helping children to learn many different techniques, skills and processes which, once mastered, can help other learning, particularly that of independence. (Moyles, 1989: 108)

Teachers can identify the skills they need to teach through observation of the play. As in Case Study 11.3, where the teacher showed the children how to snip the cardboard cylinder for ease of attachment to a flat surface, those skills can subsequently be shared with all the children. The children who identified the need for the skill can explain to the class the context in which it is needed, thereby scaffolding learning for the rest of the children. Teaching the skills the children need for play is more than likely to contribute to academic skills (Bodrova, 2008). The cutting skill for junk art is quite easily identified, but there are less obvious skills that teachers need to be aware of as they support the children to extend the affordance of the resources.

Take the example of the five year old who makes a selection of buns and cakes with playdough, and carries them over to the group who are playing picnics. This is not an uncommon occurrence (Broadhead, 2010) and most teachers happily facilitate the movement of resources around the room. What is, perhaps, less common is the recognition that this is an act of metacognition on the part of the child. Wood and Attfield (2005) identify "making connections with existing knowledge and past experience" (2005: 70) as metacognitive activity. The child bringing resources from one play area to another is making connections and combining ideas in a metacognitive act – making their thinking visible. The resources can provoke and facilitate these metacognitive acts, giving the teacher the opportunity to articulate the child's thinking by commenting on the act, modelling the language of thinking and extending the thought: "That was a good idea. It reminds me of Little Red Riding Hood bringing cakes to her Granny". Younger children are more likely to engage in such acts spontaneously, and naming those acts in terms of the language of thinking will help to progress the children's intentionality, whereas older children could benefit from a later opportunity to talk about their action.

Pause for Thought

What skills do children need to be able to tidy up the play environment?
    How could you help the children to learn those skills?

Observation

Identifying and extending the affordance of the materials provided for play is largely based on the practitioner's observation of the children's play. The benefits of observation are summed up by Wood (2013) as enabling "… practitioners to tune in to children's play activities, understand the meaning of play in their terms and identify learning potential, processes and outcomes" (2013: 103). In addition, observation allows the teacher to create connections between the children's self-directed play and teacher-led, playful activities addressing specific aspects of the Curriculum.

Observation should be systematic, meaning that each teacher needs to have routines and strategies set up so that they can be sure it will happen. Classrooms are so busy that unless an activity is planned, it may not happen. For example, *Aistear, the Early Childhood Curriculum Framework* (NCCA, 2009a: 87), designed for settings catering for children in the 0–6 age group, suggests the following routines for observation:

- Time sampling – observing children frequently for a few minutes at a time;
- Event sampling – observing children over time at an event or activity;
- Target child observations – observing one child over time.

Over a given week or month these strategies will provide a range of information about both individuals and groups. Because play is often a social activity, observation can provide insights into how the resource affords opportunities for collaborative play.

The teacher can decide, for example, to focus on a particular learning area with its associated resources for a specific period of time (event sampling) and observe how all the children, over that time, play with the resources. This will provide an overview of Curriculum engagement by the children, and the convergence/divergence between what the children do and what the teacher hoped they would do, as in Case Study 11.2. The teacher may choose to prioritise learning experiences that are consistent with their intentions, and can then plan for those children to share their learning experiences with the class. This is not to suggest that the teacher should not respond to the kind of situation described in Case Study 11.2, but with large classes it is impossible to follow through with every learning experience observed.

Recording observations is very important, and being systematic about the recording process provides the evidence for professional judgements and future planning. Whatever system you put in place, it must work for you so that you will observe and record your observations regularly. For example:

> unfortunately, I don't think I have a very good memory … In fact I use sticky labels. So I can just write down the observation and stick it onto a sheet without re-writing it. If it requires too much work then it doesn't get done. That's my record for me. (Siraj-Blatchford et al., 2002: 62)

In addition to the problem of remembering, no matter how good the memory might be, a memory is not a useable record for reflection or future reference. Jotting down observations on sticky notes means that observations that happen when the teacher is interacting with the children can be recorded for later reflection.

Another example describes using a notebook and time sampling:

> I have … a little A5 notebook and I'd stick those tiny post-its you get, stick them all down along the side with each child's initials on it. So if I was doing an observation I would open a page on, say _____ and ok what is _____ playing with today, who is she talking to, what is she doing? … And I would just pick maybe three or four kids that I'm going to look at that day and I might make a two minute observation. (Fallon, 2015b)

This strategy is useful for focusing over time on each child in the group, especially quieter children who may not come to attention often.

Notes that you generate yourself are one type of evidence, but not the only type. Digital photos of artefacts that are the outcomes of play and of the play process are particularly useful in terms of understanding the children's perspectives on the resources. They offer the opportunity to revisit the play with the children to explore their thinking and motivation in relation to the resources. This can alert you to, for example, resources the children find attractive, those they find difficult to use and why; their experience of accessing the resources they want to use; how they like to combine different resources; and whether or not they are making connections between the resources they use for play and the teacher's use of those same resources during teacher-led activity. This information contributes to planning for resource provision and is a way of ensuring that the children's perspectives are taken into account for the planning process.

Whatever system you put in place for yourself, the crucial point is that unless you record your observations, they may as well never have happened. Once observations have been recorded, the question arises as to what to do with them. Written notes should be reviewed at the end of the day, and photographs reviewed with the child/children as soon as possible. You will decide which observations will need to be followed up with a commentary. The commentary is where you reflect on what your observation means for the child(ren) and for your practice.

Pause for Thought

What strategies for recording observations would encourage you to observe regularly?

Planning

Planning is generally understood to take place across three time-frames: long-term (year); medium-term (term or a number of months); short-term (two to four weeks) (NCCA, 2009b). The long-term plan can articulate the affordance of the resources in terms of the relevant Curriculum. There is no suggestion that this is the extent of the affordance of the material, or that the Curriculum defines the children's learning through play. Rather, it is a pragmatic way for teachers to plan to connect the children's play with the Curriculum. As will be argued in relation to short-term planning, this is also more appropriate than listing themes to be covered over the course of a year.

> Planning for a rolling programme of topics or themes is not best suited to young children because their agendas may not fit in with the set topics: their interests may change, some play themes last just a few days, while others may span several weeks. (Wood and Attfield, 2005: 160)

Table 11.1 gives an example of long-term planning documentation. In this model, the affordance of the resource is expressed in terms of subject-specific objectives (in this case just three subject areas in the Primary School Curriculum (DES, 1999)). Through playing with Junk Art materials, the children will engage with the strands and strand units listed; this can be expanded into the full range of subject areas.

Table 11.1 Connecting play resources with the Curriculum

Junk Art	
Maths	
Strands	**Strand units**
Skills	Applying and problem-solving
	Communicating and expressing
	Integrating and connecting
	Reasoning
	Implementing
	Understanding and recalling
Early mathematical activities	Classifying
	Matching
	Comparing
	Ordering
Shape and space	Spatial awareness
	3-D shapes
	2-D shapes
	Symmetry
	Angles
Visual Arts	
Strands	**Strand units**
Concepts	An awareness of line
	An awareness of shape
	An awareness of form
	An awareness of texture
	An awareness of space
Construction	Making constructions
	Looking and responding
Science	
Strands	**Strand units**
Working scientifically	Questioning
	Observing
	Predicting
	Investigating and experimenting
	Estimating and measuring
	Analysing (sorting and classifying)
	Recording and communicating

(Continued)

Table 11.1   (Continued)

Junk Art	
Science	
Strands	**Strand units**
Designing and making	Exploring
	Planning
	Making
	Evaluating
Materials	Properties and characteristics of materials
	Materials and change
Environmental awareness and care	Caring for my locality

Medium-term planning is a way of organising long-term plans into the time frame of a school year to form a link between long- and short-term planning (see Table 11.2). Grouping together sets of curriculum objectives/outcomes that fit well together provides the teacher with a focus both for their provision of an "instructive play environment" (Siraj-Blatchford et al., 2002: 28) and for their direct teaching over the course of a term or a number of months.

Table 11.2   Medium-term Curriculum plan for junk art

Junk Art (Term 1, 4–5 year olds)	
Maths	
Strands	**Strand units**
Skills	**Communicating** and expressing
Early mathematical activities	**Classifying**
	Matching
Shape and space	**Spatial** awareness
	3-D **shapes**
	2-D **shapes**
Visual Arts	
Strands	**Strand units**
Concepts	An awareness of **shape**
	An awareness of **space**
Construction	Making constructions
	Looking and responding

Junk Art (Term 1, 4–5 year olds)

Science

Strands	Strand units
Working scientifically	Analysing (sorting and **classifying**)
	Recording and **communicating**
Designing and making	Exploring
Materials	Properties and characteristics of materials

However, most focus should be on the short-term plan, which must involve the children and reflect their developing interests. Themes should be chosen in consultation with the children and with respect for their interests. When short-term planning is structured around the children's evolving interests and with provision for child-led play, observation may well show additional Curriculum objectives being achieved that are over and above those envisaged by the teacher. These should be recorded in the short-term plan. This can be thought of as emergent planning, and should be seen as an integral part of planning that involves children in the process because it records the outcomes of the children's independent action.

The Planning Cycle

Observations that have been recorded systematically ensure that planning is based on evidence rather than impressions.

> Effective practitioners are good researchers of their practice through observing, listening, planning, interacting, evaluating and reflecting. (Wood, 2013: 139)

With that in mind, the action research spiral model (Figure 11.1) is helpful for planning in the classroom because it encourages building on what has gone before, with each turn of the spiral enabling greater understanding and insight (Koshy, 2010).

The spiral begins with planning, followed by action and observation, followed by reflection on the action/observations. The new cycle begins on the basis of the knowledge and understanding developed during the previous cycle. The idea of a spiral is important because it emphasises continuity from one plan to another, rather than a new plan being an entirely new beginning, disconnected from the previous one. Planning on the basis of distinct themes over a given time period can happen in a disconnected way, with each theme being a complete break from the previous one.

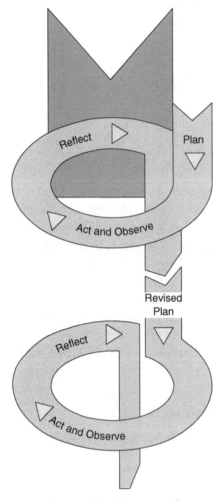

Figure 11.1   The action research spiral (Koshy, 2010: 5)

The spiral model emphasises continuity and progression, and consulting with children about the next steps is implicit in the process.

Consider the questions below to prompt planning for resource provision:

Step 1: Planning

- Why am I providing this resource, and what affordance does it provide?
- What skills will the children need to benefit from that affordance?

- What Curriculum objectives are a good fit with the affordance of the resource?
- How will I use this resource for teacher-led contexts?

Step 2: Observation on action

- What are the children doing with the resource and what affordance have they identified?
- How does that relate to the affordance I had identified?
- What is unexpected?
- Do the children have the resources they need for what they want to do?

Step 3: Reflection

- Are my Curriculum objectives relevant to what the children are doing or want to do?
- What Curriculum objectives fit with what the children are doing or want to do?
- How will I record amendments to my original plan?
- What do I need to do to extend the affordance of the resource?
- Which learning experiences do I want to pursue with the whole class?
- Why have I chosen those particular learning experiences? What are the skills, subject content, dispositions, etc., associated with them that make them significant?

Playful pedagogy is complex and this chapter has focused on just one aspect of provision for play. The intention is to encourage attention to the resources that children use to fulfil their ideas and creativity, and to acknowledge this critical aspect of professional expertise.

Key Messages

- Much (though not all) of the play in educational settings involves children interacting with concrete resources. This makes the resources central to playful learning, and planning for and providing those resources are key skills for the early years practitioner.

(Continued)

(Continued)

- Knowledge and expertise in the affordance of resources can enhance the teacher's ability to connect play and playful learning with the requirements of a specific Curriculum.
- Each teacher can enhance their knowledge and expertise of affordance through observation as part of the planning cycle. This can open up opportunities for extending the affordance of the resources either by adapting the resources or teaching children the skills they need to extend the affordance themselves.
- Providing resources is one of the main pedagogic actions undertaken by teachers in making provision for play. Teachers may not always value their own efforts in the provision of resources as a sophisticated professional activity, and perhaps do not fully appreciate the contribution this makes to children's learning. Carefully considered resources create beneficial spaces where playful teaching and learning come together, not just for Curriculum outcomes, but for happy ones.

Further Reading and Resources

Broadhead, P. (2010) 'Cooperative play and learning from nursery to year one', in P. Broadhead, J. Howard and E. Wood (eds), *Play and Learning in the Early Years*. London: Sage. pp. 43–59.

Colker, L.J. (undated) 'Block off time for learning', *Teaching Young Children*, 1 (3). www.naeyc.org/files/tyc/file/Block%20Off%20Time. pdf (accessed 9 September 2016).

Drew, W.F. and Rankin, G. (2004). 'Promoting creativity for life using open-ended materials'. *Young Children* July. www.rediscovercenter. org/pdf/promoting_creativity1.pdf (accessed 9 September 2016).

References

Bodrova, E. (2008) 'Make-believe play versus academic skills: A Vygotskian approach to today's dilemma of early childhood education', *European Early Childhood Education Research Journal* 16 (3): 357–69.

Broadhead, P. (2004) *Early Years Play and Learning: Developing Social Skills and Cooperation*. London: RoutledgeFalmer.

Broadhead, P. (2010) 'Cooperative play and learning from nursery to year one', in P. Broadhead, J. Howard and E. Wood (eds), *Play and Learning in the Early Years*. London: Sage. pp. 43–59.

Carr, M. (2000) 'Technological affordance, social practice and learning narratives in an early childhood setting', *International Journal of Technology and Design Education* 10: 61–79.

Department of Education and Science (1999) *Primary School Curriculum*. Dublin: The Stationery Office.

Fallon, J. (2015a) *Teachers' Beliefs about Play in Infant Classes in Primary Schools in the Republic of Ireland*. PhD Thesis, The University of Dublin, Trinity College.

Fallon, J. (2015b) *Teachers' Beliefs about Play in Infant Classes in Primary Schools in the Republic of Ireland: Transcript D*. Unpublished.

Kernan, M. (2014) 'Opportunities and affordance in outdoor play', in L. Brooker, M. Blaise and S. Edwards (eds), *The SAGE Handbook of Play and Learning in Early Childhood*. London: Sage. pp. 391–403.

Koshy, V. (2010) *Action Research for Improving Educational Practice* (second edition). London: Sage.

Løkken, G. and Moser, T. (2012) 'Space and materiality in early childhood pedagogy – introductory notes', *Education Inquiry* 3 (3): 303–15.

Moyles, J.R. (1989) *Just Playing? The Role and Status of Play in Early Childhood Education*. Milton Keynes: Open University Press.

National Council for Curriculum and Assessment (2009a) *Aistear, The Early Childhood Curriculum Framework, Guidelines for good practice, Supporting learning and development through assessment*. www.ncca.biz/Aistear/pdfs/Guidelines_ENG/GuidelinesIntro_ENG.pdf (accessed 9 September 2016).

National Council for Curriculum and Assessment (2009b) *Aistear, The Early Childhood Curriculum Framework, User Guide*. www.ncca.biz/Aistear/pdfs/UserGuide_ENG.pdf (accessed 9 September 2016).

Odegard, N. (2012) 'When matter comes to matter: Working pedagogically with junk materials', *Education Inquiry* 3 (3): 387–400.

Siraj-Blatchford, I., Sylva, K., Muttock, S., Gilden, R. and Bell, D. (2002) *Researching Effective Pedagogy in the Early Years – Research Report No. 356*. London: Department of Education and Skills. www.327matters.org/Docs/RR356.pdf (accessed 9 September 2016).

Wood, E. (2013) *Play, Learning and the Early Childhood Curriculum* (third edition). London: Sage.

Wood, E. and Attfield, J. (2005) *Play, Learning and the Early Childhood Curriculum*. (second edition). London: Paul Chapman.

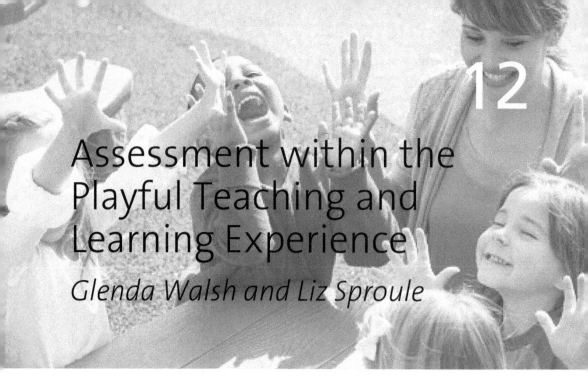

Assessment within the Playful Teaching and Learning Experience

Glenda Walsh and Liz Sproule

Chapter Overview

By the end of this chapter we hope you can:

- Recognise the importance of a socio-cultural perspective on assessment;
- Appreciate the need to embrace an holistic approach to children's assessment to include the broader goals for children's learning;
- Capitalise on the Quality Learning Instrument (Walsh and Gardner, 2005) as a potential assessment schedule for use in an early years classroom/setting.

A Socio-cultural Perspective on Assessment

The general perspective of this Playful Teaching and Learning book is aligned with post-Vygotskian theory – socio-cultural and participatory perspectives on how young children learn and develop. Yet it would appear that assessment in the early years has not undergone the same conceptual change (Fleer, 2002). In many parts of the world, there is statutory or locally mandated summative assessment of children in the early years. This assessment is very often reductionist and narrow in nature and has been widely criticised on those grounds (see, for example, Wood, 2016). Early years assessment tends to be very individualistic in approach, with the focus on what an individual child can or cannot do in isolation and on specific targets or goals. As Fleer (2002) points out, documenting individual test scores, compiling them into classroom results, or even at school or entire system level, does little to improve children's learning. Broadhead (2006) refers to such practices as convergent forms of assessment, where the emphasis is placed on target achievement rather than on learning potential. Instead, she argues for a more divergent or socio-cultural view on assessment, where the assessment is accomplished *with* the child rather than *on* the child. In this way the focus of the assessment moves beyond a deficit model, to one where the assessment lens no longer solely addresses the child, but includes the teacher's participation and mediation alongside the cultural tools (Fleer, 2002) in an effort to understand the learning process more fully and to ensure a purposeful way forward for improvement and development.

As Broadhead said when discussing assessment:

Perhaps it is now time to shift the emphasis in the early years, time to move from a position whereby starting with the child has prevailed into one where we begin from an informed understanding of learning. As we move into an era where observations in EY settings should become the norm rather than the exception, let's not think about watching the children, rather let us think about understanding their learning. (2004: 13)

Following this viewpoint, formative assessment is the much improved method of assessment, which gives the child feedback on progress and makes the teacher articulate the child's level in a way that helps her to assess the child's interests and needs. In addition, it can clarify the practitioner's thoughts about their own strategies and interactions to ensure learning along the way. As Broadhead (2006) argues, formative assessment in the form of observations and interactions provides practitioners with the potential for extending their own professional knowledge and understandings of children's learning processes and how, in response, they might enrich young children's learning experiences.

In this chapter, we aim, therefore, to present a more contextual view of assessment. Such assessment will be of value to practitioners in obtaining a richer understanding of each individual child, thus providing a basis for sensitive day-to-day interactions between adults and children, and in relating the practitioner's approaches and strategies to the child's experience.

Pause for Thought

In light of what you have just read, what does a socio-cultural perspective on assessment mean to you?

From your experience of the early years classroom/setting, to what extent do you think this approach is happening in practice?

What might some of the challenges be for you in adopting a socio-cultural approach to assessment in your classroom practice?

Towards an Holistic Approach to Early Years Assessment

Having explained the importance of a socio-cultural approach to formative assessment, what domains, as early years practitioners, should our formative assessments be tuning into? As Carr (2014) reminds us, assessment is a powerful mediator of learning and curriculum direction and if we do not assess the learning outcomes that we value, then they are not likely to survive.

Claxton and Carr (2002) recommend that education should focus not only on the cultivation of effective skills but also on positive learning dispositions to ensure real learning power. They stress the importance of considering children's dispositions as well as their capabilities in terms of learning skills, strategies and abilities. Children have to be ready and willing to embrace the learning opportunities, as well as being able to learn, as clearly articulated by Dowling and Walsh in Chapter 7 of this book and by McGuinness in Chapter 4. While Hedges and Cullen (2011) emphasise learning dispositions as a potential 'outcome' for participatory learning, they also highlight the importance of funds of knowledge and working theories. Funds of knowledge, already referred to in Chapter 1 of this book, denote the knowledge that children develop in their homes and communities which can be used and built upon in the early years setting. Hedges and Cullen (2011: 932) provide us with the example of shopping and emphasise its natural link with "Literacy, numeracy, communication and decision-making among other knowledge and skills". Working theories, on the other hand, are explained as ways in which children process everyday knowledge and how they use such spontaneous acquired knowledge to inform new information through thinking, reasoning and problem-solving.

More recent work by Carr (2014) also draws attention to the need for a richer conceptualisation of 'learning outcomes' in the early years of education, identifying five key domains of importance, namely:

- Identities and thinking (the ability to think and express own ideas);
- Skills and knowledges (e.g., shapes, letter formation, writing, mathematics, etc.);
- Social relationships (the ability to interact and learn together);
- Attunement to play as an opportunity to learn (searching for opportunities to apply one's capacities);
- Key competencies and learning dispositions (ways to approach learning).

Pause for Thought

Consider what you have just read in terms of the need to move away from an overly narrow focus on what to assess to a more holistic approach to children's learning.

In your opinion what are the advantages and disadvantages of such a change in thinking?

What challenges might teachers face in the early years context to embrace a more holistic approach to assessment and how could these be overcome?

The Quality Learning Instrument:
An Overview

The next section in this chapter will refer extensively to the Quality Learning Instrument (QLI) (Walsh and Gardner, 2005; Walsh et al., 2006). This assessment instrument was developed to assess the child's classroom experience in a novel way. Uniquely, it recognises that the child is deeply influenced by others in the early years class/setting and embraces a more holistic approach to the assessment of young children's learning,

QLI is a classroom observation schedule that is used to evaluate the quality of children's learning experience. It takes into consideration a triangle of interactions in the classroom – the children's actions, the teaching strategies and the role of the environment and resources. QLI aims to uncover how it might feel to be a child in that environment (see Katz, 1995). Thus, the QLI rating in a classroom is determined by the way in which the learning and developmental needs of the main stakeholders, the children themselves, are being met within the affective, cognitive, social and physical context. It was developed specifically for use in early years classrooms and has been subjected to considerable validity and reliability analyses (Walsh and Gardner, 2005; Walsh et al., 2006). It was later modified for application in classrooms of children up to age eight. Table 12.1 shows the nine quality indicators against which children's learning experience in a classroom can be assessed.

Table 12.1   A definition of each quality indicator from QLI (Source: Walsh et al., 2006: Table 2)

Quality indicator	Definition
Motivation	Children are interested in and inquisitive about their learning and show active signs of wanting to learn
Concentration	Children are actively engaged in the learning process, not easily distracted and attentive for reasonable periods for their age group
Confidence	Children feel secure and not under pressure in their learning environment and have confidence in their ability as learners
Independence	Children have an appropriate degree of control over their own learning and behaviour, working gradually towards being independent learners
Physical well-being	Children are happy, reasonably well behaved, appropriately nourished and physically at ease in their learning environment
Multiple skill acquisition	Children are provided with a holistic learning experience, covering a variety of skills and knowledge within an appropriate context, including, but not limited to, literacy and numeracy skills
Higher-order thinking skills (HOTS)	Children are given the opportunity to reflect on and synthesise their whole learning experience and in so doing develop their powers of such things as memory, listening, sequencing, sorting and classification
Social interaction	Children are encouraged to learn in the company of others, to get along with each other and with adults and to develop towards being able to work cooperatively with others
Respect	Children display a tolerance and respect for themselves, others and their environment

Many of the scales have been found to be important for children's progress and are highlighted throughout this book. For example, the affective and social scales (confidence, physical well-being, social interaction and respect) (see, for example, Chapter 7) and cognitive (multiple skill acquisition and higher-order thinking skills) domains (see Chapter 4), as well as the roots of children's learning dispositions (motivation, concentration and independence) (see Chapter 4 and Chapter 7).

QLI takes into consideration the inter-relatedness of young children's learning and development. The three aspects – children's actions, teaching strategies, and the environment – are rated in relation to each of the nine quality indicators. Using a best-fit model, each setting is rated against the QLI rubric on a scale of 1 (low) to 3 (high) for each aspect in each domain.

QLI is not intended to be a tick-box exercise. Instead, when using QLI, it is recommended that practitioners engage in the normal process of watching, listening and taking notes to build up rich and valid data about the child and their learning experience. It is only after the observations take place, at an opportune moment, that the practitioner will reflect on the observational data against the detail of QLI. In this way, it could be argued, QLI helps to infuse a degree of objectivity into the observational experience.

QLI can have several applications, besides rating the overall experience of the children. Each aspect – teacher, child or environment – can be rated separately. The rater may look at individual children or the class as a whole, depending on their focus. Alternatively, the teacher may concentrate on self-assessment using the teacher aspect. This approach is greatly enhanced if teachers video themselves and use the videos as the basis for assessment. Equally, the environment aspect may provoke a thorough assessment of resources and planning. Finally, the teacher may choose to concentrate on a particular quality indicator.

The next section of this chapter will allow QLI to be put into action by focusing on three key quality indicators: Motivation, Concentration and Thinking Skills and judging them against observational data gleaned from case studies from three different early years settings/classrooms.

Case Study 12.1: Rich Role Play in a Preschool Class

A group of four year olds has been learning about *The Frog Prince* during their story time sessions for the past week. The teacher has read several versions of the story to them. She has used a variety of resources to retell the story (a flipbook, hand puppets and puppet theatre, story sequencing cards). During playtime the children are provided with several activities to encourage them to explore the theme of the *Frog Prince* more fully. A group of three children

(Continued)

(Continued)

choose to go to a table in the dressing-up corner which is covered in bright fabrics, belts and grips that can hold material together. There are themed headbands for the characters from the *Frog Prince* story. Several *Frog Prince* books are in a basket, a wordless version of the story among them. There is a recording device that children may use to record themselves. Jessica puts on the headband for the frog and presses the record button. "I will fetch your golden ball" she records. Sam adopts the role of King and records, in a loud, authoritative voice, "I am the King! Let the frog eat from your plate, princess – at once!". Katie then has a go: "I will never kiss you", and starts to laugh. The three children become absorbed in changing headbands, draping themselves in fabric and recording and replaying their voices. Sam then takes the princess headband. Much giggling ensues. He turns around to record a line (semi-secretly) from the two girls. He then turns back to them and says, "Here, listen to this". He presses the play button and the two girls draw close to listen. The ICT button repeats what he has recorded, "I'm a lovely princess!". The three of them burst into peals of laughter and they all collapse in fits of giggles.

The Quality Learning Instrument in Action

After reading the case study above, turn your attention to some of the QLI indicators for motivation in Table 12.2. Examples of high and low descriptors have been included.

Table 12.2 Examples of indicators on the QLI motivation indicator across the triangle of interaction

Rating	Children's actions	Teaching strategies	Environment
High	• eager to participate in activities; • display curiosity and inquisitiveness; • show a degree of energy, creativity and imagination.	• a variety of stimulating and age-appropriate activities on offer; • activities frequently changed in accordance with children's interests; • adults show interest in children's learning; • adults extend learning when appropriate	• setting is varied and aesthetically pleasing to the learner; • resources are authentic and interesting to use; • opportunities for sensory, rich experiences

Rating	Children's actions	Teaching strategies	Environment
Low	• apathetic and unenthusiastic; • seldom ask constructive questions; • appear bored	• uninteresting activities on offer; • activities are rarely changed; • too little participation on the part of adults or become too directive of the learning situation	• dull and lacking in character; • resources available but tend to be routine and uninspiring

Pause for Thought

Based on the information in Table 12.2, how well do you think the three children were motivated throughout?

How do you rate the teacher's contribution to this activity as well as the learning environment in terms of the resources provided?

Comment

It is clear that the children are highly motivated throughout the role play, with no need for adult support. They are highly playful and creative, entering into the roles with gusto and appropriate voices. The teacher appears to recognise that she should not interrupt such a fruitful play event. When watching, she can nevertheless make a rich assessment of how well the children remember and understand the story, how they respond to the resources and how well they play together. Her contribution to this session does not need to include intervention, because she has made thorough preparation for the children and the resources. The latter are open-ended and certainly appear interesting to use.

Case Study 12.2: Number Time in Action with 5–6 Year Old Children

The teacher is working with a group of six boys. They are using a large floor mat. It has number splats on it with numbers up to 25. Children are asked to hop on to a number. Then they take football shaped beanbags to place on the number. One child needs to be refocused by the teacher. He is

(Continued)

(Continued)

rolling on the floor away from the Maths group. The teacher warmly redirects him by saying his name: "Axel, can you hop over to number 19 and leave your bean bag there?". He rejoins the group and does this. Other children take turns to identify the numbers. They are involved and enjoying the practical nature of the learning. Axel has lost focus again. The teacher places herself beside him and offers him another beanbag. She says, "Choose a number between 13 and 16 and place your beanbag on the splat. Tell us which number you have landed on". He follows the instruction.

The group move to a table where the teacher demonstrates a new game. It uses laminated footballs with numbers printed on them. It is colourful and links in to the group's current interest. After she explains the game, the children are left to play it independently. Axel starts to play with another child. The other child is engrossed and concentrating on ordering the numbers. Some degree of challenge is inherent in the game, as each row has a different starting point. Axel completes one row and leaves the table. He has ordered the numbers incorrectly. He goes to the Maths taskboard to make a choice. He selects a blank number array and takes a set of colourful gel pens to his desk. He writes the numbers to 7 and then leaves his table. The teacher has been observing and notices that he is not really involved. His level of distractibility is high. She asks him what he has chosen from the taskboard and settles beside him to get him going again with his chosen number array. She moves off to help another group. A few minutes later she notices that Axel is up from his table again and flitting from taskboard to table but not really doing anything. She says, "I'd love to see your number array. How did you get on?". He pulls a crumpled piece of paper from under his desk. It was unfinished. Without close adult support, Axel continually demonstrates a low level of involvement and a high level of distractibility. This has been observed consistently and discussed with his parents.

Pause for Thought

Now consider the relevant QLI scales in Table 12.3 and keep them in mind as you re-read the case study and then make your judgement on Axel's overall level of concentration during this scenario. Consider the relevance of the teaching strategies and the environment to determine why this might be the case.

Table 12.3   Examples of high and low descriptors on the QLI concentration indicator

Rating	Children's actions	Teaching strategies	Environment
High	• attentive/lost in what they are doing; • signs of deliberation and mental engagement, e.g., intent gaze, protruding tongue, pursed lips; • precision and care evident; • perseverance in the face of difficulty; • remain at activity until a satisfactory conclusion	• allows appropriate time for completion of activities; • ensures activities are pitched appropriately for the age-level and ability of the children; • allows for a degree of challenge and diversity of response; • adult available for intervention if and when required	• appropriate space to allow for lack of distraction and disturbance
Low	• often flits from one activity to another (butterfly behaviour); • very easily distracted; • activity completed carelessly	• frequently presents tasks/activities that are too challenging or too easy; • much too much supervision and interruption of activities	• lay-out inappropriately organised/planned to aid concentration

Comment

On later reflection the teacher notes that, without close adult support, Axel continually demonstrates a low level of involvement and a high level of distractibility. The teacher tries giving him the support of her presence and, later, lowers the difficulty of the task to test whether challenge was the issue. She expresses interest in his work in a positive way and praises his efforts. Although the teacher would score highly on the concentration scale, as would the resources, nothing has worked for very long. Axel's inability to settle and to maintain concentration remains very evident. Putting this event into the context of similar butterfly behaviour, the teacher is rightly concerned about Axel and decides to discuss him with Axel's parents and the special needs advisor. He does show evidence of making a start to activities, so motivation is less likely to be the problem, although there is some overlap between the motivation and concentration scales. Further close monitoring will be needed. It may be that, as Axel matures, he will improve naturally or some kind of extra help may be needed.

Case Study 12.3: Higher-order thinking skills (HOTS) with 6–7 year olds

The context for this case study is the topic of frogs. The class have been learning about the frog lifecycle. They have been investigating similarities and differences of frogs' skins and habitats. Camouflage

(Continued)

(Continued)

has been investigated over several playful activities. Two children are at the water tray. In the water tray is clear water. Hidden in the water tray are jelly-like clear marble-sized beads. These have formed as the result of expanding water crystals. These are not visible under the surface of the water. Toby has filled a large clear jug with water which contained about fifty beads. He swirls his hand around the material. "Oh! Put your hand in it ... put your hand in it", Toby says. He holds the jug up for the other child who puts her hand in and swishes it around. Lara says: "Oh! It's so fun". She looks closely and swirls it again. "It's like real tadpoles". Toby says: "I don't think it's tadpoles; it's like frogspawn". Both children continue to scoop out the water and beads with mini sieves. Lara continues to lift the beads in and out of the water in her hands. She looks closely again at them: "There are no black dots. Is it frogspawn?". Noticing that the beads change in appearance as they break the surface of the water, Lara says excitedly to Toby, "Look! You can't even see it. It's proper camouflaged". She calls to the teacher, "Mrs Moth, is it 'cause it is under the water? You can't see it? It's camouflaged". Mrs Moth replies, "That's a great word, camouflaged. It *does* look different under the water. I wonder why?". Toby says: "It's 'cause they are the same colour. Can they change colour?". Mrs Moth replies that you can change the colour of them. She says, "I have some that are a different colour. Would you like them?". The children nod and she goes and gets beads that are red. The children's faces have excited expressions. Lara takes the container and puts it under the water. The two children continue to explore the materials for 20 more minutes. All the time they sustain a rich conversation, collaborating, thinking and asking questions.

Now consider high and low descriptors shown in Table 12.4 from the indicator Higher Order Thinking Skills in the QLI.

Comment

The activity described in Case Study 12.3 has been well crafted to provoke the children into using their observation skills, including the rarely used

Table 12.4   Examples of descriptors on the QLI Higher Order Thinking Skills indicator

Rating	Children's actions	Teaching strategies	Environment
High	• use knowledge from other learning or activities in novel ways; • excellent observational/reporting skills and can supply a lot of detail; • offer an opinion; • make appropriate suggestions and offer alternatives; • make an attempt at solving problems for themselves	• excellent use of discourse with probing questions, amplification of children's utterances and use of thinking language; • often makes links to other learning or activities; • scaffolds children's learning	• resources are appropriately matched to children's learning and allow for appropriate extension; • is flexible but well-organised; • ample space for exploration and investigation; • many open-ended resources that are rich in possibility and adventure
Low	• make no links to other learning or activities, such as recalling part of a story with a connection to the activity; • very superficial observational and/or reporting skills, such as when asked to describe what they see in a picture	• poor use of discourse, e.g., closed questions, talking over the children, not giving children time to think of a response; • makes no links to other learning or activities; • children are closely instructed how to complete an activity, or little support provided at all	• resources in learning areas are very limited and low in quality; • space restricts exploration and investigation; • learning opportunities have not been adequately thought through to promote purposeful learning experience

sense of feel, and their thinking skills. The playful approach allows the children to experiment repeatedly and experience the thrill of discovery. As they play, they compare and contrast frog spawn with the beads, offer opinions to one another and formulate possible explanations through links with previous learning. Again, the teacher does not need to interact with the children most of the time because the previous learning and the resources provided have given them the tools to extend their learning independently. When Toby suggests his colour theory, the teacher takes the opportunity to extend the activity; she grasps the need to give him a way to investigate further, based on his question. If the coloured beads had been available at the start, it might have distracted the children from comparison with frog-spawn. The teacher's use of "I wonder why" is another example of the good use of discourse mentioned in Table 12.4. It encourages the children to think for themselves, whereas a direct answer might have closed down the thinking opportunity.

Pause for Thought

How might the activity be adapted if the quality of the HOTS experience across the three domains was rated as low?

Key Messages

- This chapter has encouraged a broadly based view of assessment, one that envisages the early years as a time of preparation for later school years in a number of ways other than progress in Literacy and Numeracy.
- There is increasing emphasis internationally on building good learning dispositions, acquiring systematic thinking skills and preparing children for teamwork in the early years.
- Such an early learning experience prepares children to get the most out of their later schooling as proactive and well-motivated students who have the confidence to cope with any challenges they encounter.
- QLI gives the teacher a tool that will enable her to weigh up the experience of her children against a standard frame of reference with a view to providing the children with such skills and competences.
- In addition QLI provides an opportunity to tune into the entire quality of the learning experience, enabling professionals to engage in a process of self-reflection on their own playful teaching and learning environment in an effort to respond to the needs of the children more fully.

Further Reading and Resources

Carr, M. (2002) *Assessment in Early Childhood Settings: Learning Stories*. London: Paul Chapman.

The International Baccalaureate Primary Years Programme: www.ibo.org/programmes/primary-years-programme/ (accessed 10 September 2016).

References

Broadhead, P. (2004) *Early Years Play and Learning: Developing Social Skills and Cooperation*. London: RoutledgeFalmer.

Broadhead, P. (2006) 'Developing an understanding of young children's learning through play: The place of observation, interaction and reflection', *British Educational Research Journal* 32 (2): 191–207.

Carr, M. (2014) 'Play and playfulness: Issues of assessment', in L. Brooker, M. Blaise and S. Edwards, *The Sage Handbook of Play and Learning in Early Childhood*. London: Sage. pp. 264–75.

Claxton, G. and Carr, M. (2002) 'A framework for teaching learning: The dynamics of disposition', *Early Years* 24 (1): 87–97.

Fleer, M. (2002) 'Sociocultural assessment in early years education – myth or reality?' *International Journal of Early Years Education* 10 (2): 105–20.

Hedges, H. and Cullen, J. (2011) 'Participatory learning theories: A framework for early childhood pedagogy', *Early Child Development and Care* 182 (7): 921–40.

Katz, L.G. (1995) *Talks with Teachers of Young Children: A Collection*. Norwood, NJ: Ablex.

Walsh, G. and Gardner, J. (2005) 'Assessing the quality of early years learning environments', *Early Childhood Research and Practice* 7: 1.

Walsh, G., Sproule, L., McGuinness, C., Trew, K., Rafferty, H. and Sheehy, N. (2006) 'An appropriate curriculum for the 4–5 year old child in Northern Ireland: Comparing play-based and formal approaches', *Early Years: An International Journal of Research and Development* 26 (2): 201–21.

Wood, E. (2016) 'Professional knowledge, assessment and accountability: A perspective from England', *Early Education Journal* 78: 13–15.

Towards the Playful Professional

Dorothy McMillan

13

Chapter Overview

Adults who work with young children need to have a clear understanding of what is involved in high-level play, along with a clear grasp of their own role as playful professionals in the process of children's learning. The first section of this book has reinforced this dual message at a conceptual level, and the central section has explored how playful teaching and learning can be applied within and across various areas of the curriculum. The third section has focused on the importance of rigorous implementation of the planning cycle for effective learning within a playful environment. This leads us to the final consideration of the book: What does a playful professional actually look like? In this chapter I will attempt to answer this question by exploring personal qualities that tend towards playfulness; specific roles to be played and others to be avoided; appropriate training for the playful professional and guidance for leading a playful team. I hope that by the end of this chapter you will be able to follow the storyline of the book, recognise the links between the sections and, above all, be inspired to be a playful professional.

Personal Qualities

Working alongside young children ought to be, overall, a happy experience. Kane (2004), in his book advocating a more playful societal landscape for the enrichment of both adults and children, defines adult playfulness in terms of "a joyful readiness for anything" (2004: 181). The same emotion is highlighted by Rose (2007) when she outlines "...ways in which you can help to ensure your teaching is joyous for both yourself and the young children with whom you work" (2007: 70). Rose (2007) focuses on the interplay between the affective and conceptual domains, arguing that effective teachers need to be skilled in both emotional intelligence and critical reflection. For some professionals, this combination appears to come naturally, whilst others lean more towards one or other domain. It seems that certain personal characteristics enable playfulness in adults more than others. So what are some of the personal qualities that make a playful professional?

Sense of Humour

Closely related to joyfulness is the possession of a sense of humour; in fact, Peterson and Seligman (2004: n.p.) regard playfulness and humour as synonymous. They define humour in terms of "liking to laugh and tease; bringing smiles to other people; seeing the light side; making (not necessarily telling) jokes". In an online study of 268 adults, using three adult playfulness scales – including Peterson and Seligman's (2004) *Values in Action* inventory – Proyer and Ruch (2011) found that adult playfulness was best predicted by a sense of humour. We have seen throughout the central section of this book how humour can be used to encourage children's engagement and enjoyment of learning within and across the curriculum. In Chapter 10, for example, the authors explore the potential for aspects of STEM learning where children and adults share in humorous play exchanges. In Chapter 6, the writer documents in detail a humorous approach to literacy development, and she encourages early years teachers to engage actively with children's sense of humour by joining in their 'nonsense' word games and jokes. She also advocates humour right from the planning stage, urging teachers to select humorous material such as poetry and funny stories as part of the literacy diet for young children. We should not underestimate the value of humour on a wider level: Proyer and Ruch (2011) argue that playfulness as a concept is located within the field of positive psychology and that humour is hugely beneficial for many work-related activities, team efforts and, ultimately, for all-round adult wellbeing.

Flexibility and Ambiguity Tolerance

Based on observations and interviews with teachers in Northern Ireland, Walsh et al. (2011) identified three features of the playful professional:

preserving a light-hearted tone (related to the sense of humour discussed above); being outgoing, energetic and active in style; and leaving room for spontaneity. The ability to be spontaneous and cope with the unexpected is a key characteristic of the playful professional. Tegano et al. (1999) investigated the relationship between teachers' personality types, their level of playfulness and their ability to tolerate ambiguity, such as "classroom confusion, disarray or activities that have no apparent point of closure" (1999: 292). In their study they used a personality type indicator, an adult behaviour inventory and a test to measure "ambiguity tolerance". They found a close relationship between playfulness and ambiguity tolerance and concluded that playful teachers will tend to be perceptive and intuitive and display traits such as being curious rather than decisive; flexibility, adaptability and tolerance; and easy adjustment to the accidental and unexpected. Teaching professionals who can display these traits are, according to Goouch (2008), becoming rarer, partly due to the pedagogical demands of closely prescribed curricula and the policy demands of accountability. But, even in terms of personal disposition, a sense of willingness to "enter a state of confusion" (Claxton, 2000: 49) with regard to flexibility and tolerance of ambiguity is attractive to some individuals but rather alien to others. Note that flexibility does not mean that teachers should be unprepared in terms of planning and organisation. In Chapter 8 of this book, the author emphasises the importance of giving children the freedom to make play choices in the outdoor environment within a context of careful planning and purposeful organisation. In Chapter 11, we see the deceptively dichotomous relationship between planning and children's choices, as in the case of the Bungee Jumping Farmers. The flexible professional who can tolerate ambiguity must balance this with careful planning; conversely, the well-prepared professional must add a measure of ambiguity tolerance so that both become truly playful professionals.

Warmth and Affection

In addition to having a sense of humour and being flexible in the face of ambiguity, the playful professional must be someone who displays genuine warmth to the children and other adults involved in the setting. Literature across the field of early childhood education and care abounds with references to the importance of the quality of the relationship between teacher and learner. Goouch (2008), for example, refers to the "pedagogy of relationships" (2008: 94) that pervades the Reggio Emilia philosophy. Similarly, in Chapter 3 of this book, the author contends that establishing caring yet nurturing relationships is foundational to the concept of playful teaching and learning. There is often a perceived contradiction between professionalism and warm caring. Griffin (2008) highlights the reluctance of some childminders to present themselves as professionals, since they prefer to be known for their "warmly affectionate level of care for children" (2008: 67). Yet there need not be any contradiction, since warmth and affection are essential components of playful teaching and learning. Thus Mitchell and Lloyd (2013) reject the idea that qualities "allied to motherliness" are a disadvantage in the context of early years education and care and pose the rhetorical question: "Surely possessing qualities which enable a worker to relate to young children and build effective relationships should be celebrated rather than used as a reason to inhibit professional recognition for such a role?" (2013: 128). In Chapter 7 of this book, we see the need for strong emotional attachments between child and teacher in order to 'grow' the child. Genuine warmth and affection are fundamental elements of such attachment. Furthermore, Rose (2007) relates this quality of personal warmth to Goleman's (1995) theory of emotional intelligence and contends that it is essential not only to good interpersonal relationships with both adults and children, but also to good decision-making, since the emotionally intelligent person will be sensitive to the needs and signals of others, leading to better-informed reflection and ultimate outcomes.

Curiosity and Love of Learning

During my career as an early years teacher, I occasionally encountered a child who was 'un-curious' – who asked few if any questions, and seemed to lack a desire to make sense of their world. I learned that one of the most effective ways to overcome this problem is to persist in demonstrating a personal quality of genuine curiosity and desire to learn. Most of us can recall the irresistible influence of at least one teacher from our own schooldays who exuded enthusiasm for learning and, more specifically, for their subject area. In Chapter 5 of this book, the authors demonstrate their passion for mathematical learning and state their aim to promote positive mathematical dispositions within young children. Similarly, in Chapter 4, we recognise a passionate commitment to cultivating thinking skills within early years settings. The potentially harmful impact of the professional who, even though possessing other playful personal qualities, lacks curiosity in a specific area of learning is touched upon in Chapter 9, where readers are urged to reflect on how their own disposition towards ICT affects their provision for the children in their setting. A similar challenge is posed in Chapter 8 in regard to adult dispositions to outdoor play and this is applicable to every area of the curriculum. The truly playful professional possesses a genuinely curious disposition and love of learning, shares it with most of the children they teach and models it to the 'un-curious' few.

In this section we have considered four key personal qualities which facilitate playfulness in the early years professional. It is crucial to note, however, that these qualities are not necessarily present from birth: professionals can learn to be playful. Walsh et al. (2011) acknowledge that some teachers are not naturally playful, but contend that "at least some aspects of playfulness are open to teacher education" (2011: 116). We will return to the issue of professional training later in this chapter. However, perhaps the most effective trainers in playfulness are the children themselves – the experts in this field. Caldwell (1985) somewhat humorously describes the 'play paradox', whereby adults, who often do not know how to play, teach children, who are generally proficient in play, how to play. From a similar perspective, Goouch (2008) suggests that children as young as three and four years of age move easily between the roles of learner, play-partner and teacher as required. Perhaps we need to listen more and learn from all the experts in our early years settings.

Pause for Thought

Which of the personal qualities above do you possess? Are there others you consider equally important? How do they affect your playfulness?

Discuss the 'play paradox' in relation to your own professional experiences.

Playful Professional Roles

The role of the adult in children's learning is difficult to define, since it has many possibilities and variations. Based on a social constructivist view of learning, there are central principles on which the playful professional will base their interactions with children. These include the belief that learning occurs in scenarios that are meaningful to the child; that development cannot be separated from its social context; and that language plays a central role in conceptual development. These convictions mean that the complex role of the playful professional will include acting as co-player/play partner; co-learner/co-explorer; facilitator; listener/decoder; co-planner; commentator and observer (Dunkin and Hanna, 2001). Considering the wide diversity of professional roles required to support children's learning, Rose and Rogers (2012) refer to "the plural practitioner" and suggest at least seven roles: critical reflector; carer; communicator; facilitator; observer; assessor and creator. However, when we use the specific term '*playful* professional', there are some potential areas of misunderstanding in regard to the roles played. During interviews carried out with teachers of children aged four to five years in Northern Ireland, Walsh et al. (2011) found that teachers "held a variety of competing mental models of early years pedagogy and child learning that led to confusion and tensions in their pedagogy" (2011: 107–8). In Chapter 2 of this book, the author explores this problem further and helps playful professionals develop a clearer mental model of their role. Three specific areas of possible confusion and tension regarding appropriate roles for the playful professional are considered below.

Enthusiast, Not Clown

Playfulness is often ascribed only to children and associated with silliness or frivolity. However, the argument throughout this book is that it can be applied equally to both children and adults and that it has a more positive connotation. Kane (2004) extols the benefits of playfulness for the psychological wellbeing of all age groups, even calling adult playfulness a "fitness indicator" (2004: 68). However, exercising a sense of humour and "preserving a light-hearted tone" (Walsh et al., 2011: 112) does not imply that the playful professional should simply play the role of the clown. Silliness is one tool in the playful toolbox and the discerning playful professional will use it as one of a variety of approaches. For example, in Chapter 5 of this book, silliness is advocated as a pedagogical strategy in playing mathematical estimation games with children. According to Wood (2010), playful ways of interacting with others will include humour, jokes, mimicry, riddles, rhymes and singing; however, playful moods will range from wild and boisterous to moments of focused contemplation. The writers of the central section of this book make a compelling case for fun and enthusiasm rather than clownery; for example, in Chapter 6, the author demonstrates how passion and enthusiasm for learning, for the specific curricular area and for the children with whom we work are key to playful professionalism. Edgington (2005) reinforces this idea succinctly when she says that "young children deserve to be surrounded by optimism and enthusiasm" (2005: 8).

Partner, Not Follower

One of the most visible outcomes of taking a social constructivist approach to children's learning is the adoption by the professional of an intentionally collaborative role – co-learning, co-playing, co-exploring, co-planning, co-constructing. Goouch (2008) speaks of "following children into play" and being willing to "pursue children's play objectives" (2008: 95). This type of language is entirely consistent with a Vygotskian approach, but there is a danger that it is misinterpreted so that the professional adopts a passive, tentative or supervisory role within the learning environment. Early years teachers who have undergone major change during their career in regard to educational policy and practice may have abandoned the familiar didactic elements of their teaching style and consequently find themselves uncertain about their 'new' role. Others may resist playfulness as a pedagogical strategy, equating it with a "loss of authority" (Walsh et al., 2011: 111). These valid concerns have been addressed in Chapter 2 of this book. It is helpful to recall Siraj-Blatchford's (1999) identification of three equally important elements of effective pedagogy – creating learning environments, direct instruction and scaffolding – and to balance these three in our playful practice. A later study (Siraj-Blatchford and Sylva, 2004) revealed that the most effective early years settings provide a balance of child-led and adult-initiated activities, including direct instruction; in other words, a partnership. Sometimes the adult is the 'more knowledgeable other' in the partnership and at other times, as illustrated by the exploration of playful approaches to ICT in Chapter 9 of this book, it is the child who has greater expertise. This commitment to working in partnership with children is an important mindset for the playful professional and leads to the building of what Wenger (1998) refers to as a "community of learners", which stretches beyond professionals and children to encompass parents, families and the wider community.

Professional, Not Amateur

An emphasis on playful teaching and learning can lead to the public misapprehension that there is no particular skill or expertise involved. The title of a book chapter by Mitchell and Lloyd (2013) "She's only going to work with little children" encapsulates this disparaging attitude to early years professionalism. However, the three chapters in the first section of this book delineate the robust theoretical underpinning, rigorous conceptual understanding and complex array of professional skills that are required to promote children's learning and development through a truly playful approach. According to Proyer and Ruch (2011: 113), "Playfulness is 'a highly skilled task'". All the authors in the central chapters of this book address the demanding nature of playful professionalism and demonstrate that it is not a task for the amateur. In Chapter 8, for instance, we see the complicated balancing act of playful professionalism, with so many roles and interactions needing to be managed simultaneously; in Chapter 11, the author declares that planning for children's learning is a sophisticated act of professionalism. The 'external' approach to professionalism – involving debates about appropriate qualifications and recognition – is important and will be considered in the next section. However, this should not distract us as playful professionals from adopting the 'internalised' approach, whereby all staff members – whatever their position on the qualifications and experience continuum – are regarded as professional in terms of how they carry out their work, including their amenability to continuous improvement and development (McMillan et al., 2012).

Pause for Thought

Think of all your roles as a 'plural practitioner'. Are there areas of contradiction or confusion?

Try to explain your 'mental model' of the playful professional role in one or two sentences.

Training the Playful Professional

Earlier in this chapter we noted the dual nature of playful teaching and learning: understanding the concept of high-level play and having a clear grasp of the playful professional's role in practice. This combination of theoretical and practical knowledge is crucial to effective playful teaching and learning. Rinaldi (2006) speaks of early years training in terms of supporting students as they find the connection between theory and practice, within a process she terms 'formazione' – professional and personal development. How can this 'formation' be achieved in the experience of the playful professional?

Level of Training

The challenging nature of playful professionalism has been discussed throughout this chapter and lends weight to the argument for a graduate leader in every setting (McMillan and Walsh, 2011). However, early years policy across the United Kingdom has tended recently to move away from a commitment to graduate leadership and has largely reverted to the cheaper system of employing graduates only in statutory settings and using lower-qualified staff in voluntary sector settings. We have argued elsewhere that this system should be abandoned in favour of one where graduate playful professionals would lead in all early years settings and the artificial education/care divide would be abolished (McMillan and Walsh, 2011).

It is often assumed that those with high-level academic qualifications will not wish to 'waste' their talents by working with the youngest children. This is an assumption not applied to other areas of professionalism: for example, the general public is pleased to have the highest qualified minds working in the field of paediatric medicine. However, in a reflective colloquium article, Bentley (2011) relates her experience in almost being rejected for the post of early years teacher because she had a doctorate and the interviewer considered her to be over-qualified for the job. Moreover, the interviewer was not alone in her assumptions: they were shared by friends and family of the would-be teacher. Reflecting on this experience, Bentley poses some piercing questions:

> What does it mean to be 'too qualified' to teach? What does it mean that classroom teaching is not considered to be a fit occupation for someone with a doctoral degree? What does this mean for the field of early-childhood education (ECE) in terms of the voices coming from within the classroom? (2011: 285)

I argue that the early years workforce would benefit greatly from the recruitment of higher-ability graduates (and, indeed, those with postgraduate qualifications) who can meet the demands of the complex and varied roles of the effective playful professional.

Content of Training

We have already established that effective early years professional training involves a combination of two main elements: subject knowledge (theory) and subject-specific skills (practice). The core subject knowledge area for early years professionals is most simply expressed as 'the child'. A holistic approach to understanding the child will necessarily highlight the key role of play within children's learning and development. This leads logically to the two foundational issues of playful teaching and learning theory: the concept of high-level play and the playful professional's role in the process of children's learning, which make up the first section of this book. In a study comprising interviews with 22 students from a range of early years training courses (McMillan, 2008), students were asked to suggest areas of subject knowledge gained during their course. One student's comment that "children should interact and be excited about learning" (2008: 226) reflects the core of playful teaching and learning theory.

When considering the subject-specific skills needed by the playful professional, Chapters 11 and 12 of this book highlight observation, planning, assessment and reflection. Each of these is a complex and high-level skill and the central section of the book illustrates how these can be integrated into playful practice on an everyday basis. In Chapter 4, the author makes a compelling case for explicitly teaching thinking skills and it is clear that the playful professional must develop expertise in this foundational area of practice. When student interviewees were asked to suggest skills they had developed through their course (McMillan, 2008), skills specific to playful teaching included "model play"; "set children a challenge"; "take a caring approach"; "see the world from the eyes of a child". These and a wider array of subject-specific skills can be seen in practice throughout the central chapters of this book. For example, in Chapters 5 and 6 the authors outline strategies for modelling play in the contexts of Maths and Literacy; in Chapter 10 there are numerous examples of how playful teachers may set Science challenges for children; in Chapter 7 a caring approach is portrayed as foundational to all learning and to 'growing' the child; in Chapters 8 and 9 playful teachers are encouraged to see the outdoor world and the world of ICT respectively through the eyes of a child.

Earlier in this chapter we considered the key personal qualities that make a playful professional: a sense of humour; flexibility and ambiguity tolerance; warmth and affection; curiosity and a love of learning. These might be seen as generic skills, all of which could be developed incidentally through any process of effective professional learning. However, Walsh et al. (2011) argue convincingly that, although some teachers are not naturally playful, they can learn to be so and effective training of the playful professional should include intentional development of these vital characteristics.

Pause for Thought

How would you respond to the questions posed by Bentley (2011: 285) above?

   To what extent has the content of your training formed you as a playful professional?

Leading a Playful Team

So far we have considered the personal qualities and roles that facilitate playful teaching and learning. Aspects of the process of developing these qualities and becoming equipped to carry out these roles have also been addressed. However, in focusing on the formation of the individual playful professional, there is a danger of forgetting that early years professionals do not work in isolation; they work in teams. The process of building and leading a playful team is vital to the success of consistent and ongoing playful professionalism. Being a leader, according to Rodd (2006), involves a range of skills such as giving direction; offering inspiration; building teamwork; gaining respect and setting an example – a combination of both 'being' and 'doing'. Leading a playful team, therefore, involves more than understanding high-level play and the professional's role within it; it also involves a dual intentional strategy of teaching playfulness and growing a playful team.

Teaching Playfulness

The social constructivist approach places emphasis on constructing professional identity at both individual and corporate levels. A "reflective competence" model of training (McMillan et al., 2012) is entirely consistent with this approach and requires the team leader to take responsibility for teaching playfulness within the setting. The strategy of modelling playfulness is the most effective means of demonstrating its strength to the other members of the staff team, and this means undertaking an ongoing 'in-house' process of professional development. Whalley (2011) supports this leadership responsibility: "To lead involves influencing the behaviour of others" (2011: 17). This does not mean, of course, that only the team leader can model playfulness. It is the leader's role to facilitate this through the optimum means, whether by personal modelling, delegation to more playful staff members or use of external resources, such as funding in-service training.

Warford (2011) proposes a practical application of Vygotsky's (1978) Zone of Proximal Development (ZPD) to teacher education. This may be a useful model for the playful team leader who wants to increase the playfulness of the staff team. First, staff members reflect on and express their personal views and approaches (stage one: self-assistance); then demonstrations of playfulness are observed within the setting (stage two: teacher-assistance); these are discussed by the staff team, leading to opportunities for imitation and reinforcement of the demonstrations (stage three: internalisation); finally, adjustments may be made to policies and procedures so that playfulness becomes the norm within the setting (stage four: recurrence).

This approach assumes a "climate of reciprocal relationships" (Rodd, 2006: 33) within the setting, so that observation, reflection and discussion occur easily within a collaborative ethos. The playful team leader will be committed to the concept and practice of playful teaching and learning and find the most effective means by which to communicate this to their staff team, as well as to parents and the wider community. In practice, being an active advocate for playfulness may involve activities such as leading playful workshops; writing explanatory blog posts or articles in newsletters or local papers; giving talks at local events or at parents' evenings within the setting.

Growing a Playful Team

The process of teaching playfulness (individual professional development) runs in parallel with the process of playful team growth (corporate professional development). As the individual team member increases in playfulness, acquiring the personal characteristics that facilitate playful teaching and learning, they reflect together with other team members on how the setting can continue on this journey of improvement. In this way both personal and corporate development are inextricably connected.

According to Whalley (2011), it is the role of the early years setting leader to establish an effective team which is characterised by a shared sense of purpose; a collective focus on children's learning; purposeful collaborative activity; de-privatised activity and reflective dialogue. But how is this to be done? The key to creating such a team is, in Murray and McDowall Clark's (2013) phrase, "practising leadership in community" (2013: 298). Most writers agree that a collaborative, interactive and distributed style of leadership, in which responsibility is shared and hierarchies are minimised, is most appropriate to early years practice. It is important to remember that the same personal qualities that facilitate playful teaching and learning with young children – sense of humour; flexibility and ambiguity tolerance; warmth and affection; curiosity and love of learning – also facilitate adult learning and so these should be evident in the interactions amongst the members of the playful team.

The playful team will only be truly effective if all its members identify with the principles and practice of playfulness; playfulness should not be an optional extra for those staff members who seem to have 'natural' playful characteristics. Open discussion about the meaning of shared vision, values and beliefs is fundamental to the ongoing growth of the healthy playful team, despite the challenges that may occur during this process. Edgington (2005) suggests that there are three types of team in early years settings: the cosy team, whose members have worked together for a long time and are not open to change; the turbulent team, whose members appear to agree but express disagreement outside the setting, making change dialogue difficult; the rigorous and challenging team, whose members like to discuss issues critically and are open to agreed change. The leader of a playful team aims to build a rigorous and challenging team, characterised by reflection, discussion, openness and professional passion, well-prepared to undertake truly playful teaching and learning.

Pause for Thought

How might you plan to 'teach' playfulness to parents and carers of the children in your setting?

Which type of team (Edgington, 2005) do you belong to? How does this affect your setting's playfulness?

Key Messages

- In this chapter I have attempted to answer the question: What does a playful professional actually look like? I have painted a picture of the playful professional and set this profile within the context of the playful team.
- I have suggested personal qualities that tend towards playfulness; specific roles to be played and others to be avoided; appropriate training for the playful professional and guidance for leading a playful team.
- Reflective questions have been posed throughout to prompt individual thought and group discussion, so that you may apply what you have learned to your own practice.

Further Reading

Proyer, R. and Ruch, W. (2011) 'The virtuousness of adult playfulness: The relation of playfulness with strengths of character', *Psychology of Well-Being: Theory, Research and Practice* 1 (4): 1–12.

Whalley, M. (2011) *Leading Practice in Early Years Settings* (second edition). Exeter: Learning Matters.

References

Bentley, D. (2011) 'Banished from the classroom: An over-educated educator?', *Contemporary Issues in Early Childhood* 12 (3): 284–89.

Caldwell, B.M. (1985) 'Parent–child play: A playful evaluation', in C.C. Brown and A.W. Gottfried (eds), *Play Interactions: The Role of Toys and Parental Involvement in Children's Development*. Skillman, NJ: Johnson & Johnson. pp. 167–78.

Claxton, G. (2000) 'The anatomy of intuition', in T. Atkinson and G. Claxton (eds), *The Intuitive Practitioner*. Buckingham: Open University Press. pp. 32–52.

Dunkin, D. and Hanna, P. (2001) *Thinking Together: Quality Child Interactions*. Wellington, New Zealand: New Zealand Council for Educational Research.

Edgington, M. (2005) *The Foundation Stage Teacher in Action* (third edition). London: Paul Chapman.

Goleman, D. (1995) *Emotional Intelligence*. New York: Bantam Books.

Goouch, K. (2008) 'Understanding playful pedagogies, play narratives and play spaces', *Early Years* 28 (1): 93–102.

Griffin, S. (2008) 'The 'P' word and home-based child carers', in L. Miller and C. Cable (eds), *Professionalism in the Early Years*. London: Hodder Education. pp. 65–74.

Kane, P. (2004) *The Play Ethic*. London: Macmillan.

McMillan, D. (2008) *Education and Care: Implications for Educare Training in Northern Ireland*. Unpublished PhD thesis, Queen's University Belfast.

McMillan, D. and Walsh, G. (2011) 'Early years professionalism – issues, challenges and opportunities', in L. Miller and C. Cable (eds) *Professionalization, Leadership and Management in the Early Years*. London: Sage. pp. 47–61.

McMillan, D., Walsh, G., Gray, C., Hanna, K., Carville, S. and McCracken, O. (2012) 'Changing mindsets: The benefits of implementing a professional development model in early childhood settings in Ireland', *Professional Development in Education* 38 (3): 395–410.

Mitchell, H. and Lloyd, I. (2013) 'Professionalism – raising the stakes in the early years: "She's only going to work with little children"', in M. Wild and A. Street (eds), *Themes and Debates in Early Childhood*. London: Learning Matters/Sage. pp. 126–40.

Murray, J. and McDowall Clark, R. (2013) 'Reframing leadership as a participative pedagogy: The working theories of early years professionals', *Early Years* 33 (3): 289–301.

Peterson, C. and Seligman, M.E.P. (2004) *Character Strengths and Virtues: A Handbook and Classification.* Washington, DC: American Psychological Association. www.viacharacter.org/www/Character-Strengths/VIA-Classification (accessed 13 September 2016).

Proyer, R. and Ruch, W. (2011) 'The virtuousness of adult playfulness: The relation of playfulness with strengths of character', *Psychology of Well-Being: Theory, Research and Practice* 1 (4): 1–12.

Rinaldi, C. (2006) *In Dialogue with Reggio Emilia: Listening, Researching and Learning.* London: Routledge.

Rodd, J. (2006) *Leadership in Early Childhood* (third edition). Maidenhead: Open University Press.

Rose, J. (2007) 'Enjoyment in the early years through critical reflection', in D. Hayes (ed.), *Joyful Teaching and Learning in the Primary School.* Exeter: Learning Matters. pp. 70–8.

Rose, J. and Rogers, S. (2012) *The Role of the Adult in Early Years Settings.* Maidenhead: Open University Press.

Siraj-Blatchford, I. (1999) 'Early childhood pedagogy: Practice, principles and research', in P. Mortimore (ed.), *Understanding Pedagogy and Its Impact on Learning.* London: Paul Chapman. pp. 20–45.

Siraj-Blatchford, I. and Sylva, K. (2004) 'Researching pedagogy in English pre-schools', *British Educational Research Journal* 30 (5): 713–30.

Tegano, D., Groves, M. and Catron, C. (1999) 'Early childhood teachers' playfulness and ambiguity tolerance: Essential elements of encouraging creative potential of children', *Journal of Early Childhood Teacher Education* 20 (3): 291–300.

Vygotsky, L. (1978) *Mind in Society: The Development of Higher Psychological Processes* (trans.). Cambridge, MA: Harvard University Press.

Walsh, G., Sproule, L., McGuinness, C. and Trew, K. (2011) 'Playful structure: A novel image of early years pedagogy for primary school classrooms', *Early Years* 31 (2): 107–19.

Warford, M. (2011) 'The zone of proximal teacher development', *Teaching and Teacher Education* 27 (2): 252–8.

Wenger, E. (1998) *Communities of Practice.* Cambridge: Cambridge University Press.

Whalley, M. (2011) *Leading Practice in Early Years Settings* (second edition). Exeter: Learning Matters.

Wood, E. (2010) 'Developing integrated pedagogical approaches to play and learning', in P. Broadhead, J. Howard and E. Wood (eds), *Play and Learning in the Early Years.* London: Sage. pp. 9–26.

Index

Tables and Figures are indicated by page numbers in bold print. The abbreviation *bib* indicates bibliographical information in a Further Reading section.